JULIE GOODWIN'S

Essential Cookbook

hachette
AUSTRALIA

This book is for you, our three beautiful sons
Joseph Brian, Thomas Roy and Patrick Tony,
and for the families in your future, whatever shape they may take.
Dad and I look forward to it all.

CONTENTS

Introduction

Cooking has brought so much to my life. Not just my cooking either, but my friends, my family, and even my children's cooking. It has brought me countless wonderful meals, which are a little bit about the food and a lot about the people who share that food. Cooking has brought me new friends, people I never would have met if I hadn't been struck with this passion for food. It has brought me satisfaction, fun and joy. It has brought me experiences I will never, ever forget.

Most importantly, cooking has brought me closer to the people I love. I treasure the connections I feel with the beautiful cooks in my life who aren't with us physically any more, especially my nan, Edna White; Mick's mother, Kathleen Goodwin; his grandmother, Imelda Henebery; and my friend Julie Wilson. They live on in my cooking and in my memory. Cooking has also given me connections with the family and friends who are with me, the ones I see often and the ones I see rarely; there is no occasion where food is not an integral part of the gathering or the occasion.

The point I find myself at at the moment is as the parent of three sons who are new adults. They are all still at home right now but I guess the clock is ticking, and although I have taught them what cooking knowledge I could over the years, I feel an almost desperate need to get all the important recipes, information and tips together so that when they go, they're set.

That's what this book is. It's a collection of everything I think is important to know in order to be able to nourish yourself and the people you love; it's the recipes that bring back childhood memories for myself and my kids; it's the little bits of kitchen wisdom that have been handed down through generations, or passed on from friends, or discovered by accident or through trial and error. It's the book I want my boys to have for when they have families of their own.

I want them to have these recipes not just so they can cook well but so they can cook for the people in their lives and, through that act of love, draw them closer and make them feel valued. So they can create new memories of their own, and by doing that be truly connected to the patchwork of our family through generations. So they can have family meals like we have – gathered around a table, appreciating the food, laughing and talking about the day. So their children might develop their own passion for cooking and pay it forward to their children.

It's a lot to hope for from a book of recipes, but there's more. I hope this book can do those things for your family, too.

With love,

Julie

Cook's note

I try wherever possible to source fresh ingredients that are in season and locally grown. If I cannot source locally, I use Australian produce wherever possible.

When my recipes call for shallots, I am referring to the long green onions that are sometimes called spring onions or eschallots. I do not mean the little brown French shallots.

Many of my recipes call for the use of a chef pan. This is similar to a large frying pan, but has deep sides, a non-stick surface and an oven-proof handle or two small handles, one on either side. My chef pan is 32 cm across and 7.5 cm deep. It's great for cooking without overcrowding the pan and I recommend investing in one.

Where I have specified olive oil, I am referring to extra virgin Australian olive oil. It is the freshest option available to us, and also supports our producers.

To cook well, there are a few things that are particularly helpful. My favourite kitchen items are listed below and are mentioned throughout this book. However, if you don't have all the equipment listed, don't despair – there's not too much that can't be done if you have a good pan, a good knife, a whisk and a wooden spoon!

Electrical:	Oven (temperatures are not fan-forced unless specified), oven grill, microwave, food processor, mini food processor, toaster, kettle, hand-held stick mixer
Cookware:	Chef pan with lid, large pot with lid, medium pot, wok, medium frypan, baking dish (heavy-based, non-stick), baking tray (flat tray, non-stick), grill plate, microwave rice cooker (microwave-safe with a lid)
Measuring:	Measuring jug, cup measures, measuring spoons (check that they are Australian; the tablespoon should be 20 ml or 4 teaspoons)
Mixing:	Bowls of various sizes – stainless steel or heat-proof glass, shallow dish, narrow jug
Large utensils:	Chopping board (bamboo is my pick), wire rack, colander, wire mesh strainer, mandolin/v-slicer with plain and julienne attachments
Small utensils:	Knives – large chef knife, paring knife, serrated knife; fine grater, can opener, citrus squeezer, silicone spatula, big spoon, slotted spoon, wooden spoon, tongs, vegetable peeler, egg flip, ladle, meat mallet, pasta server, pastry brush, pizza cutter, wire whisk, timer, grater, kitchen scissors, oven mitt, long metal skewers
Consumables:	Baking paper, foil, paper towel, plastic wrap, snap-lock bags

Eggs

Introduction

I think if I could only have one ingredient for the rest of my life, it would be eggs. They are so versatile and contain protein, vitamins, minerals, good fats and trace nutrients. Also, they are delicious.

You get the very best eggs when you keep chickens. Not everyone can do that, though, so the next best thing is to find a neighbour who sells their chooks' eggs, or a local farmers' market that sells free-range organic eggs. If these options aren't available, read the label carefully at the supermarket. Choose free range eggs over cage eggs. Happy chickens make the best-tasting eggs. I hope that one day there won't be cage eggs as an option; I much prefer the idea of our feathered friends having a happy life.

These recipes all call for large eggs – 60 grams or more – at room temperature.

Perfect poached eggs

Breaking into a perfectly poached egg is one of the most satisfying eating moments in my view. But there does seem to be a lot of contention and anxiety around how to best cook them. Some people create a whirlpool in the pot, some people put vinegar in the water, some people use silicone poach pods, or wrap the eggs in plastic wrap, or use electric egg cookers. The method I use is as simple as it gets and is pretty fail-proof if you are using good fresh eggs.

Eggs from the supermarket can be hard to poach because the white doesn't hold together. Find somewhere in your area where freshly laid eggs are sold – you won't believe the difference. We're lucky enough to have our own chooks, but when they're off the lay we have a number of options including roadside sellers and the local weekly farmers' market.

Cooking time: approximately 2 minutes

1 In a large non-stick chef pan, bring about 4 cm of water to the boil then reduce the heat so that the water is barely simmering.

2 Crack the first egg gently on the side of the pan and, as carefully as you can, lower it into the water. Then leave it alone! The egg will gather the bulk of its white to itself. Any stringy floaty bits can be ignored. If the eggs are really fresh, not too much will get away.

3 Repeat with remaining eggs – don't do more than 4 in a large pan at a time. The water may need to be strained or replaced every few batches.

4 When the white looks cooked through, carefully lift each egg with a slotted spoon. If the white is still translucent or wobbly, set it back in the water until it cooks. If you prefer your egg yolks to be firm, leave the eggs in the water until the yolk lightens in colour. After removing from the water, rest briefly on paper towel (still in the slotted spoon) to remove excess water, then slide straight onto the serving plate.

Boiled eggs

Cooking time: 5–6 minutes

1 Bring a pot of water to a rolling boil. Gently lower the eggs into the water with a spoon. Boil for 5 minutes then remove the eggs from the water.

2 For soft-centred eggs, crack the top off immediately to prevent them from cooking further and serve straight away in an egg cup. If using whole, plunge them into cold water to prevent further cooking. For a firmer yolk, allow the eggs to cool in their shells. For hard-boiled eggs, cook for 6 minutes then remove from the water and allow them to cool in their shells.

Scrambled eggs

Serves 2   Prep time: 1 minute   Cooking time: 2–3 minutes

4 eggs   50 g cold butter, cubed
¼ cup cream

1 In a bowl, whisk the eggs gently together with the cream.

2 In a non-stick frypan over low heat, add the cold cubed butter and pour in the egg mixture. This needs to be done over a low heat so that the eggs will set without browning. Once the eggs have just started to firm up, gently run a spatula across the bottom of the pan and around the sides, in effect turning the mixture 'upside down'. Repeat this process until the eggs are done to your liking. Try not to agitate the eggs too much and don't cook until they are completely dried out or they will be rubbery instead of soft.

Note: Some lovely variations are to add fresh herbs, or a little feta or parmesan cheese.

Fried eggs

Not everyone likes their eggs cooked the same way, and this is true of fried eggs too. For many years my husband Mick used to like his yolks popped and the eggs flipped and cooked on both sides. This changed over time and now he likes the yolks runny! This method of frying will give you a slightly crisp edge and a runny yolk. If you want your eggs 'over easy' (flipped with a still-runny yolk), you'll need a very good non-stick pan, a silicone spatula and a steady hand.

Cooking time: 2–3 minutes

1 tablespoon olive oil   2 eggs

1 Preheat a heavy-based, non-stick frypan over medium-high heat. Heat the olive oil in the pan. Once the oil is hot, crack the eggs into the pan. Use a spatula to gently loosen around the edges of the egg. After about 2–3 minutes, the whites will be just set and the yolks runny.

Basic cheese omelette

Prep time: 5 minutes   Cooking time: 2–3 minutes

2 eggs   Salt and pepper
1 tablespoon thickened cream   Generous handful of grated
½ teaspoon olive oil   tasty cheese (about ¼ cup)
   or olive oil spray

1 Preheat a heavy-based, non-stick frypan over medium-high heat. (On my gas cooktop, this means high heat on the smallest burner. On an electric cooktop, practice until you know what works.)

2 Break the eggs into a bowl, add the cream and beat with a fork. Don't over-beat the eggs – they just need to be combined.

3 Heat the olive oil in the pan. Pour the egg mixture into the pan. Allow it to set for a few moments, then, using a spatula, push the mixture from the edge to the centre of the pan. Turn the pan from side to side to make sure the base is covered with the egg mixture. Wait a few moments then repeat. When there isn't enough runny egg to keep coating the base of the pan, stop agitating it and let it set. Use the spatula to go around the edge of the omelette and make sure that the edges are tidy. Season with salt and pepper and throw a handful of cheese across it. Carefully lift one side of the omelette and check for colour – it should be a light golden brown. If it is, fold in half. Slide onto a plate and serve.

Filling suggestions: For an omelette with a filling that needs to be cooked, such as bacon, mushrooms, asparagus, cherry tomatoes or chorizo, cook the filling first then set aside. Fillings that don't need pre-cooking include fresh herbs, chopped shallots (spring onions), baby spinach leaves, shaved ham or smoked salmon. Sprinkle the filling across half the omelette before folding the other half over the top.

Egg salad

This salad is absolutely lovely on sandwiches or just on its own as part of a lunch box.

Makes 4 sandwiches   Prep time: 10 minutes   Cooking time: 5 minutes

4 eggs, at room temperature
3 shallots (spring onions), white
  and pale green parts only,
  finely sliced

1 tablespoon tomato sauce
2 tablespoons mayonnaise
Salt and ground black pepper

1 Bring a small pot of salted water to a rapid boil. Use a spoon to lower the eggs one by one into the water. Boil for 5 minutes. Remove the eggs from the water and leave them to cool in their shells. When cool, peel and chop the eggs.

2 In a bowl, mix the chopped egg with the shallots, tomato sauce and mayonnaise. Season with salt and pepper to your liking.

Devilled eggs

Makes 24   Prep time: 20 minutes   Cooking time: 5 minutes

12 eggs, at room temperature
2 tablespoons tomato sauce
1 teaspoon Worcestershire sauce
1 tablespoon mayonnaise

1 teaspoon curry powder
¼ teaspoon salt
¼ teaspoon ground black pepper
½ teaspoon sweet paprika

1 Bring a medium pot of salted water to a rapid boil. Use a spoon to lower the eggs one by one into the water. Boil for 5 minutes. Remove the eggs from the water and leave them to cool in their shells. When cool, peel them, being very gentle to keep the whites intact. Cut the eggs in half lengthways, remove the yolks and place them in a bowl.

2 Place the tomato sauce, Worcestershire sauce, mayonnaise, curry powder,

salt and pepper in the bowl with the cooked yolks and mash with a fork to combine. Arrange the egg whites on a serving platter and spoon the yolk mixture back into the cavity. Sprinkle each egg with a little pinch of paprika.

Scotch eggs

Makes 8   Prep time: 20 minutes   Cooking time: 15 minutes

10 eggs
500 g good-quality sausage mince
250 g beef mince
3 cups homemade or
   panko breadcrumbs
¼ cup tomato sauce

1 tablespoon French mustard
1 tablespoon curry powder
1 teaspoon salt
1 teaspoon white pepper
2 cups plain flour
Oil, for deep-frying

1 Bring a pot of water to a rolling boil. Gently lower 8 eggs into the water and boil for 4 minutes. Remove with a slotted spoon and put into a bowl of cold water. When cool, gently peel. The eggs will be quite soft but this is needed as they will be cooked a second time.

2 In a bowl, place the sausage and beef minces, 1 cup breadcrumbs, tomato sauce, mustard, curry powder, half of the salt and half of the pepper. Using your hands, work the mixture very well until all combined. Divide into 8 equal portions and form into thin flat oval shapes.

3 Preheat a deep-fryer to 180°C.

4 Beat the remaining 2 eggs in a shallow dish. Combine the flour with the remaining salt and pepper in another shallow dish. Place the remaining breadcrumbs in a third shallow dish.

5 Dip a peeled egg into the flour and place it on a meat patty. Using damp hands, gently wrap the meat around the egg. Dip into the flour mixture, coating evenly. Then dip into the beaten egg; allow the excess egg to drain. Coat all over with the breadcrumbs. Repeat with the remaining eggs.

6 Deep-fry 4 eggs at a time until quite a deep gold colour.

7 Set aside to drain on paper towel while you cook the next batch.

Shakshuka

There's a fair bit of heated debate about the origins of this dish, so I'll just call it Middle Eastern and let you decide where its roots are! All I know is that it is delicious for brunch and even goes all right as a quick and economical dinner.

Serves 4   Prep time: 10 minutes   Cooking time: 20 minutes

1 tablespoon olive oil
2 small red chillies, seeded
  and finely chopped
1 green capsicum, seeded
  and cut into strips
2 cloves garlic, chopped
1 brown onion, chopped
1 teaspoon ground cumin seed

1 teaspoon smoked paprika
2 x 400 g tins chopped tomatoes
2 teaspoons salt
1 tablespoon sugar
4 eggs
Ground black pepper
⅓ cup chopped fresh parsley
Crusty baguette, for serving

1 In a 28 cm frypan, heat the oil over a medium heat. Add the chilli, capsicum, garlic and onion and stir until soft and translucent. Add the cumin and paprika and stir for a further minute. Stir in the tomatoes, salt and sugar, then simmer for 10 minutes. The sauce will be thickened and the flavours more intense.

2 Crack the 4 eggs gently into the sauce. Partially cover with a lid and simmer for a further 5 minutes, or until the whites have set but the yolks are still soft. Remove the pan from the heat, grind over some black pepper and sprinkle with parsley.

3 Serve the eggs to the table in the pan, with a crusty baguette.

Variations: Chop a chorizo sausage into cubes and fry with the chilli and onion. You could serve this dolloped with some thick plain Greek yoghurt if you wish.

Chinese prawn omelette, recipe
page 9

Chinese prawn omelette

Serves 4   Prep time: 15 minutes + marinating time
Cooking time: 15 minutes

2 teaspoons cornflour
2 tablespoons Shaoxing wine
   (Chinese cooking wine)
1 tablespoon soy sauce
¼ teaspoon white pepper
24 green (raw) banana prawns,
   shelled and deveined
¼ cup peanut oil
1 red capsicum, seeded and
   cut into thin strips

½ bunch shallots (spring onions),
   cut into 3 cm lengths
8 eggs
Ground white pepper (optional)
Oyster sauce, bean sprouts,
   coriander leaves and crispy
   fried shallots, to serve

1 In a bowl, combine the cornflour, cooking wine, soy sauce and white pepper. Add the prawns and marinate, covered in the fridge, for 1 hour.

2 Heat a quarter of the oil in a 28 cm frypan over high heat and stir-fry 8 prawns, then remove to a bowl. Repeat twice more.

3 Add a dash more oil and stir-fry the capsicum and shallots for a minute or until soft. Remove and set aside.

4 Beat 2 eggs together with 1 tablespoon water. Heat ½ teaspoon oil in the frypan, then pour the egg in and swirl to coat the base of the pan. Reduce the heat to medium.

5 When the egg has almost set (after 2–3 minutes), lay 6 prawns and a quarter of the vegetable mixture over half of the omelette. Season with ground white pepper, if desired. Using a spatula, carefully fold the omelette in half. Cook for a further minute or so. Invert onto a plate, then repeat for the remaining 3 omelettes.

6 Serve with oyster sauce on the side, and top with bean sprouts, coriander and crispy fried shallots.

Asparagus and cheese frittata

Serves 4   Prep time: 5 minutes   Cooking time: 10 minutes

1 teaspoon olive oil
6 shallots (spring onions),
  sliced into 1 cm pieces
1 bunch asparagus
  (preferably young, thin
  spears), cut into 3 cm pieces
8 eggs

½ cup milk
¼ teaspoon salt
¼ teaspoon ground white pepper
50 g baby spinach leaves
½ cup grated mozzarella cheese
½ cup grated tasty cheese
½ bunch dill

1   Preheat the oven grill to 200°C.

2   Place a 28 cm frypan with a heat-proof handle over medium heat with the oil in it. Sauté the shallots and asparagus for 1 minute.

3   In a mixing bowl, beat the eggs and milk together with a wire whisk. Whisk in the salt and pepper. Pour into the frypan, then scatter over the spinach and half the mozzarella and tasty cheese. Tear a few dill leaves into the pan and stir with a spatula, lifting the egg from the bottom. When the mixture is starting to thicken, arrange the ingredients so they are fairly evenly distributed over the base of the pan. Scatter the other half of the cheeses over the top and place the pan on the bottom shelf of the oven.

4   After about 6 minutes the frittata will be golden brown on top and just set in the middle. Remove from the oven using an oven mitt as the handle will be very hot. Put a plate over the top of the pan and invert to remove the frittata. Place a plate over the bottom of the frittata and invert again, so that it is right side up.

Eggs Benedict

Serves 2   Prep time: 10 minutes   Cooking time: 20 minutes

2 English muffins, lightly toasted
Small handful of baby spinach
  leaves or rocket
150 g shaved leg ham (or smoked
  salmon or crisp cooked bacon)

4 eggs, poached (see page 2)
½ cup Hollandaise sauce
  (see page 142)
⅓ cup parsley leaves, lightly
  chopped

1 Lightly butter the toasted muffins and place on 2 warm plates. Top with the spinach then the ham, and gently rest the poached eggs on top of this. Spoon the Hollandaise sauce over the top and sprinkle with the parsley.

Note: If using smoked salmon, replace parsley with finely chopped dill.

Asparagus with poached egg and warm bacon vinaigrette

Serves 4   Prep time: 10 minutes   Cooking time: 15 minutes

1 tablespoon olive oil
4 rashers bacon, rind removed,
  very finely diced
¼ cup red wine vinegar
2 bunches (about 16 spears)
  fresh green asparagus,
  woody ends removed

4 eggs
4 slices toasted sourdough
  bread, for serving

1 In a frypan over medium-high heat, place the olive oil and chopped bacon. After a few minutes the bacon will become golden and crispy. A few little pieces might jump around in the pan so be careful. Add the vinegar and remove the pan from the heat. Mix well.

2 Place about 5 cm of salted water into a large, deep frypan or chef pan. Bring to a fast simmer. Simmer the asparagus for roughly 1½ minutes, or until bright green and tender but still crisp. (The exact time will depend on the thickness of the spears.) Remove the asparagus and drain on paper towel.

3 Reduce the heat in the frypan to a gentle simmer and poach the eggs following the directions on page 2.

4 Serve the asparagus on a slice of toasted sourdough, topped with the poached egg and generously drizzled with the bacon vinaigrette.

Big green breakfast
plate, recipe page 13

Big green breakfast plate

Serves 4   Prep time: 20 minutes   Cooking time: about 6 minutes

4 slices sourdough bread
2 tablespoons olive oil
2 ripe avocados
½ cup quinoa, cooked to
  packet directions
100 g baby spinach leaves,
  finely chopped
4 shallots (spring onions),
  finely sliced

Handful of herbs from the
  salsa verde
½ teaspoon salt
Juice and zest of 1 lemon
4 eggs
Salsa verde (see page 138)
¼ cup pistachio kernels,
  roughly chopped

1 Fill a chef pan to 5 cm with salted water and bring to a gentle simmer over medium heat. Toast the sourdough in a toaster. Drizzle with olive oil and set aside.

2 Prepare the avocado by running a knife around its circumference and cutting in half. Remove the seed by lodging the knife in it and giving it a gentle twist. While the avocado is still in its half-shell, run a knife lengthways through the flesh down to the skin. Use a spoon to scoop out the flesh, which will be neatly sliced. Arrange the avocado slices on the sourdough on 4 plates.

3 In a bowl, mix the prepared quinoa, spinach, shallots, herbs, salt and lemon juice and zest. Spoon evenly over the top of the avocado.

4 Poach the eggs following the directions on page 2. Drain the eggs and place on top of the toast.

5 Spoon the salsa verde generously over the plates, scatter with chopped pistachios, and serve.

Brioche bruschetta with avocado, poached eggs and dukkah

Serves 4   Prep time: 20 minutes (unless making dukkah)
Cooking time: about 8 minutes

4 slices brioche bread,
   sliced 2 cm thick
1 tablespoon olive oil, plus a
   drizzle for serving
2 ripe avocados
Juice of 1 lemon

8 eggs
¼ cup dukkah (see page 167)
⅔ cup tomato relish
Sea salt flakes
Freshly ground black pepper

1   Heat a char-grill pan over high heat. Fill a chef pan to 5 cm with salted water and bring to a gentle simmer over medium heat.

2   Brush the brioche slices on both sides with olive oil. When the char-grill pan is very hot, place the brioche in the pan and cook for about a minute or until dark golden char marks score the bread. Turn and repeat on the second side. Remove from the pan and set aside.

3   Prepare the avocado by running a knife around its circumference and cutting in half. Remove the seed by lodging the knife in it and giving it a gentle twist. While the avocado is still in its half-shell, run a knife lengthways through the flesh down to the skin. Use a spoon to scoop out the flesh, which will be neatly sliced. Squeeze the lemon juice over the avocado to prevent it from turning brown.

4   Arrange 1 brioche slice on each of 4 plates. Layer the sliced avocado over the bread. Poach the eggs following the directions on page 2. Drain the eggs and place on top of the brioche and avocado.

5   Drizzle the eggs with olive oil and scatter with the dukkah. Dollop the tomato relish around the plate. Season with salt and pepper, and serve.

Quiche Lorraine

Serves 4   Prep time: 15 minutes   Cooking time: 40 minutes

1 quantity of savoury shortcrust
   pastry (see recipe on page 232)
   or two sheets plain frozen
   shortcrust (if you have it in
   the freezer)
4 rashers bacon, rind removed, diced
1 large brown onion, diced

6 eggs
¼ cup cream
Salt and pepper to taste
Any fresh herbs that you may
   have in the garden or fridge,
   chopped (optional)
1 cup grated tasty cheese

1 Preheat the oven to 170°C. Spray a 23 cm pie dish (or quiche tin) with olive oil and line with pastry. Prick the pastry with a fork. Place a sheet of baking paper over the pastry and fill with baking weights or rice. Bake for 15 minutes then remove from the oven and take out the weights and paper. Set the pastry case aside.

2 In a frypan over medium-high heat, sauté the bacon and onion until starting to brown.

3 Place the eggs, cream, salt and pepper in a bowl and beat with a fork or whisk until just combined.

4 Arrange the bacon and onion mixture evenly over the base of the pastry case, followed by chopped herbs if using, and top with grated cheese.

5 Carefully pour the egg mixture into the pastry case. Bake for 25 minutes or until the egg has just set.

Spinach and feta quiche

This is an easy and very economical family dinner.

Serves 4   Prep time: 15 minutes   Cooking time: 40 minutes

1 quantity of savoury shortcrust
   pastry (see recipe on page 232)
   or two sheets plain frozen
   shortcrust (if you have it in
   the freezer)
6 eggs
½ cup cream
Salt and pepper
100 g baby spinach leaves

4 shallots (spring onions),
   very finely sliced
100 g feta, crumbled into
   large chunks
Any fresh herbs that you may
   have in the garden or fridge,
   chopped (optional)
1 cup grated tasty cheese

Salmon quiche, recipe page 17

1 Preheat the oven to 170°C. Spray a 23 cm pie dish (or quiche tin) with olive oil and line with the pastry. Prick the pastry with a fork. Place a sheet of baking paper over the pastry and fill with baking weights or rice. Bake for 15 minutes then remove from the oven and take out the weights and paper. Set the pastry case aside.

2 Place the eggs, cream, salt and pepper in a bowl and beat with a fork or whisk until just combined.

3 Arrange the spinach, shallots and feta evenly over the base of the pastry case, followed by chopped herbs if using, and top with grated cheese.

4 Carefully pour the egg mixture into the pastry case. Bake for 25 minutes or until the egg has just set.

Salmon quiche

Serves 10–12   Prep time: 25 minutes   Cooking time: 40 minutes

1 quantity savoury shortcrust pastry (see recipe on page 232) or two sheets plain frozen shortcrust (if you have it in the freezer)
1 cup grated mozzarella cheese
50 g baby spinach leaves
400 g skinless, boneless salmon fillet, cut into 2 cm cubes

1 bunch shallots (spring onions), finely sliced
1 bunch dill, leaves chopped
10 eggs
½ cup cream
½ teaspoon salt
¼ teaspoon pepper

1 Preheat the oven to 170°C. Grease a 26 cm loose-based flan tin with butter or spray oil. Lay the pastry into the flan tin and trim the edges. Prick the pastry with a fork. Place a sheet of baking paper over the pastry and fill with pastry weights or rice. Bake for 15 minutes or until starting to turn golden. Remove from the oven and take out the weights and paper.

2 Arrange half the mozzarella cheese evenly over the base of the pastry case. Arrange the spinach over the top, followed by the salmon cubes, then scatter with the shallots and half of the dill leaves.

3 In a bowl, beat the eggs then add the cream and beat well. Season with salt and pepper. Carefully pour the egg mixture into the pastry case and top with the remaining mozzarella.

4 Bake for 25 minutes or until golden brown on top and just firm in the middle. Remove from the oven and set aside to cool a little before serving.

Meat

Introduction

In this chapter, you'll find my favourite go-to recipes that use the most popular cuts of meat and different methods of cooking them. Here's a run-down of cooking methods and some great tips on how to achieve the best results from different cuts and cooking styles.

Grilling, barbecuing and pan-frying

These are all methods of cooking where the meat is cooked with a direct, usually high heat. They're best suited to smaller cuts of meat.

Best cuts of red meat for grilling, barbecuing and pan-frying

Beef – rump, sirloin, T-bone, skirt, eye fillet and (my pick) scotch fillet.
Lamb – eye fillet, backstrap, mid-loin chops, leg chops, cutlets. (Mid-loin chops are my pick, unless lamb cutlets are on a very good special.)
Pork – fillet, chops, loin steak or medallions, scotch fillet steak (shoulder). (Pork chops are my pick.)

Tips for achieving beautifully cooked steaks and chops

Allow the meat to come to room temperature before cooking. Super-cold meat placed on a super-hot grill will 'tense up'. It's also harder for the heat to penetrate to the centre of the meat. Very cold meat can also release juices, meaning the meat will start to steam or stew.

It's important to have the grill or pan very hot. On an underheated surface, the meat will start to stew in its own juices and won't develop that beautiful dark golden crust that has so much flavour. For the same reason, don't overcrowd the pan or hotplate – it will cool down the cooking surface too much.

Drizzle the meat with oil before putting it on the hot surface. If you're pan-frying, the oil can go into the pan instead, but on a char grill or grill pan, it needs to go directly on the meat. Sprinkle on some salt just before putting the meat into the pan or onto the grill.

Cooking methods vary widely between cooks – for steak, some say it should be only cooked once on each side, others say to flip it every 30 seconds. My method is different to both of those but it works for me. I leave my steak on one side until it is beautifully dark and crusty. I then oil the top and sprinkle salt on, then turn and leave until the second side looks the same as the first. I then turn it once more on each side to achieve the right amount of 'doneness'.

A final, critical and often overlooked step is to rest the meat. It needs to be removed from the heat and placed in a warm place under foil for about half of its cooking time. This allows the fibres of the meat to relax and the juices to be evenly distributed throughout.

Cooking time for steak, chops and fillets varies widely depending on the cut, the thickness, the ferocity of the heat and many other factors. Learning to cook meat the way each person likes it is a matter of trial and error at first but you will gain in experience. Pay attention to how the meat looks, feels and smells when it is right. When rare, it will feel very soft; when medium it will have slight resistance and when well done it will feel firm. It's best to err on the side of underdone – you can always cook it a little bit more, but you can't uncook it!

In summary:

- **Get friendly with the butcher.**
- **Choose the right cut for the job.**
- **Take the meat out of the fridge 30 minutes before cooking.**
- **Oil and season the meat just before cooking.**
- **Cook on a very high heat.**
- **Turn it once to develop the outer crust, and once more to cook it to your liking.**
- **Rest the meat. Don't skip this step!**
- **Err on the side of underdone.**

Roasting

Roasting is one of the simplest and most satisfying methods of cooking whole joints of meat. The meat is cooked in dry heat, such as in an oven or a covered barbecue. If your barbecue is one of the kettle-shaped ones designed more for roasting than grilling, then you're set. If you have a normal hooded barbecue you can still make a great roast dinner. To roast in the barbecue, turn on the outer gas elements and place the pan in the middle of the barbecue plate with no direct heat underneath it, and close the lid.

For rare beef or lamb, remove the roast when the internal temperature reads 55–57°C. For medium rare, remove at 60–62°C. And for medium, remove at 68–70°C. For well done, remove at 75°C or above. Pork should reach 71°C in the centre. As with all meat, be sure to rest it before carving. For a large roast, rest under foil for half an hour or so. Rest pork uncovered so the crackle stays crispy.

The best cuts for roasting

Pork – leg, rolled loin, belly (belly is my pick; see the recipe on page 51).

Beef – whole rump, blade, bolar, topside, whole eye fillet (rump or eye fillet are my picks; see the recipe on page 27).

Lamb – whole leg, boneless leg, rolled loin, shoulder for slow roasting (whole leg and shoulder are my picks; see the recipe on page 43).

Pork: achieving great pork crackle

There are a few things you can do to make sure your crackle is crisp and crunchy. Firstly, the skin of the pork should be very dry. Leave it in the fridge overnight with no plastic wrapping on it. Sprinkle it with salt, and as the salt draws the moisture out, pat it dry with a paper towel. Let it come to room temperature before cooking.

Score the rind with a very sharp small knife – a retractable utility knife, such as a Stanley or Mickey knife, does a great job. Cut through the skin to the fat, but not all the way to the flesh, to allow the fat to render out, basting the skin as it goes. If the flesh is cut, blood/juices will seep out, and the rind will be rubbery instead of crackly.

Preheat the oven to 220°C. Massage the skin with a little oil and plenty of salt and cook for about 20–30 minutes or until the skin starts to bubble up. Turn the oven down and finish cooking.

When the roast is cooked, if there are areas of skin that have not crackled you can place them under a hot grill or use a kitchen blowtorch. Be careful in either case as these methods can easily burn the crackle. To avoid burning under the grill, place the pork on the lowest shelf of the oven, turn the grill up high and leave the door open. Watch it like a hawk. Crackle will harden up as it cools as well.

Lamb and beef: season and brown before roasting

For the best flavour when roasting red meat, the roast should be seasoned at least with salt and pepper before cooking, and browned. There are two ways to brown the roast. The first is for smaller roasts such as beef eye fillet and rolled lamb loin. Brown these on the stove top in a large chef pan, or the heavy-based baking dish you will be roasting it in. When browned on all sides place in the oven to finish cooking. The second method is for larger cuts like whole leg of lamb or rump roast, which won't overcook with a bit of a heat blast at the start of cooking. Give the roast 15 minutes or so at a higher temperature – add about 20°C and then turn it down to the temperature in the recipe once the outside has browned.

At the end of cooking, use the beautiful pan juices to make a jus or gravy. (See recipes on pages 136 and 137.)

Braising and slow cooking

Braising and slow cooking are methods that cook the ingredients with liquid. This can be done in a covered pot large enough to hold the ingredients (cast-iron enamel pots are great because of their evenly distributed heat), in a heavy-based baking dish tightly covered in the oven, or in a slow cooker. The best cuts of meat for slow cooking are secondary cuts – these are the cheaper cuts of meat that contain some fat and sinew. It is the breaking down of the fat and sinew that makes the meat moist and tender. Lean cuts of meat are not suitable for slow cooking.

Best cuts of meat for slow cooking:

Beef – beef shin, chuck steak, gravy beef, osso bucco, short ribs, ox tail (shin beef is my pick: see the recipe on page 40).

Lamb – shank, whole shoulder, diced shoulder, neck (shank is my pick; see the recipe on page 45).

Pork – ribs, diced shoulder, whole shoulder, belly, rashers (diced shoulder is my pick; see the recipe on page 59).

Top tips for braising and slow cooking

Brown the meat before putting it in the pot or slow-cooker with the liquid. This will greatly enhance the final flavour. If braising on the stovetop in a pot, make sure you keep the pot to a very slow simmer. My nan always said, 'Boil a stew, spoil a stew!' If you boil the pot, the meat will be tough and chewy. A good way to regulate the temperature is to brown the meat on the stovetop, then transfer the pot to the oven on a low temperature, or transfer the contents to the bowl of a slow-cooker which is especially designed to keep your food at the correct temperature for slow cooking.

Once the meat is cooked, if the sauce isn't thick or rich enough for your liking, you can remove the meat to a bowl using a slotted spoon, and allow the sauce to continue to reduce, uncovered, until it thickens up. Return the meat to the sauce.

Stir-frying

Stir-frying is a method of cooking small, thinly sliced pieces of meat or vegetables in very hot oil, while stirring or tossing continuously. The high heat allows the food to maintain great colour, flavour and texture.

Best cuts for stir-frying
Most lean, tender cuts of meat are good for stir-frying.

Beef – rump, sirloin, scotch fillet, skirt

Lamb – backstrap, fillet, leg steak

Pork – fillet, scotch fillet steak, loin steak

Top tips for stir-frying

Stir-frying is a very quick method of cooking, so it's important that you do all the prep before you start cooking. Vegetables should be cut into similar sizes as each other so that they cook rapidly and evenly. The meat should be sliced very thinly so that it cooks quickly. One way to do this is to place the meat flat on a plate in the freezer until it starts to solidify When it is firm, but not frozen solid, it's possible to slice it very thin. Make sure the meat comes back to room temperature before you stir-fry.

To cook, use a thin wok with a wooden handle. The large, non-stick heavy-based woks you find in homewares stores take a long time to react to changes in heat so I prefer to use the thin metal kind that you can buy inexpensively at any Asian grocery store. The lighter wok also allows you to toss the ingredients together.

Heat the wok over a high heat and add a splash of oil – rice bran, peanut or canola oil work well. First cook the meat in small batches, stirring all the time, then transfer to a bowl. Then cook the vegetables in batches, add whatever sauces and flavourings you are using and toss it all together in the wok. The key is fast, small batches and high heat.

Beef

Rib-eye on the bone

I love to serve this steak sliced on a board, with the bones, generously covered in chimichurri (see page 139) or salsa verde (page 138).

Serves 4   Prep time: 10 minutes   Cooking time: 20 minutes

2 rib-eye steaks, on the bone (about 500–600 g per steak)

¾ cup olive oil
Sea salt flakes

1 Heat a grill pan to a high heat and preheat the oven to 180°C.

2 Brush olive oil generously over the steaks and season with salt. Cook on the grill pan for 3–4 minutes on each side or until rich golden brown and char-marked. Using tongs, hold every surface of the steaks against the grill pan until browned all over, including the fat on the edge.

3 Place the pan in the oven for about 10 minutes for medium rare. Time will vary depending on the thickness of your steak and how you like it cooked. Remove the pan from the oven and rest the steaks on a board under foil for 8–10 minutes before serving.

Steak Diane

This was a hit on the menu back when I was a waitress at the Black Stump in Pennant Hills. It seems to have disappeared from steak houses and pub fare these days, but I'm leading a one-woman charge to bring it back.

Serves 4   Prep time: 15 minutes   Cooking time: 10 minutes

4 eye fillet steaks (about 180 g each)
2 tablespoons olive oil
½ teaspoon sea salt
4 cloves garlic, chopped
¼ cup brandy
2 tablespoons Worcestershire sauce

1 tablespoon Dijon mustard
¼ teaspoon freshly ground black pepper
½ cup thickened cream
½ cup flat-leaf parsley, finely chopped

1 Cut the fillet steaks in half horizontally, to make 8 thinner medallions of

meat. Place the medallions between 2 sheets of plastic wrap and pound gently with a meat mallet until about 5 mm thick.

2 In a large, non-stick frypan over high heat, place 2 teaspoons olive oil. Season the steak with a sprinkle of sea salt, and when the oil is hot, place 4 medallions in the pan. Cook for about 1 minute, or until a lovely golden crust has started to form. Flip and cook on the second side for another minute. Remove from the pan, cover and set aside, then repeat with the remaining 4 medallions of steak.

3 Reduce the heat to medium. Place the remaining olive oil in the pan and sauté the garlic for about a minute or until soft and fragrant. Pour in the brandy and allow it to reduce. Place ½ cup of water in the pan, along with the Worcestershire sauce, mustard and pepper and stir to combine well. Allow the sauce to reduce until dark and becoming thick. Add the cream and stir well. Bring to the boil and allow to simmer for another 2 minutes. The sauce is ready when it is a little thickened, mid-brown and very flavoursome.

4 Serve the steak with the sauce poured over the top and sprinkled with fresh parsley.

Beef bourguignon

Serve this French-style casserole with mashed potato, or cauliflower puree (see page 190).

Serves 6   Prep time: 30 minutes   Cooking time: 2½ hours

½ cup plain flour
½ teaspoon salt
¼ teaspoon ground white pepper
⅓ cup olive oil
1.5 kg stewing beef (shin or
    gravy beef), cut into 3 cm cubes
12 pearl onions, peeled (see notes)

250 g tiny button
    mushrooms (see notes)
4 cloves garlic, chopped
¼ cup tomato paste
3 bay leaves
1 cup red wine
1 cup beef stock

1 Preheat the oven to 160°C.

2 Combine the flour, salt and pepper in a bowl.

3 In a large enamel pot on the stove top, heat a tablespoon of oil over high heat. Toss a third of the meat in the flour and shake off the excess – take care with this step as loose flour will burn in the pot. Place the meat in the pot and brown on all sides then remove to a bowl. Take your time with this step to ensure a good golden colour, as this is important to the flavour of the finished

dish. Repeat with the rest of the meat, using a further tablespoon of oil with each batch. If the pot has any burnt flour, wipe it clean with a paper towel before moving on to the next step.

4 Reduce the heat to medium and add the remaining oil. Sauté the onions and mushrooms for 3–4 minutes until light golden. Add the garlic and sauté until soft but not brown. Add the tomato paste and stir for a further minute.

5 Return the meat to the pan, then add the bay leaves. Pour in the red wine, followed by the beef stock. Cover and bake in the oven for 2 hours or until the meat is soft. If the sauce needs to thicken, cook without the lid for 30 minutes.

Note: If you can't buy pearl or pickling onions, buy the smallest brown onions you can find; then peel and halve them before using. If the button mushrooms are larger than 2 cm across the top, halve them.

Marinated eye fillet roast

This is a great recipe for the barbecue.

Serves 6   Prep time: 10 minutes + marinating time
Cooking time: 25–50 minutes

1 tablespoon ground fennel seeds	¼ cup Dijon mustard
1 tablespoon ground coriander seeds	1.5 kg eye fillet of beef (thick end)
1 tablespoon ground cumin seeds	¼ cup olive oil
2 teaspoons ground red chilli	Horseradish cream or
3 cloves garlic, crushed	hot mustard, for serving

1 Preheat the oven or hooded barbecue to 180°C.

2 Combine the spices, chilli, garlic and mustard and rub all over the beef fillet. Place in a snap-lock plastic bag and refrigerate for at least 6 hours or overnight.

3 In a large chef pan, heat olive oil over medium-high heat. Brown the fillet on all sides.

4 Place the pan in the oven or the barbecue, covered with the hood. Roast the beef for 20 minutes for rare, 30 minutes for medium, or 45 minutes or more for medium–well done. Rest, under foil, for at least 10 minutes.

5 Serve with a good-quality horseradish cream or hot mustard.

Roast beef with red wine jus

Serves 8   Prep time: 20 minutes   Cooking time: up to 2½ hours

3 cloves garlic
1 bunch thyme, leaves picked,
  stalks reserved for jus
  (see page 137)
1 tablespoon olive oil

1 teaspoon sea salt flakes
½ teaspoon ground black pepper
2.5 kg whole beef rump
Red wine jus, to serve
  (see page 137)

1 Preheat the oven to 180°C.

2 Combine the garlic, thyme leaves, olive oil, salt and pepper in a bowl. Spread all over the top and sides of the beef roast. Bake on a rack over an oven tray for the desired time: allow 1¼ hours for rare, 1¾–2 hours for medium, 2¼–2½ hours for well done. Times will vary according to your oven, too.

3 Remove the beef from the roasting tray to a warm place and cover with foil to rest for at least 30 minutes before serving. Serve with red wine jus.

Roast beef with Yorkshire pudding

Serves 6   Prep time: 10 minutes   Cooking time: 2 hours 20 minutes

2.5 kg bolar beef roast
1 head garlic, halved crossways
1 teaspoon olive oil
1 teaspoon sea salt
½ teaspoon ground black pepper
1 teaspoon dill seeds

2 eggs
½ cup milk
½ cup flour
For serving: your favourite roast
  vegetables and gravy
  (see pages 136 and 137)

1 Preheat the oven to 220°C (200°C fan-forced). Place the beef in a non-stick baking tray and place the garlic, cut side up, alongside. Drizzle both with the oil. Sprinkle the salt, pepper and dill seeds over the beef. Bake for 30 minutes or until the top of the beef browns. Reduce the temperature to 170°C (150°C fan-forced) and cook for a further 1½ hours. Remove from the oven and rest under foil. After resting, the beef should be about medium; reduce or increase the cooking time according to your taste. Pour any fat from the pan into a jug and reserve for the puddings. Reserve the pan juices, too, if you wish to use them for gravy. Squeeze the flesh from the garlic head and season with a little salt. Set aside to serve with the beef.

2 Increase the oven temperature to 220°C (200°C fan-forced).

3 In a small bowl, whisk together the eggs and milk. Add the flour and beat well to ensure there are no lumps.

4 Place 1 teaspoon beef dripping (fat) into each base of a 6-hole Texas (large) muffin tin. (If there is not enough fat from the beef roast, you can use vegetable oil instead.) Place the tin into the hot oven until the fat is very hot. When the fat is hot, carefully remove the tin from the oven and place ¼ cup batter into each hole. The batter should start to sizzle immediately. Place the tin back in the oven and bake for 10 minutes, until golden brown.

5 Serve the roast beef and puddings immediately with your favourite roast vegetables and gravy.

Curried beef rice

Serves 4   Prep time: 10 minutes   Cooking time: up to 20 minutes

1½ cups basmati rice
2¾ cups beef stock
½ cup slivered almonds
2 tablespoons olive oil
500 g beef mince
2 brown onions, peeled and
  quartered
2 cloves garlic
2 long green chillies, seeded

1 tablespoon curry powder
2 medium zucchinis,
  quartered lengthways then
  cut into 1 cm chunks
400 g tin tomatoes
1 cup plain Greek yoghurt
¼ cup coriander leaves
¼ cup harissa (see page 144)
1 lemon, cut into 8 wedges

1 Place the rice and beef stock in a rice cooker, or microwave on high for 16 minutes.

2 Heat a chef pan over medium-high heat and add the almonds. Toast until they are a light golden brown then remove from the pan and set aside.

3 Add 1 tablespoon oil to the hot pan. Sauté the beef mince until starting to brown, stirring with a wooden spoon and squashing any lumps. Reduce the heat to medium-low.

4 While the beef is cooking, place the onion, garlic and chilli in the bowl of a mini food processor. Blitz until finely chopped. Add the onion mixture and curry powder to the pan and stir through the beef. Cook for a further 1–2 minutes until soft and fragrant.

5 Add the zucchini, tomatoes and half of the yoghurt to the pan and stir through. Increase the heat to high and bring to the boil. Place the lid on the pan and cook for about 5 minutes.

6 When the rice is cooked, remove from the rice cooker or microwave and add to the beef in the pan. Stir through and cook until the mixture is quite dry. Serve to the table scattered with the almonds and coriander leaves, with the remaining yoghurt, harissa and lemon wedges on the side.

Oxtail stew

Serves 4   Prep time: 20 minutes   Cooking time: 2 hours

1 cup plain flour
2 teaspoons table salt
1 teaspoon ground white pepper
1.5 kg oxtail
¼ cup olive oil
2 brown onions, finely chopped
3 cloves garlic, finely chopped

200 g Swiss brown mushrooms,
 thinly sliced
2 sprigs thyme leaves
2 bay leaves
1 cup red wine
3 cups beef stock
Mashed potato, for serving
 (see page 190)

1 Preheat the oven to 160°C.

2 Combine the flour, salt and pepper in a bowl. Trim the oxtail of any really big pieces of visible fat. Toss the meat through the flour.

3 In a heavy, enamel casserole pot (with lid), heat 1 tablespoon olive oil. Shake the excess flour off the oxtail and place half in the pot. Brown the meat – take your time doing this to ensure all the surfaces of the meat are golden, this is important for the flavour. Remove the meat to a bowl and repeat with another tablespoon of oil and the remaining meat. Reserve the excess flour.

4 Wipe out the pot and return to the heat. Place the last tablespoon of oil in the pot and sauté the onions and garlic for 2 minutes or until golden and translucent. Add the mushrooms and sauté for a further 5 minutes, until soft and browned. Add the thyme and bay leaves.

5 Pour the red wine into the pot, followed by the stock, and return the meat to the pot. Put the lid on and place in the oven for 1½ hours. After this time the meat should be very tender.

6 With a slotted spoon, remove the meat to a bowl and place the pot back on the stovetop. Add enough water to the reserved flour to make a mixture about the consistency of cream. Whisk this into the pot. Bring the sauce to a boil and cook, stirring, until it is rich and has the thickness of gravy. Return the meat to the pot and serve the pot to the table with mashed potato.

Cottage pie

A cheap and cheerful dinner that tastes just as lovely reheated for lunch the next day.

Serves 6   Prep time: 10 minutes   Cooking time: 40–50 minutes

4 Sebago or Dutch cream
  potatoes (about 800 g)
50 g butter
⅓ cup milk
1 teaspoon salt
1 teaspoon vegetable oil
2 small brown onions, chopped

2 medium carrots, diced
3 celery stalks, diced
750 g lean beef mince
½ cup tomato paste
¼ cup plain flour
1 cup beef stock
Ground black pepper

1 Preheat oven to 180°C. Peel the potatoes and boil in a large pot of salted water until tender. Drain and mash immediately with half the butter, the milk and half the salt. Set aside.

2 In a large frypan or chef pan, heat the oil over a medium-high heat and add the onion, carrot and celery. Sauté for 5 minutes or until transparent and fragrant. Add the beef and cook for a further 6–8 minutes, stirring and breaking up any lumps with a spoon, until all the meat has browned.

3 Add the tomato paste and sauté for a further minute. Sprinkle the flour over the meat mixture and stir to mix through. Stir in the stock, a little at a time, until all incorporated. The meat mixture should be a lovely dark brown colour, and the gravy will be rich. Season with remaining salt and pepper to taste.

4 Place the meat mixture into a 22 cm square glass or ceramic baking dish. Carefully spread the mashed potato over the top and rough it up with a fork – this will help to create lovely crispy bits on top. Dot the top with the remaining butter.

5 Bake for 30–40 minutes or until the top is a deep golden brown.

Korean barbecue beef,
recipe page 33

Korean barbecue beef

Serves 4   Prep time: 20 minutes   Cooking time: 15 minutes

1 kiwi fruit or 1 small pear,
  peeled
800 g beef eye fillet, sliced
  3–4 mm thick
3 cloves garlic, crushed
2 tablespoons soy sauce
1 tablespoon sesame oil
2 tablespoons Shaoxing wine
  (Chinese cooking wine)

2 tablespoons brown sugar
½ teaspoon freshly ground
  black pepper
2 tablespoons peanut oil
For serving: oak leaf lettuce
  leaves, cooked jasmine rice,
  thinly sliced long red chillies,
  lime wedges

1 Place the kiwi fruit or pear into the bowl of a mini food processor and blitz until it forms a paste. Toss the paste through the beef and allow to stand for 10 minutes.

2 In a small bowl, combine the garlic, soy sauce, sesame and peanut oil, Shaoxing wine, brown sugar and pepper. Stir through the beef and marinate for 30 minutes.

3 Heat a barbecue or grill pan to a very high heat. When the grill is smoking, cook the beef for 1 minute on each side. You should get good char marks.

4 Serve the beef in a lettuce leaf with a little rice and sliced chillies and a squeeze of lime.

Veal scallopini alla funghi

Serves 4   Prep time: 15 minutes   Cooking time: 20 minutes

4 large or 8 small
  veal schnitzels (about 800 g)
3 tablespoons butter
1 tablespoon olive oil
2 cloves garlic, finely chopped
400 g button mushrooms, sliced
1 tablespoon plain flour

½ cup brandy
½ cup beef stock
½ cup thickened cream
2 teaspoons Dijon mustard
Salt and ground
  white pepper to taste

1 Place the veal schnitzels between 2 sheets of plastic wrap and beat with a rolling pin or meat mallet until very thin.

2 Place 1 tablespoon butter and olive oil in a chef pan over medium-high heat.

Veal parmigiana,
recipe page 35

Cook the veal quickly, only about 2 minutes each side. Set aside on a plate and cover.

3 Into the same pan, add the remaining butter, garlic and mushrooms. Sauté until the mushrooms are browned. (They will release a lot of fluid, then the fluid will evaporate and they will go brown.)

4 Sprinkle the flour over the mushrooms and pour in the brandy. Stir until well combined. Stir in the stock, cream and mustard and simmer until the sauce reduces slightly. Taste, and season with salt and pepper. Serve the sauce over the veal.

Veal parmigiana

To make this meal very quick and easy, use a good quality store-bought pasta sauce instead of making the tomato sauce. Thinly sliced chicken breast can be substituted for the veal.

Serves 4   Prep time: 20 minutes   Cooking time: about 25 minutes

2 teaspoons olive oil
1 brown onion, chopped
2 cloves garlic, crushed
2 x 400 g tins chopped tomatoes
1 tablespoon sugar
½ teaspoon salt
½ teaspoon dried oregano leaves
½ cup plain flour
¼ teaspoon salt
¼ teaspoon ground
  white pepper

2 eggs, beaten with
  1 tablespoon water
3 cups homemade or
  panko breadcrumbs
4 large or 8 small veal
  schnitzels (about 800 g)
Vegetable oil, for frying
½ cup grated tasty cheese
½ cup grated mozzarella cheese

1 Heat the oil in a medium saucepan and gently sauté the onion and garlic until it is soft and fragrant but not brown. Stir in the tomatoes, sugar, salt and oregano and simmer for 15 minutes or until it has reduced and thickened slightly.

2 Meanwhile, combine the flour, salt and pepper in a shallow dish. Place the beaten egg and the breadcrumbs in separate shallow dishes. Working with 1 piece at a time, dip the veal into the flour, then the egg and then into the breadcrumbs. Place it on a clean plate.

3 Heat a large chef pan or frypan over a medium-high heat, add the vegetable oil and fry the veal for 2–3 minutes each side or until golden brown. Only fry a couple of pieces at a time to avoid overcrowding the pan.

4 Preheat the griller to a high heat. Arrange the cooked veal on a lined baking tray and top each piece with a couple of generous spoonfuls of tomato sauce and a good handful of the tasty and mozzarella cheese. Place under the grill for 2 minutes, or until the cheese begins to turn golden. Serve immediately.

Note: You can also serve the veal as a plain schnitzel but make sure you provide a few lemon wedges!

Veal Oscar

Serves 4   Prep time: 20 minutes   Cooking time: 15 minutes

4 large or 8 small
  veal schnitzels (about 800 g)
3 tablespoons butter
1 tablespoon olive oil
2 cloves garlic, crushed

12 green (raw) prawns, shelled
  and deveined, tails intact
2 bunches asparagus, trimmed
1 quantity bearnaise sauce
  (see page 138)

1 Place the veal schnitzels between 2 sheets of plastic wrap and beat with a rolling pin until very thin.

2 Place 1 tablespoon butter and olive oil in a chef pan over medium-high heat. Cook the veal quickly, only about 2 minutes each side. Set aside on a plate and cover with foil to rest.

3 Into the same pan, add the remaining butter, garlic and prawns. Sauté until the prawns are just cooked through. Remove from the pan. Add the asparagus to the pan and sauté for 1–2 minutes until tender but still vibrant green and al dente.

4 Serve the veal topped with the prawns and asparagus and drizzled generously with the bearnaise sauce.

Bacon-wrapped glazed meatloaf

Serves 4–6   Prep time: 20 minutes   Cooking time: 1¼ hours

1 teaspoon olive oil
2 brown onions, diced
750 g beef mince
400 g (about 4) pork sausages,
  skin removed
2 cups breadcrumbs
⅓ cup tomato paste
1 tablespoon dried oregano leaves

1 cup grated tasty cheese
½ bunch parsley, roughly chopped
1 egg
½ teaspoon salt
¼ teaspoon pepper
6 whole rashers bacon,
  rind removed

For the glaze
⅓ **cup tomato sauce**
⅓ **cup apricot jam**

¼ **cup soy sauce**

1 Preheat the oven to 180°C.

2 Heat the oil in a frypan over medium heat and sauté the onion until soft. Remove from the pan to cool.

3 In a large bowl, combine the beef mince, sausage, breadcrumbs, tomato paste, oregano, cheese, parsley, egg, salt and pepper. Using your hands, mix the ingredients. Really massage the meat until it is sticky.

4 Place a wire rack in a baking dish and lay the bacon vertically across it, alternating the eye end of the rasher. Place the beef mixture along the bacon and shape it into a cylindrical loaf. Bring the bacon up and over to wrap the beef.

5 For the glaze, combine the tomato sauce, apricot jam and soy sauce in a microwave-safe jug and heat for 1 minute on high or until the jam melts and the glaze can be stirred to combine.

6 Paint the glaze over the meatloaf and bake for 1–1¼ hours, basting every 15 minutes with the glaze.

7 Slice thickly to serve.

Beef Wellington

Serves 4   Prep time: 45 minutes   Cooking time: 35 minutes

500 g beef eye fillet, thick end
1 teaspoon salt
½ teaspoon ground black pepper
2 tablespoons olive oil
50 g butter
500 g button mushrooms,
  finely chopped
4 cloves garlic
2 teaspoons fresh thyme leaves

12 slices prosciutto (see note)
2 tablespoons Dijon mustard
2 quantities rough puff pastry
  (see page 234) or 2 sheets frozen
  puff pastry
2 eggs, lightly beaten
Red wine jus (see page 137),
  for serving

1 Sprinkle the beef fillet with salt and pepper. Place a large, non-stick chef pan over medium-high heat and heat the olive oil. Brown the eye fillet thoroughly on all sides. Remove from the pan and set aside to rest.

Rissoles, recipe
page 39

Meat

38

2 Add the butter, mushrooms, garlic and thyme. Sauté for 7–8 minutes or until the liquid has evaporated and mushrooms are starting to brown.

3 Lay a 50 cm piece of plastic wrap vertically on the bench in front of you. Lay the prosciutto slices, vertically and slightly overlapping on the long edge, along the bottom edge of the plastic wrap. Carefully spread the mushroom mixture over the prosciutto. Spread the mustard over the beef fillet and place it at the bottom of the prosciutto. Using the plastic wrap to help lift and roll, tightly wrap the beef in the prosciutto. Wrap the entire roll tightly with another sheet of plastic wrap and place in the fridge for 30 minutes to chill.

4 Preheat the oven to 200°C.

5 Join the 2 sheets of puff pastry together (or roll out your 50 cm x 20 cm rough puff rectangle to 3–4 mm thickness). Remove the plastic wrap from the beef and prosciutto roll and place it on the pastry, then roll the pastry up tightly. Place the roll seam side down on a lined baking tray and cut some small vents in the top. Brush thoroughly with the beaten eggs and bake for 35 minutes. Rest, uncovered, for 15 minutes before carving to serve. The ideal gravy is the red wine jus (see page 137).

Note: Ask your deli server to slice the prosciutto paper-thin for you.

Rissoles

Serves 4   Prep time: 15 minutes   Cooking time: 20 minutes

500 g beef mince
1 egg, lightly beaten
½ cup grated tasty cheese
2 large garlic cloves, crushed
1 medium carrot, grated
1 brown onion, grated

1 cup fresh breadcrumbs
2 tablespoons Dijon mustard
¼ cup tomato sauce
¼ teaspoon salt
¼ teaspoon pepper
1 teaspoon oil, for frying

1 Preheat the oven to 180°C.

2 In a bowl, combine all the ingredients except the oil. Using your hands, mix thoroughly. Form into 8 equal patties.

3 Heat an ovenproof frypan over medium-high heat, add the oil and brown the rissoles on both sides. Place the pan into the oven and bake for 20 minutes or until the rissoles are golden brown and cooked through.

Osso bucco

This can be done in the oven in an ovenproof casserole dish, or started in a pan and finished in the slow cooker. Either way, it will fill the house with beautiful aromas.

Serves 4   Prep time: 20 minutes   Cooking time: up to 3 hours

½ cup plain flour
¼ teaspoon salt
¼ teaspoon ground
  white pepper
4 veal osso bucco (about 1.2 kg)
3 tablespoons oil
2 carrots, diced into 1 cm pieces
3 celery stalks, cut in half
  lengthways and cut into
  1 cm pieces

2 onions, diced
4 cloves garlic, chopped
¼ cup tomato paste
1½ cups white wine
1½ cups veal or beef stock
800 g tin chopped tomatoes
2 bay leaves

For gremolata

½ cup flat-leaf parsley,
  finely chopped
1 clove garlic, chopped

1 tablespoon finely grated
  lemon zest
¼ teaspoon cracked black pepper

1 Preheat the oven to 150°C.

2 Combine the flour, salt and pepper in a large bowl. Coat the osso bucco in the flour. Be careful to shake off the excess flour, otherwise it will burn in the pot. Reserve the excess seasoned flour to add to the sauce.

3 Heat 1 tablespoon oil in an enamel casserole pot over a medium-high heat. Brown 2 osso bucco until golden, and transfer to a plate. Repeat with the remaining 2 pieces. Make sure you get good golden colour as this will be important for the flavour. If there is any burnt flour in the pot after this process, carefully wipe it out with a paper towel.

4 Reduce the heat to medium. Heat the remaining tablespoon of oil, add the carrot, celery, onion and garlic. Sauté for 3–4 minutes or until the onion is translucent but not brown. Add the tomato paste to the vegetables and sauté for a further minute.

5 Into the pot, add the wine, stock, tomatoes and bay leaves. Add any of the leftover flour from coating the osso bucco and stir through.

6 Return the veal to the pot. Make sure it is all submerged in the liquid – any meat poking out the top will be tough and dry. Put the lid on the pot and bake

Osso bucco, recipe
page 40

in the oven for 2–3 hours. Check from 2 hours onwards, and when the veal is soft and falling away from the bone, it is ready.

7 When the meat is cooked, if the sauce needs to be thickened further, remove the meat and keep under foil. Place the pot on a medium-low heat on the stove top and boil until the sauce is as thick as you like it. Make sure you keep stirring so nothing burns.

8 For the gremolata, combine the ingredients and sprinkle over the osso bucco before serving.

Note: Serve this simply on mashed potato (page 190), Milanese risotto (page 184) or soft polenta.

Bolognese sauce

This is such a versatile recipe. We usually make a double batch as it freezes so well. Not only great with the traditional spaghetti, this is lovely on baked potatoes with sour cream, or baked into a puff pastry parcel.

Serves 6–8   Prep time: 15 minutes
Cooking time: 4–5 hours in slow cooker or 2 hours on stovetop

1 teaspoon olive oil
2 brown onions, chopped
2 cloves garlic, crushed
500 g beef mince
500 g pork mince

2 x 800 g tins crushed tomatoes
1 tablespoon dried oregano leaves
2 tablespoons sugar
1 teaspoon salt

1 In a large non-stick chef pan, heat the olive oil over a medium heat. Add the onion and garlic and stir until soft but not brown. Add the mince to the pan and brown. Using a wooden spoon, make sure you get rid of any lumps.

2 If you have a slow cooker, put the mince in along with the tomatoes, oregano, sugar and salt. Simmer uncovered on the high setting for 4–5 hours, stirring occasionally. The sauce initially appears quite runny and not a very rich colour. As it cooks and reduces, it achieves a thick consistency and a beautiful red colour. You will know when it's ready – it becomes very aromatic. To make the recipe on the stovetop is equally effective, but you need to make sure it doesn't burn on the bottom of the pot. Keep it over a very low heat, uncovered, and stir it frequently, for about 2 hours.

Lamb

Roast leg of lamb

Serves 6–8   Prep time: 5 minutes   Cooking time: 1½ hours

2.5 kg lamb leg
3 cloves garlic, sliced lengthways

2 rosemary sprigs, leaves removed
Salt and ground black pepper

1 Preheat the oven to 180°C.

2 Using a small sharp knife, pierce the lamb every 3 cm or so. Stuff each incision with a slice of garlic and a few rosemary leaves. Sprinkle the lamb with salt and ground black pepper.

3 Roast for 1¼–1½ hours for medium lamb. Remove from the oven and rest in the pan under foil for 30 minutes.

Note: A rule of thumb for roasting lamb is 15 minutes, then add 15 minutes per 500 g. Drain some but not all of the fat and use the pan juices to make a gravy or jus (pages 136 and 137).

Lamb chop tray bake

Serves 4   Prep time: 10 minutes   Cooking time: 1 hour

½ cup plain flour
½ teaspoon salt
¼ teaspoon ground
  white pepper
12 lamb forequarter chops
  (about 1.2 kg)
3 large brown onions,
  sliced ½ cm thick
3 large carrots, peeled and
  cut into 2 cm thick slices
2 large Sebago potatoes, peeled
  and cut into wedges

¼ cup Worcestershire sauce
¾ cup tomato sauce
¼ cup whole grain mustard
2 cloves garlic, crushed
⅓ cup brown sugar
3 large zucchini, cut into
  2 cm thick slices
½ bunch flat-leaf parsley,
  roughly chopped

1 Preheat the oven to 180°C.

2 Mix the salt and pepper into the flour and dust the chops.

Lamb chop tray bake,
recipe page 43

3 Lay the onion and carrot slices over the base of a large baking dish. (It must be large enough to contain the chops in a single layer.) Lay the floured chops over the onions. Nestle the potatoes around the chops.

4 In a jug, combine the Worcestershire sauce, tomato sauce, mustard, garlic and sugar with ½ cup of water and pour over the contents of the baking dish. Cover tightly with foil and put into the oven.

5 After 20 minutes, remove the foil and, using a spoon, baste the meat and potatoes with the liquid in the dish. Cover again, and return to the oven for a further 20 minutes.

6 Remove the foil and, using the oil that has rendered out of the chops, baste the potatoes again. Add the zucchini to the baking dish, making sure it is nestled in among the chops and potatoes. Return the dish, uncovered, to the oven for 20 minutes. The potatoes will brown and the sauce will thicken and become beautifully rich. Serve scattered with the parsley.

Meat

45

Lamb shank cacciatore

Serves 4   Prep time: 15 minutes   Cooking time: 4 hours

½ cup plain flour
½ teaspoon salt
¼ teaspoon ground white pepper
4 lamb shanks, frenched
3 tablespoons olive oil
2 brown onions, diced
4 cloves garlic, crushed
1 teaspoon dried oregano leaves
1 cup red wine

2 cups beef stock
800 g tin crushed tomatoes
2 teaspoons salt
24 pitted Kalamata olives
½ bunch flat-leaf parsley,
  roughly chopped
Mashed potatoes, for serving
  (see page 190)

1 Turn the slow cooker on to the high setting.

2 Place the flour, salt and pepper in a large bowl and mix well. Toss the lamb shanks in the flour and shake off any excess.

3 Heat a large, non-stick chef pan over medium-high heat and add the oil. Place the shanks in the pan and turn until brown on all sides. Remove from the pan and place in the bowl of the slow cooker.

4 Reduce the heat to medium and add the onions, garlic and oregano to the pan. Sauté for 3–4 minutes until the onion is starting to soften. Add the red wine and simmer for a few seconds before adding this mixture to the slow cooker. Add the beef stock, crushed tomatoes and salt to the slow cooker and cook with the lid on for 2 hours. Remove the lid and cook for a further 2 hours. Add the olives in the last hour of cooking.

5 The lamb is cooked when it is buttery soft and falling off the bone. The sauce should be quite rich in flavour. Serve the lamb with the chopped parsley over the top, with mashed potatoes.

Lamb and pine nut sausage rolls

Makes 96 cocktail sausage rolls   Prep time: 10 minutes
Cooking time: 25 minutes

1 kg lamb sausage mince
  (buy lamb sausages and
  remove the skins)
500 g lamb mince
2 brown onions, finely chopped
2 cloves garlic, finely chopped
2 cups fresh breadcrumbs
¼ cup French mustard
2 tablespoons ground cumin seed
2 tablespoons ground coriander seed

1 tablespoon dried oregano leaves
¾ cup pine nuts, toasted and
  roughly chopped
Zest of 1 lemon
1 teaspoon salt
½ teaspoon pepper
6 sheets frozen puff pastry
1 egg, beaten with
  1 tablespoon water

1 Preheat the oven to 200°C. Line a baking tray with baking paper.

2 In a bowl, place all the ingredients except for the pastry and egg. Using your hands, work the mixture until very well combined.

3 Lay the pastry out on a work surface and cut each sheet in half. Work with the pastry still a little bit firm from the freezer as it is easier to handle.

4 Divide the sausage mixture into 12 pieces and place a piece lengthways on each pastry half-sheet. Fold the 2 pastry sides over the sausage mixture and gently press to join.

5 Turn the rolls over, and cut each into 8 pieces using a sharp knife. Place the sausage rolls seam side down on the baking tray. Brush the pastry with the beaten egg.

6 Bake for 20–25 minutes until the pastry is puffed and golden.

Crumbed cutlets

This was my favourite meal as a kid but, of course, that was back when lamb was the cheap meat! Lamb cutlets are more of a treat these days.

Serves 4   Prep time: 15 minutes   Cooking time: 20 minutes

12 lamb cutlets (about 1.2 kg)
1 cup plain flour
Salt and pepper
2 eggs

2 cups fresh breadcrumbs
2 tablespoons olive oil
Lemon wedges, to serve

1 With a meat mallet, gently hammer the lamb cutlets until they are just less than 1 cm thick.

2 Combine the flour with salt and pepper in a shallow dish. Beat the eggs with ¼ cup of water in another shallow dish. Place the breadcrumbs in a third shallow dish.

3 Set up the cutlets to the left of the other three dishes, to create a production line. Dip each cutlet into the flour, then bathe in the egg mix, and toss generously in the breadcrumbs. Place onto a clean plate.

4 Meanwhile, heat 1 tablespoon olive oil in a large heavy-based chef pan over medium-high heat. Cook 6 cutlets for 4 minutes each side or until golden brown and cooked to medium. Clean out the pan, add the remaining olive oil and cook the remaining cutlets.

5 Rest the cutlets for 5 minutes or so before serving on the plate. But no longer!

Stuffed eggplant

Serves 4   Prep time: 10 minutes   Cooking time: 30 minutes

2 eggplants
2 teaspoons salt
¼ cup olive oil
500 g lamb mince
3 brown onions, diced
4 cloves garlic, chopped
½ teaspoon ground cumin seed

½ teaspoon cinnamon
¼ teaspoon nutmeg
½ teaspoon pepper
4 slices bread, processed to
  a coarse crumb
1⅓ cups grated tasty cheese

1 Preheat the oven to 200°C.

2 Cut the eggplants in half lengthways and scoop the flesh out of each half, leaving a thin layer of flesh in the skins. Cut the removed flesh into 2 cm cubes and sprinkle with half the salt.

3 Heat the olive oil in a large frypan over medium-high heat and fry the mince until brown and cooked through. Rinse the eggplant cubes and squeeze dry then add to the mince, along with the onion, garlic, spices, remaining salt

and pepper. Stir until the onion and garlic are fragrant and translucent. Stir through the crumbed bread.

4 Pile the mixture into the eggplant halves and top each half with ⅓ cup cheese. Place on a lined baking tray and bake for 20 minutes or until the cheese is golden and bubbling.

Roasted lamb rump with garlic, thyme and mustard

Serves 4   Prep time: 15 minutes   Cooking time: about 15 minutes

3 lamb rumps (about 350–400 g each)
4 cloves garlic, chopped
¼ cup whole grain mustard
2 tablespoons fresh thyme leaves

½ teaspoon garlic powder
½ teaspoon salt
Freshly ground black pepper
Olive oil, for drizzling

For the sauce
½ cup white wine
½ cup chicken stock (see page 152)

1 clove garlic, halved
1 rosemary sprig

1 Turn the lamb rump upside down on a chopping board. Carefully create a split lengthways, only cutting about two-thirds of the way through the rump.

2 Combine the garlic, mustard and thyme leaves, and stuff a quarter of the mix into the incision of each rump. Tie the rump with cooking twine to create a neat cylindrical shape.

3 Combine the garlic powder with salt and plenty of pepper and scatter on a tray. Roll a lamb rump through the seasoning to coat thoroughly. Repeat with the remaining rumps.

4 Seal the rumps in a frypan with olive oil over high heat, until all sides are golden brown. Reduce the heat to medium and continue to cook, turning, until cooked to your liking. Depending on your pan and the thickness of the rumps, this will be about 10 minutes. Test by piercing with a skewer: pink juices indicate medium; bright red indicates a little further cooking time is required. Remove the meat from the pan and rest under foil for 10 minutes before serving.

5 Meanwhile, deglaze the pan with white wine. Stir in the chicken stock, garlic and rosemary. Simmer until the sauce is reduced to about ⅔ cup, and thickened, then strain into a serving jug.

Stuffed eggplant,
recipe page 47

Slow-roasted lamb shoulder

Serves 4   Prep time: 15 minutes   Cooking time: 4 hours 20 minutes

6 cloves garlic, crushed
1 tablespoon dried oregano leaves
1 tablespoon dried ground
 cumin seed
¼ teaspoon ground black pepper
1 teaspoon sea salt flakes

1 teaspoon olive oil
Zest of 2 lemons
1.5–2 kg butterflied
 lamb shoulder
1 cup red wine

1 Preheat the oven to 200°C (180°C fan-forced).

2 In a small bowl, combine the garlic, oregano, cumin, pepper, salt, olive oil and lemon zest.

3 Place the lamb shoulder, skin side up, in a large baking tray. Rub the spice mixture all over the skin. Bake for 20 minutes, or until the spiced lamb is becoming golden and fragrant. Remove the tray from the oven and reduce the temperature to 140°C (120°C fan-forced). Pour the red wine into the base of the tray, cover very tightly with foil and bake for 3½–4 hours.

4 Remove the tray from the oven and take the lamb out. It will be very soft. It can be served immediately. If you are cooking the day before, place the lamb onto another tray then place a tray with a weight on top. Refrigerate overnight. This will enable neat carving while cold and a gentle reheat before serving.

5 Use the pan juices to create a sauce according to directions for a jus on page 137.

Rack of lamb with rosemary and mustard crust

Serves 4   Prep time: 20 minutes   Cooking time: 15 minutes

3 cloves garlic, crushed
Zest and juice of 1 lemon
2 tablespoons olive oil
Freshly ground black pepper
4 racks of lamb (each rack
 with 4 chops), trimmed

¼ cup Dijon mustard
1 tablespoon rosemary leaves,
 finely chopped
½ teaspoon salt

1 Preheat the oven to 200°C.

2 Combine the garlic, lemon zest, 2 teaspoons olive oil and a twist of black pepper in a bowl. Put the lamb racks into the bowl and turn several times to ensure the meat is coated. Set aside for 10 minutes.

3 In a small bowl, combine the mustard, rosemary and salt and spread over the meat. In a large baking tray, place the racks in pairs with their bones intertwined, so that they stand up. Bake for 10–15 minutes for pink-centred lamb, or until cooked to your liking. Rest under foil for 5 minutes before serving.

Pork

Slow-roasted pork belly with apricot sauce

Serves 4   Prep time: 10 minutes   Cooking time: 3 hours

2 kg piece of pork belly, bones removed
Olive oil
Salt

¼ cup arrowroot or cornflour
3 cups chicken stock (see page 152) or store bought
3 cups apricot nectar

1 Make sure the pork skin is very dry. If required, leave it uncovered in the fridge for 24 hours before cooking.

2 Using a Stanley knife or a Mickey knife, score the rind. Cut into the fat but not into the flesh. I like to score the rind in lines about ½–1 cm apart. Make sure the belly has no stray bristles on it. Rub the rind with a little olive oil and massage salt thoroughly into it.

3 Preheat the oven to 220°C.

4 Place the pork on a rack in a roasting pan, and bake for 30 minutes or until the skin begins to puff up and look crisp. Reduce the oven to 140°C and continue to roast, uncovered, for a further 2½ hours. Remove from the oven and rest well. (See note.)

5 Place the roasting pan on the stovetop over medium heat and stir the arrowroot into the pan juices. Use a spatula to scrape up any tasty brown bits from the bottom of the pan. Add about ¼ cup chicken stock and stir until the arrowroot is incorporated and thickened. Add another ¼ cup stock and stir again, then keep repeating this process until the sauce is becoming looser.

Stir in the apricot nectar and boil for 5 minutes or until thickened. Strain the gravy into a jug for serving.

Note: If you are making this for a dinner party, you can cook the pork the day before and chill it in between 2 baking trays with weights on top. When chilled it's easier to carve. Reheat in a gentle oven, and if needed refresh the crackling by putting the pieces skin side down in a hot frypan before serving.

Roast loin of pork

Roast pork is a traditional favourite for Christmas and my boys love it. Whenever I roast pork, I ask the butcher if he has any extra rind, and if he does, I cook it separately. It ensures that everyone has as much crackling as they want!

Serves 4–6   Prep time: 10 minutes   Cooking time: 2 hours

1 boned rolled loin of
  pork (about 2 kg)

Olive oil, for rubbing
1 tablespoon sea salt

1 Preheat the oven to 220°C.

2 Using a Stanley or Mickey knife, score the rind of the pork in lines about ½–1 cm wide. Cut into the fat but not into the flesh. Rub with oil. Massage the salt very thoroughly into the skin. Place on a rack in an oven tray.

3 Roast for 30 minutes, then reduce the temperature to 160°C and roast for a further 1½ hours. Test the pork to make sure it is cooked by inserting a bamboo skewer into the roast. The juices that come out should be clear, not dark pink. The crackling should be crunchy.

4 Remove the pork from the baking tray and rest in a warm place.

Pork noodle stir-fry

Serves 4   Prep time: 20 minutes   Cooking time: about 15 minutes

¼ cup light soy sauce
2 teaspoons sesame oil
600 g pork fillet, thinly sliced
2 tablespoons cornflour
440 g packet shelf-fresh
  Singapore noodles
2 tablespoons peanut oil
2 cloves garlic, finely chopped
3 cm knob ginger, peeled and
  finely julienned
2 long red chillies, thinly sliced
  on the diagonal

1 bunch broccolini
  (or Chinese broccoli),
  cut into 3 cm lengths
½ cup char siu sauce
¼ cup rice wine vinegar
  (or white vinegar)
2 tablespoons crispy fried garlic
  (see note)
4 shallots (spring onions),
  finely sliced on the diagonal
1 bird's eye (small red) chilli,
  sliced finely on the diagonal

1 In a bowl, combine 2 tablespoons soy sauce with the sesame oil and toss the pork through. Sprinkle the cornflour over and toss again.

2 Prepare the noodles according to the packet directions.

3 Place about one-third of the oil in a very hot wok and stir-fry half of the pork. Remove from the wok and set aside. Repeat with the other half of the pork.

4 Add the remaining oil and stir-fry the garlic, ginger and chillies until soft and fragrant. Add the broccolini and 2 tablespoons water. Toss until the broccolini is tender but still a little bit firm and the water has evaporated.

5 Return the pork to the pan along with the noodles. Add the remaining soy sauce, char siu sauce and rice wine vinegar, and mix well. Serve scattered with crispy fried garlic, shallots and bird's eye chilli slices.

Note: Crispy fried garlic can be found in the Asian section of the supermarket or at the Asian grocer.

Honey mustard glazed pork chops

Serves 4   Prep time: 10 minutes
Cooking time: 15 minutes + marinating time

⅓ cup honey
⅓ cup whole grain mustard
⅓ cup white wine
2 cloves garlic, crushed

4 pork loin chops
 (about 250 g each)
1 tablespoon olive oil
⅓ cup cream

1 Combine the honey, mustard, wine and garlic in a bowl. Add the pork chops, ensuring they are coated all over, and marinate for 10 minutes.

2 Heat the oil in a large chef pan over medium-high heat. Remove the chops from the bowl, reserving the marinade, and cook for about 4–5 minutes on each side or until golden and just cooked through. Remove from the pan and rest under foil.

3 Place the reserved marinade in a small saucepan and bring to the boil. Cook for 2–3 minutes until reduced by half. Stir in the cream and simmer for about 2 minutes or until thickened to a saucy consistency.

4 Drizzle the chops with the honey mustard sauce and serve.

Maple-glazed pork ribs

Serves 4–6 as a main, 10–12 as part of a shared table
Prep time: 10 minutes   Cooking time: 2 hours

1 teaspoon salt
1 teaspoon white pepper
1 teaspoon garlic powder
½ teaspoon ground dried chilli
1 teaspoon smoky paprika
4 American-style pork rib racks
 (about 500 g each)

¾ cup apricot jam
½ cup maple syrup
¼ cup Dijon mustard
¼ cup malt vinegar
½ cup light soy sauce
2 teaspoons cracked black pepper

1 Preheat the oven to 160°C.

2 Combine the salt, 1 teaspoon pepper, garlic powder, chilli and paprika in a small bowl. Place the rib racks in 2 baking dishes and sprinkle with the mixture. Cover the baking dishes tightly with foil and bake for 1½ hours.

Honey mustard glazed pork chops, recipe page 54

Cheese-stuffed meatballs,
recipe page 57

3 Combine the jam, maple syrup, mustard, vinegar, soy sauce and 2 teaspoons cracked black pepper in a pot over medium-high heat. Boil for 5–10 minutes, making sure it does not boil over. The sauce should be slightly thickened.

4 Remove the baking dish from the oven and take the foil off. Using tongs to handle the racks, run a knife between each bone so that they are individual ribs. Increase the temperature of the oven to 180°C.

5 Pour the sauce over the ribs. Bake for a further 15 minutes, turning the ribs to coat with sauce every few minutes. The ribs will be falling-apart tender and have a lovely thick, sticky glaze.

Cheese-stuffed meatballs

Serves 6   Prep time: 20 minutes
Cooking time: 1 hour if simmering in sauce; 10 minutes if frying

For the meatballs
750 g pork mince
250 g premium beef mince
4 eggs
1 cup grated parmesan
1 large garlic clove, crushed
1½ cups fresh breadcrumbs

Salt and freshly ground
  black pepper
200 g mozzarella cheese,
  cut into 1 cm cubes
Vegetable oil, for frying
Spaghetti, for serving

For the sauce
1 tablespoon olive oil
2 cloves garlic, finely chopped
2 brown onions, finely chopped
2 x 600 ml jars tomato passata
½ teaspoon dried ground oregano

1 teaspoon salt
½ teaspoon black pepper
2 teaspoons sugar
2 teaspoons red wine vinegar

1 Combine all the meatball ingredients except the mozzarella in a large bowl, and use your hands to mix thoroughly. Using damp hands, roll into meatballs about the size of a golf ball, keeping the size uniform. Press a cube of mozzarella into the meatball and make sure it is completely covered with the mince mixture. Place on a plate and refrigerate for at least 30 minutes before cooking.

2 To make the sauce, heat the oil in a large chef pan over medium-low heat. Add the garlic and onion and sauté gently until the onion becomes transparent. Be careful not to brown it. Stir in the passata, oregano, salt, pepper, sugar and vinegar. Simmer the sauce for 5 minutes or until it thickens slightly. Taste, and add more salt, sugar or vinegar as required.

3 Drop the chilled meatballs into the sauce and simmer for 1 hour.

4 Serve with spaghetti cooked to packet instructions.

Note: Instead of cooking the meatballs in the sauce, they can be sautéed for about 10 minutes in a chef pan over medium-high heat.

Apricot-glazed ham

Serves as many people as you can invite over!
Prep time: 15 minutes   Cooking time: 3 hours

7 kg leg of ham
1½ cups apricot nectar
½ cup brown sugar
½ cup apricot jam

¼ cup Dijon mustard
¼ cup soy sauce

1 Preheat the oven to 160°C. Line a large baking dish with baking paper.

2 Carefully remove the rind from the ham, leaving a good layer of fat intact, but leave the rind around the shank of the leg. Score the fat in a diamond pattern, being careful not to cut all the way through to the meat or the fat will dislodge during cooking. Make a few deep incisions into the meat using a small sharp knife.

3 Combine the apricot nectar, brown sugar, jam, mustard and soy sauce in a large saucepan. Bring to the boil, and stir, then boil for about 15 minutes or until reduced to about 1⅓ cups. The mixture will thicken as it cools and should have the consistency of a thick syrup. Be vigilant, as the mixture can bubble up to the brim of the pot. Allow to cool.

4 Baste the ham generously with the glaze, making sure that some gets into the deep incisions. Place the ham in the baking dish and bake for 3 hours, basting with the marinade several times. Serve straight to the table or refrigerate and serve cold.

Slow-cooked pork curry

Serves 6   Prep time: 10 minutes   Cooking time: about 2 hours

2 tablespoons vegetable oil
1 large onion, chopped
4–5 garlic cloves, crushed
1 tablespoon finely grated ginger
10 dried curry leaves
2 teaspoons chilli powder
3 tablespoons curry powder
  (see below)

2 teaspoons salt
1 kg pork (such as shoulder or
  scotch fillet), cut into 3 cm cubes
1 tablespoon tamarind puree
1 tablespoon honey

1 Heat the oil in a large saucepan over medium heat and fry the onion, garlic, ginger and curry leaves for about 6–8 minutes, stirring often, until golden brown.

2 Mix the chilli powder, curry powder and salt with a little water to make a paste. Add the paste to the pan and continue to fry, stirring often, for about 2 minutes, until fragrant. Add the pork to the pan and stir to coat thoroughly with the spice mixture. Add the tamarind puree and stir again.

3 Cover and bring to a simmer over low heat. Cook for 1½ hours, until the meat is very tender. Stir in the honey and cook uncovered for 15–20 minutes, or until the gravy thickens.

Curry powder

Prep time: 5 minutes   Cooking time: 3 minutes

¼ cup fennel seeds
2 tablespoons cumin seeds
½ cup coriander seeds
1 teaspoon fenugreek seeds

2 handfuls dried curry leaves
5 cm cinnamon stick, broken up
5–6 cardamom pods (seeds only)

1 Combine the fennel, cumin, coriander and fenugreek seeds with the curry leaves in a large frying pan. Dry-fry over low heat for about 3 minutes, until fragrant and dark brown (not black!). Make sure you keep stirring regularly so that the seeds do not burn.

2 Transfer to a bowl to cool, then place into a small food processor or spice grinder with the cinnamon and cardamom seeds. Blend to a fine powder, and store in an airtight container.

Poultry

Introduction

Chicken is by far the most consumed meat in Australia. It's not surprising given how economical, versatile and delicious it is. This chapter looks at the many ways of enjoying chicken and other popular poultry. For more details about methods of cooking please look at the introduction to the meat chapter.

Grilling, barbecuing and pan-frying

The best cuts for grilling, barbecuing and pan-frying
Chicken – breast fillet, thigh fillet, tenderloin.
Duck – breast (see the recipe on page 87).

Roasting

The best cuts for roasting
Chicken – whole, butterflied, breast on the crown, maryland, drumsticks, thigh cutlets, wings. (Whole roast chicken is my pick; see the recipe on page 65).
Turkey – whole, buffe (breast). (Whole turkey is my pick; see the recipe on page 90.)
Duck – whole, legs.

Poaching

Poaching is a method of cooking where the ingredient is cooked in liquid, usually over a gentle heat.

The best cuts for poaching
Chicken – whole, breast (see the recipe on page 84).
Duck – whole, breast.

Tips for poaching

Poultry can be poached in stock, in water, in wine or even in buttermilk. Flavour the liquid with whatever aromatics will go with the dish you are creating. Keep the heat nice and gentle, and allow your poultry to cool for a while in its poaching liquid.

Stir-frying

The best cuts for stir-frying
Chicken – breast fillet, thigh fillet.
Duck – breast fillet.
Turkey – breast fillet.

Braising and slow cooking

The fattier parts of the poultry are the best parts for slow cooking.

The best cuts for braising
Chicken – whole, maryland, drumsticks, thigh cutlets, thigh fillets, wings.
Duck – legs.
Turkey – drumsticks, wings.

How to joint a chicken

1 To remove the leg and thigh, cut through the skin and meat between the thigh and the body, then feel for the joint and cut through to remove it fully. Keep as much skin as possible on the breast. If desired, separate the drumstick from the thigh cutlet by cutting through the joint between those two bones.

2 Pull the wing out and feel for the joint where it attaches to the breast. Put your knife through the joint between the bones and remove.

3 Take a pair of kitchen scissors or a knife and remove the back of the chicken by cutting up either side of the spine. You should be left with the double breast still attached to the rib cage.

4 Use a small sharp knife to separate the ribs from the flesh and cut them with kitchen scissors. Turn the chicken breast side up. Run a sharp knife down either side of the breast bone and carefully remove the breast meat from the bones. The carcass can be used to make stock.

Herbed roast chicken,
recipe page 65

Chicken

Herbed roast chicken

Serves 4   Prep time: 10 minutes   Cooking time: 1 hour

1.7–1.8 kg chicken – try to buy
  organic or free range
50 g unsalted butter,
  at room temperature
½ cup chopped fresh herbs
  (e.g. parsley, sage, basil,
  tarragon – you choose)

1 clove garlic, crushed
1 lemon, zest finely grated
  and cut in half
½ teaspoon salt
½ teaspoon ground black pepper
1 large brown onion,
  peeled and halved

1 Preheat the oven to 180°C. Rinse the chicken and pat dry with paper towel.

2 In a bowl, combine the butter, fresh herbs, garlic, lemon zest, salt and pepper. Using your fingers, starting at the neck end, separate the skin from the breast of the chicken, including the tops of the thighs/drumsticks.

3 Push the butter mixture under the skin and spread it evenly over the breast and tops of the thighs. Place the halved lemon and onion into the cavity of the chicken, along with any herb stalks. Put the chicken on a baking tray. Place in the oven with the breast facing the back of the oven. About 30 minutes later, spin it around so that the legs/thighs are facing the back.

4 An hour is a subjective cooking time – depending on your oven, on whether the chicken's legs are trussed shut, even the size of the baking dish can have an impact on cooking time. To check that the chicken is cooked, pierce the thickest part of the thigh with a skewer and the juices should run clear. Another way to tell is if the leg joint feels loose in its socket, or when the chicken is picked up with tongs by its cavity, the juices run clear. The breast should be golden brown with a lovely layer of herbs underneath the skin.

Chicken and chorizo paella

Serves 4   Prep time: 30 minutes   Cooking time: 1 hour

2 chorizo (about 200 g),
   sliced 5 mm thick
2 chicken thigh fillets
   (about 280 g), cut into strips
1.5 litres chicken stock
   (see page 152) or store bought
400 g tin crushed tomatoes
1 medium brown onion,
   peeled and cut into quarters
1 red capsicum, seeded and
   cut into large pieces

3 cloves garlic, peeled
2 tablespoons olive oil
2 teaspoons smoked paprika
2 cups carnaroli or arborio rice
A little extra olive oil
½ cup roughly chopped
   flat-leaf parsley
2 lemons, cut into wedges

1 Heat a paella pan or a large, shallow chef pan or frypan over medium-high heat. Cook the chorizo slices for a minute on each side or until golden brown. Remove to a bowl, leaving any oil they released in the pan.

2 Sauté the chicken strips for 2–3 minutes or until golden. The chicken doesn't have to cook all the way through, as it will cook further in the stock later; it's just important to brown it at this stage. Remove to the bowl with the chorizo.

3 In a medium saucepan over medium-high heat, bring the chicken stock to the boil. Once boiling, reduce the heat to a very low simmer.

4 Place the tomatoes, onion, capsicum and garlic in a food processor and puree until smooth. Add 2 tablespoons olive oil to the pan and then the tomato mixture. Stir until most of the moisture has evaporated. This will take about 5 minutes. The mixture will start to crackle and become more paste-like when it is ready. Add the paprika and stir for a further minute. Add the rice and stir to combine.

5 Pour in about a third of the stock and stir to mix everything together. Add the chicken and chorizo and distribute evenly in the pan. Pour in the rest of the stock and reduce the heat to very low. Cook for about 40 minutes. As time goes by, the rice absorbs the liquid and a crust should form on the bottom and around the sides of the pan. The dish is ready when the rice is cooked through.

6 Serve the paella to the table in the pan, drizzled with a little extra olive oil and scattered with parsley and lemon wedges.

Chicken and chorizo paella,
recipe page 66

Chicken korma

Serves 4–6   Prep time: 20 minutes + marinating time
Cooking time: 2½ hours

⅓ cup plain Greek yoghurt
1 tablespoon ground coriander seed
2 teaspoons ground cumin seed
1 teaspoon ground cardamom
1 teaspoon ground turmeric
1.2 kg chicken thigh fillets,
   cut into 2.5 cm cubes
2 large red onions, peeled
5 cm knob ginger, peeled and
   roughly sliced

3 cloves garlic
½ cup almond meal
2 tablespoons vegetable oil
5 whole cloves
1 cinnamon stick
1 teaspoon salt
400 ml tin coconut cream
Basmati rice, for serving

1 Place the yoghurt in a bowl and add the ground spices. Add the chicken and stir through thoroughly. Marinate for at least 30 minutes (the longer the better; overnight is ideal).

2 Coarsely chop 1 onion and place in a mini food processor along with the ginger, garlic and almond meal. Process until a smooth paste forms, adding a little water if needed to bring the mixture together.

3 Heat the oil in a large non-stick chef pan over medium-low heat. Thickly slice the remaining onion and cook for 10 minutes, stirring occasionally, until deep golden brown and completely softened. Stir in the almond meal mixture and continue cooking for a further 2–3 minutes or until fragrant and the paste has dried out a little. Remove from the pan to the bowl of the slow cooker.

4 Add the chicken mixture, whole spices, salt, coconut cream and ¾ cup of water to the slow cooker and mix well. Cover and bring to a simmer. Cook, uncovered, for 2 hours or until the curry has thickened. Taste and season with salt if required. Serve with basmati rice.

Chicken fricassee

A fricassee is traditionally a light stew, made with white meat. This version is stripped down to its simplest form, and is essentially succulent simmered chicken in a lovely chicken gravy. It can have all kinds of vegetables and herbs added to it, or serve it as is with lots of crusty bread to sop up the gravy.

Serves 4   Prep time: 10 minutes   Cooking time: 30 minutes

25 g butter
4 chicken marylands,
  cut into 2 pieces each
2 brown onions, sliced

¼ cup flour
1 litre chicken stock (see page 152)
  or store bought
Salt and pepper

1 Melt the butter in a chef pan over medium heat. Place the chicken pieces in the pan and turn until lightly browned. Add the onion and sauté until translucent and aromatic. Sprinkle the flour over the chicken and onion and stir for 1 minute. Stir in the stock, adding a little bit at a time. Simmer for 20 minutes, uncovered, turning the chicken pieces occasionally, until the chicken is cooked through and the gravy has thickened.

2 I like the gravy fairly thick, and I achieve that by removing the chicken from the pan once it is cooked, turning up the heat and reducing the gravy further. Put the chicken back in the pan before serving.

Lemon chicken meatballs

We like these with steamed long-grain rice and a garden salad.

Serves 4   Prep time: 20 minutes   Cooking time: about 15 minutes

800 g chicken mince
2 cloves garlic, chopped
1 lemon, zested and juiced
1 egg
1 cup breadcrumbs
1 tablespoon ground cumin seed
½ teaspoon salt

¼ teaspoon ground
  black pepper
¼ cup finely chopped
  mint leaves
2 teaspoons olive oil
½ cup plain Greek yoghurt
¼ cup thick mint sauce

1 In a large bowl, place the chicken mince, garlic, lemon zest, egg, breadcrumbs, cumin, salt, pepper and mint. Using clean damp hands, mix thoroughly until well-combined and sticky. Keeping your hands damp, form the mixture into balls the size of golf balls.

2 Heat half the oil in a large non-stick frypan over medium-high heat and add half the meatballs, cooking for 6–7 minutes or until golden brown and cooked through. Repeat with the remaining oil and meatballs.

3 In a small bowl, combine the yoghurt, mint sauce and 1 tablespoon lemon juice. Serve the meatballs with the dressing on the side.

Portuguese-style chicken pieces

I have used chicken thigh cutlets for this recipe, which is the thigh on the bone with the skin on. Chicken maryland (the leg and thigh together) could also be used, but separate the leg from the thigh first. Just drumsticks would also work well. Chicken takes a long time to cook on the barbecue, and it requires both grilling to seal the skin and roasting under the hood to make sure it cooks through. There's a bit of chilli kick in this spice mix, tone it down if you don't like heat.

Serves 4   Prep time: 5 minutes   Cooking time: 40 minutes

2 teaspoons paprika
2 teaspoons chilli powder
2 teaspoons ground cinnamon
2 teaspoons garlic powder
2 teaspoons onion powder

2 teaspoons salt
8 chicken thigh cutlets
  (about 1.6 kg), patted dry
  with paper towel
¼ cup olive oil

1 Combine all the dry spices and salt in a snap-lock bag. Place the chicken in the bag, a few pieces at a time, and coat evenly.

2 Heat the whole barbecue to high. Drizzle the chicken with oil and place on the char grill for 6 minutes or so, turning until all sides have char marks and are starting to crisp.

3 Move all the chicken to one half of the barbecue and turn off the burners on that half. Leave the burners on the other half going at a medium-high heat, so that there is no direct heat under the chicken. Lower the hood on the barbecue and leave to cook for about 25 minutes. Check that the chicken is cooked by piercing the thickest part of the biggest piece with a skewer. If the juices run clear, it will be cooked through. If not, lower the hood and check at 5-minute intervals. Cooking time will depend on the size of your chicken pieces and also on the heat of your barbecue.

Lemon and garlic chicken pot roast

Serves 4   Prep time: 10 minutes   Cooking time: 1 hour 10 minutes

1 tablespoon olive oil
1 whole chicken (about 1.6 kg),
  patted dry
1 lemon, halved
1 head garlic, halved crossways

2 large rosemary sprigs
½ cup white wine
1 cup chicken stock (see page 152)
  or store bought
Salt and pepper if necessary

1 In a large flame-proof casserole pot with a lid, heat the oil over medium-high heat. Brown the chicken, breast side down first, then turn over and brown the back. Carefully remove the chicken from the pot.

2 Place the lemon and garlic, cut side down, in the pot, and add the rosemary. Pour in the white wine and allow to cook for 1 minute. Pour in the chicken stock and return the chicken to the pot, breast side up, on top of the garlic and lemon. Bring to the boil then reduce to a low simmer. Place the lid on the pot and reduce the heat to low. Cook for an hour. The chicken is cooked when the legs are loose in their joints and the juices run clear when a skewer is inserted into the thickest part of the thigh.

3 Remove the chicken from the pot and carve. Remove the lemon, rosemary and garlic. Squeeze the soft garlic flesh back into the pot and mix well. Taste and season if necessary – this will depend on the saltiness of your stock. Serve the chicken with the pot juices poured over.

Note: Some carrots, cut large, and whole baby chat potatoes can be cooked in the pot with the chicken. Just add a little more stock.

Chicken tenders with plum dipping sauce

Serves 6 as a snack   Prep time: 15 minutes
Cooking time: 10 minutes

Vegetable oil to fill
  frypan to 5 mm
½ cup plain flour
½ teaspoon salt
1 egg, beaten
1 cup homemade or
  panko breadcrumbs

1 kg chicken tenderloin pieces,
  or 1 kg chicken breast fillets
  cut into strips lengthways
Plum dipping sauce
  (see page 134)

1 In a wide frypan, heat the oil over a medium-high heat.

2 Place the flour and salt in a shallow bowl. In another shallow bowl, combine the beaten egg with 1 tablespoon water. Place the breadcrumbs in a third shallow bowl.

3 Dip each piece of chicken into the flour, then the egg, then the breadcrumbs, pressing the crumbs gently so they stick. Place the pieces into the frypan and cook for 3–4 minutes on each side or until golden brown and crunchy.

Apricot chicken tagine,
recipe page 73

Don't overcrowd the pan – cook in 2 or 3 batches if necessary. Serve with the plum dipping sauce.

Note: These can be deep-fried at 190°C instead of pan-frying.

Apricot chicken tagine

Serves 4   Prep time: 15 minutes   Cooking time: 45 minutes

2 teaspoons sea salt
1 tablespoon ground turmeric
1 tablespoon ground cumin seeds
1 teaspoon ground cinnamon
⅓ cup olive oil
1 large onion, peeled and quartered
3 cloves garlic, peeled
5 cm knob ginger, peeled
 and cut into 1 cm pieces
4 chicken marylands,
 cut into drumsticks
 and thigh cutlets

½ cup chicken stock (see page 152)
 or store bought
1 cup apricot nectar
12 dried Turkish apricots,
 chopped
1 cup pearl (Israeli) couscous
½ bunch parsley, roughly
 chopped
¼ cup slivered almonds, toasted
Crusty bread and green salad,
 for serving

1 Place the salt, turmeric, cumin, cinnamon, 3 tablespoons oil, onion, garlic and ginger into a food processor and blitz until a smooth thick paste is achieved. Place in a large snap-lock bag with the chicken and massage to ensure all the chicken is coated.

2 Place the remaining olive oil in the tagine base (see note) over medium-high heat. Add the chicken pieces, skin side down, and cook for about 3 minutes without turning or until they are a lovely caramel brown. Turn the chicken over, and pour in the chicken stock and apricot nectar. Scatter the chopped apricots around the tagine. Bring to the boil then reduce the heat to low. Place the tagine on a heat diffuser if you have one, to ensure a very low heat. (Alternatively place the tagine in an oven preheated to 160°C.) Cook for 40 minutes.

3 Remove the tagine lid, and carefully lift the chicken pieces one by one and scatter the couscous around and under them. Turn off the heat. After 5 minutes the couscous will swell and be ready to eat. Scatter the parsley and almonds over the tagine and serve to the table with crusty bread and salad.

Notes: Chicken maryland is the drumstick with the thigh cutlet still attached. They are very inexpensive to buy. Thigh fillets can also be used but reduce the cooking time by 15–20 minutes. If a tagine is not available, a large chef pan with a fitted lid or tented foil over the top will work.

Chicken in peanut sauce

Serves 4   Prep time: 15 minutes   Cooking time: 20 minutes

½ bunch coriander
1 brown onion
4 cloves garlic
2 limes, zested and juiced
1 tablespoon peanut oil
800 g chicken thigh fillets,
    cut into 2 cm thick strips

1 teaspoon ground turmeric
¼ teaspoon ground dried chilli
400 ml tin coconut cream
1 cup crunchy peanut butter
¼ cup fish sauce
¼ cup brown sugar
Cooked rice, for serving

1   Wash the roots and stems of the coriander and place in a food processor along with the onion, garlic and lime zest. Process until very fine. Alternatively, crush in a mortar and pestle. Reserve the coriander leaves for serving.

2   Heat the oil in a large non-stick chef pan over medium-high heat. Place the chicken strips into the hot pan and allow to brown on one side, without moving them – this will take 4–5 minutes. Turn and allow to brown on the other side. Remove from the pan and set aside.

3   Reduce the heat to medium. Add the onion mixture to the pan and fry until soft and fragrant. Be careful not to let it 'catch' or start to burn. Add the turmeric and ground chilli and stir for a further minute or so.

4   Add half the coconut cream and the peanut butter, stir through then bring to a simmer. Simmer for about 5 minutes. The sauce will split – this is okay.

5   Reduce the heat to low and stir in the fish sauce, brown sugar and half the lime juice. Taste to see if the sauce needs any more of these three things – this is very dependent on personal taste. Add the chicken and simmer for a further 5 minutes or until cooked through.

6   Stir in the rest of the coconut cream, taste again and adjust seasoning if needed. Remove from the heat, garnish with coriander leaves and serve with rice.

Oven-fried chicken wings with sticky sauce

Serves 4   Prep time: 20 minutes   Cooking time: 50 minutes

1 cup plain flour
2 tablespoons smoked paprika
1 tablespoon garlic powder
1 tablespoon onion powder
2 teaspoons ground dried oregano
½ teaspoon ground chilli
1 teaspoon finely
  ground white pepper
1 teaspoon freshly
  ground black pepper
2 teaspoons fine table salt

Olive oil cooking spray
2 kg chicken wings, jointed,
  tips discarded or kept for stock
½ cup tomato sauce
½ cup sweet chilli sauce
¼ cup light soy sauce
¼ cup white vinegar
Sliced shallots (spring onions)
  and small red chillies,
  to garnish

1 Preheat the oven to 200°C and line 2 baking trays with baking paper. In a large mixing bowl, combine the flour, all the dried spices and salt.

2 Working with a few at a time, dip the wings into the spiced flour mixture. Spray the wings with cooking spray, coating all sides. Dip the wings in the flour once more and place them on the lined baking trays. When all the chicken is coated and on the trays, give it one more spray and bake for 45 minutes or until golden brown, crisp and cooked through.

3 In a small saucepan over medium-high heat, combine the tomato sauce, chilli sauce, soy sauce and white vinegar. Bring to the boil and allow to boil for 2 minutes.

4 When the chicken is cooked, place it on a serving platter and drizzle the sauce over. Garnish with shallots and chilli and serve.

Thai-style chicken burger

Makes 4 burgers   Prep time: 15 minutes   Cooking time: under 15 minutes

For the patties
500 g chicken mince
1 egg, beaten
½ cup breadcrumbs
1 tablespoon fish sauce
1 tablespoon red curry paste
½ bunch coriander, stems and
  roots thoroughly washed and
  chopped, leaves reserved

1 small red chilli, finely chopped
4 shallots (spring onions), sliced
1 lime, zested and juiced
1 teaspoon peanut oil, for frying

For the burger
¼ cup sweet chilli sauce
¼ cup Kewpie (Japanese-style)
  mayonnaise

4 brioche buns
4 butter lettuce leaves

1 In a bowl, combine all the patty ingredients including the lime zest but not the lime juice or peanut oil. Work the mince with your hands until it is holding together. Using damp hands, form the mince into 4 large, thin patties. Make sure they are bigger than your burger buns as they will shrink when they cook.

2 In a large chef pan over medium-high heat, heat the peanut oil and cook the patties for 3 minutes each side or until just cooked through. Remove from the pan and set aside, covered with foil.

3 In a small bowl, combine the sweet chilli sauce, mayonnaise and lime juice.

4 To assemble the burgers, spread chilli mayonnaise generously over the bottom bun, then add the lettuce and some coriander leaves. Top with the chicken patty and top bun, and serve.

Chicken and cheese strudel

Serves 6   Prep time: 15 minutes   Cooking time: about 40 minutes

1 tablespoon olive oil
800 g chicken thigh fillets,
   cut into 3 cm cubes
200 g button mushrooms, sliced
3 cloves garlic
2 tablespoons plain flour
1¼ cups milk
1 tablespoon Dijon or
   French mustard

½ teaspoon sea salt
¼ teaspoon ground white pepper
1 cup grated tasty cheese
2 sheets frozen puff pastry
1 egg, beaten
4 shallots (spring onions),
   finely sliced

1 Preheat oven to 200°C. Heat 1 teaspoon oil in a large, heavy-based frypan over medium-high heat and brown half of the chicken. Remove to a bowl and repeat with another teaspoon of oil and the remaining chicken. The chicken only needs to have some golden colour; it doesn't need to be cooked all the way through at this stage.

2 Heat the remaining oil in the pan and sauté the mushrooms and garlic until the garlic is fragrant and translucent, and the mushrooms are a light golden colour. The mushrooms will release liquid as they cook, so continue to cook until this liquid evaporates.

3 Return the chicken to the pan and sprinkle the flour over the top. Stir to coat the chicken. Stir in the milk, ¼ cup at a time, allowing the sauce to cook and thicken between each addition. When all the milk is added, bring the sauce to a simmer and stir in the mustard, salt, pepper and two-thirds of the

Chicken and cheese strudel,
recipe page 76

cheese. Simmer for a few minutes or until the chicken is cooked through. Remove to a bowl and allow to cool.

4 Preheat the oven to 200°C. Place 2 sheets of puff pastry on a sheet of baking paper on a large cutting board. Brush 1 cm of the edge of one sheet with a little beaten egg, and overlap another sheet over it. Press the edge to join the sheets together into a large rectangle. Turn the rectangle so it is vertical on the bench. Using the back of a butter knife or a skewer, make faint lines on the pastry to divide it into equal thirds lengthways. Cut off the top two corners of the large rectangle to form a point. At the base of the large rectangle, cut a square out of the left and right thirds of the pastry. It should now resemble the shape of a big straight Christmas tree.

5 On the left and right thirds of the large rectangle (not the middle third), make incisions about 1.5 cm apart, following the angle of the upper point of the pastry and going to each edge. These will form your pastry braids for the strudel. Once the pastry is cut, lift it, still on the baking paper, onto a large baking tray.

6 Place the cooled chicken mixture along the middle third of the pastry, stopping short of the pointy and square-cut end. Sprinkle with the sliced shallots and the remaining cheese. Fold the pointy end over the chicken mixture, then fold the square end of the pastry over. Then, alternating from left to right, fold the strips of pastry over the chicken mixture. It will look a bit like a braid. Brush liberally with egg and bake for 20–25 minutes or until a deep golden brown. This is lovely served hot or at room temperature.

Flat-out Lebanese chicken

Serves 4   Prep time: 15 minutes   Cooking time: about 40 minutes

1 whole chicken (about 1.9 kg)
60 g butter, at room temperature
1 tablespoon sumac
1 tablespoon whole cumin seeds
¼ teaspoon ground hot chilli
1 teaspoon dried oregano leaves

3 cloves garlic, finely chopped
½ cup chopped flat-leaf parsley
½ teaspoon sea salt
¼ teaspoon ground black pepper
1 lemon, zested
Lemon wedges, for serving

1 Preheat the oven to 180°C.

2 To butterfly the chicken, use a sharp knife or kitchen scissors to cut down either side of the backbone. Remove the backbone. Open the chicken outwards and using a sharp knife, remove the rib bones. Wipe the bird with paper towel.

3 Turn the chicken over and give it a good thump in the middle of the chest

to flatten it out. Starting at the neck end, insert your fingers between the skin and the flesh of the breast. Carefully create a pocket in the breasts, thighs and drumsticks.

4 Mix the butter with the sumac, cumin, chilli, oregano, garlic, parsley, salt, pepper and lemon zest. Spread the butter mixture under the skin.

5 Cut the lemon in half, and place the halves, cut side down, in a baking dish. Place the chicken on top of the lemon. Roast for 45–50 minutes or until the skin is richly golden. Carefully remove the chicken and lemon from the pan. Pour most of the pan juices into a microwave-safe jug and microwave on high for about 3 minutes until reduced and thickened.

6 Brush the chicken with the pan juices before serving with lemon wedges.

Chilli chicken with cashews

Serves 4   Prep time: 20 minutes   Cooking time: 10 minutes

⅓ cup roasted salted cashews
2 tablespoons peanut or
   vegetable oil
800 g chicken thigh fillets,
   trimmed and cut into strips
4 cm knob ginger, peeled and
   sliced very thinly
2 cloves garlic, sliced very finely
1 red onion, sliced thinly

½ cup sweet chilli, garlic and
   ginger jam (see page 216,
   and note below)
¼ cup soy sauce
1 teaspoon cornflour
¼ cup white vinegar
1 long red chilli, sliced finely
¼ bunch coriander, leaves only
Cooked rice, for serving

1 Place the wok over a high heat and dry-fry the cashews, tossing, until dark patches appear. Set aside for garnish.

2 Place 1 teaspoon oil in the wok over high heat and stir-fry a quarter of the chicken until cooked. Remove from the wok and repeat 3 more times until all the chicken is cooked.

3 Reduce the heat to medium and add another 2 teaspoons oil. Stir-fry the ginger, garlic, red onion and chilli jam until soft and fragrant. Return the chicken to the pan and add the soy sauce. Dissolve the cornflour in the vinegar and add to the chicken, stirring. Cook for a further 2 minutes or until the sauce has thickened and darkened. Scatter the chilli, coriander leaves and cashews over the top and serve immediately with rice.

Note: You can use store-bought sweet chilli sauce, if you prefer.

Chinese five-spice wings

Serves 6 as a main meal; also makes a huge platter for a party
Prep time: 5 minutes   Cooking time: 40 minutes

2 tablespoons sesame seeds
1 tablespoon Chinese five-spice
2 teaspoons ground dried chilli
1 tablespoon garlic powder
1 tablespoon onion powder

1 tablespoon salt
3 kg chicken wing pieces
  – the drumettes and the
  wingettes, not the tips
¼ cup olive oil

For serving: plum sauce (see page 134), garlic chilli dipping sauce
(see page 140) or hoisin peanut sauce (see page 142)

1 Preheat the oven to 200°C.

2 Combine the sesame seeds and all the dry spices in a large bowl. Working
with a few at a time, toss the chicken pieces in the mixture, coating all over,
and place onto 2 large, lined baking trays. It's important that the chicken
pieces are not overcrowded on the tray, or they will boil in their own juices
rather than going golden and crispy. Drizzle the wings with oil and bake in
the oven for 40 minutes or until golden brown and cooked through. The time
will vary according to the size of the wings.

3 Serve with plum sauce, garlic chilli dipping sauce or hoisin peanut sauce.

Greek-style chicken tray bake

Serves 4   Prep time: 10 minutes   Cooking time: 45 minutes

4 chicken marylands, cut into
  drumstick and thigh cutlets
¼ cup olive oil
2 teaspoons sea salt flakes
½ teaspoon freshly
  ground black pepper
1 tablespoon dried oregano leaves
Juice and finely grated
  zest of 1 lemon

2 red onions, peeled and
  quartered
12 large green olives
12 baby chat potatoes
2 heads garlic, unpeeled,
  top chopped off to reveal
  the tips of the cloves

1 Preheat the oven to 200°C.

2 In a large, heavy-based baking dish, arrange the chicken pieces. Drizzle
with olive oil, then sprinkle with the salt, pepper, oregano and lemon zest.
Nestle the onions around the chicken and bake for 20 minutes.

3 Remove the tray from the oven and add the lemon juice, olives, baby chat potatoes and garlic heads. Return to the oven and roast for a further 20–25 minutes, or until the chicken is cooked through and the potatoes and garlic are tender.

4 Before serving, squeeze the garlic out of its skin into the pan. Serve to the table in the baking dish.

Note: Chicken maryland is the drumstick with the thigh cutlet still attached. They are very inexpensive to buy. Thigh fillets can also be used but reduce the cooking time by 15–20 minutes.

Coq au vin

Serves 4   Prep time: 30 minutes   Cooking time: 2 hours 10 minutes

¼ cup plain flour
½ teaspoon salt
¼ teaspoon ground white pepper
1.2 kg chicken pieces
 – legs, thighs, wings, jointed
1 tablespoon olive oil
150 g speck, cut into batons
20 pearl onions (or 6 French/brown
 shallots, peeled and sliced)

16 small Swiss brown
 mushrooms, sliced
2 cloves garlic, chopped
1 teaspoon thyme leaves,
 finely chopped
1 tablespoon tomato paste
30 ml brandy
1½ cups red wine
1 bay leaf

1 Preheat the oven to 140°C.

2 Combine the flour, salt and pepper in a bowl. Coat the chicken pieces thoroughly in the flour.

3 Place the olive oil in an enamel casserole pot over medium-high heat, and when it is hot, brown the chicken on all sides. Transfer the chicken to a plate.

4 Place the speck in the casserole pot and cook for about a minute, until it starts to turn golden. Add the onions, mushrooms, garlic and thyme leaves and sauté for 3–4 minutes, until softened and fragrant. Add the tomato paste and cook, stirring, for a further minute. Pour the brandy into the pot, followed by the red wine. Bring to the boil, then return the chicken to the casserole pot. Add the bay leaf. Cover with a lid and bake for 1½ hours in the oven. Remove the lid and bake for a further 30 minutes.

5 If the sauce is too thin, at this stage you can remove the chicken pieces and turn the oven up to 180°C. Cook the sauce, uncovered for another 10–15 minutes before returning the chicken to the casserole pot to serve.

Hainanese chicken rice,
recipe page 84

Hainanese chicken rice

Serves 4   Prep time: 15 minutes
Cooking time: 2 hours (including cooling time)

1 litre chicken stock (see page 152)
  or store bought
1 whole chicken (about 1.4 kg)
½ cup soy sauce
5 cm knob ginger, sliced
½ bunch shallots (spring onions),
  cut into 3 cm lengths

2 cups jasmine rice
2 Lebanese cucumbers,
  sliced, for serving
Lime wedges, for serving
Ginger and shallot oil
  (see page 141), optional

For the chilli sauce
Juice of 1 lime
6 long red chillies, stalks removed
3 cloves garlic
2 cm knob ginger, peeled

2 teaspoons sugar
2 tablespoons reserved
  chicken broth

1 Place the chicken stock in a pot large enough to submerge the chicken. Add the chicken to the pot and top up with water so it is submerged. Add the soy sauce, ginger and shallots. Bring to the boil then reduce the heat so that the liquid is barely simmering. Place a lid on the pot and cook for 50 minutes. Remove the pot from the heat and allow the chicken to finish cooking as it cools in the pot.

2 Gently remove the chicken from the pot using a pair of tongs in the bird's cavity. Strain the cooking liquid and discard the solids. Put the stock back on the heat and bring to the boil. Skim any froth off the top. Taste and season with soy sauce if it needs more salt.

3 Place the rice in a microwave-safe container with a tight-fitting lid and add 3 cups cooking liquid from the chicken. Cook on high for 18 minutes.

4 For the chilli sauce, place all the ingredients in a mini food processor and blitz to a paste.

5 Carve the chicken and serve with rice, bowls of chicken broth, cucumber slices, lime wedges and chilli sauce, plus some ginger and shallot oil if desired.

Roast crown of chicken

Serves 4   Prep time: 10 minutes + 30 minutes chilling time
Cooking time: 40 minutes

100 g unsalted butter,
  room temperature
Zest of 1 lemon
¼ cup finely chopped fresh
  sage leaves

2 crown roasts of chicken
  (double breast)
Salt and white pepper to taste
2 teaspoons olive oil

1 Preheat the oven to 180°C.

2 Mix the butter, lemon zest and sage until well combined. Carefully separate
the skin of the chicken breasts from the flesh and spread the butter with your
fingers over the flesh. Tuck the skin around the edges of the crown roast.
Season all over with salt and white pepper.

3 In an ovenproof chef pan, heat the oil and brown the crown roasts, skin side
down. This takes about 5 minutes. Turn the crown roasts over, skin side up,
then place the pan in the oven for 30 minutes or until the chicken is tender.
Baste the skin with juices periodically during cooking.

Sticky chicken drumsticks

Serves 6   Prep time: 15 minutes + 30 minutes standing time
Cooking time: 50 minutes

2 kg chicken drumsticks
½ cup light soy sauce
½ cup honey
½ cup char siu sauce
2 tablespoons rice wine vinegar,
  or white vinegar
3 cloves garlic, chopped
3 cm knob ginger, finely julienned

½ teaspoon freshly
  cracked black pepper
1 teaspoon sesame oil
1 tablespoon peanut or
  vegetable oil
½ teaspoon Chinese five-spice
½ teaspoon salt

1 Place the chicken drumsticks on a board over the sink and pour boiling
water from the kettle over them. This will help the skin to shrink and to dry
out. Leave the chicken to air dry for 30 minutes.

2 Preheat the oven to 200°C.

3 In a medium pot over medium-high heat, combine the soy sauce, honey,

char siu, garlic, ginger and pepper. Bring to the boil. Reduce to a simmer and simmer for 10 minutes or until the sauce has thickened to a syrupy consistency. Watch the pot to make sure it doesn't boil over.

4 Combine the sesame and peanut oils in a small dish and brush over the skin of the drumsticks. Sprinkle the drumsticks with five-spice and salt. Place the drumsticks on a wire rack in a large baking tray.

5 Bake the chicken for 10 minutes, until the skin starts to go a light golden brown. Remove from the oven and baste generously with the marinade. Bake for a further 20 minutes, basting every few minutes. When the drumsticks are ready, the marinade will be cooked onto the chicken; it will be dark golden brown and sticky. The juices will run clear if a skewer is inserted into the thickest part of the leg down to the bone.

Duck

Confit duck legs with orange sauce

Serves 4   Prep time: 15 minutes + curing time
Cooking time: 2½ hours

4 duck marylands (drumstick and thigh attached)

For the salt cure
½ cup sea salt flakes
½ teaspoon ground white pepper

Finely grated zest of 1 orange
1 tablespoon thyme

For the oil
**Vegetable oil, for the confit
  (see note)**
3 cloves garlic, halved
3 star anise

4 slices ginger
4 sprigs thyme
**3 strips orange peel, made using
  a vegetable peeler**

For the sauce
1 tablespoon olive oil
2 cloves garlic, sliced
**1 small brown onion,
  peeled and sliced**
3 sprigs thyme
1 cup orange juice

¼ cup Grand Marnier
1 star anise
2 cm knob ginger, thinly sliced
**1 cup chicken stock (see page 152)
  or store bought**
1 tablespoon soy sauce

1 In a small bowl, combine the sea salt, pepper, orange zest and thyme. Rub the mixture all over the skin of the duck marylands and refrigerate for 6 hours or overnight.

2 Preheat the oven to 120°C.

3 Rinse the skin of the duck and pat dry. Place the marylands in a single layer in a baking dish just big enough to fit them. Pour in vegetable oil to just cover, and nestle the garlic, star anise, ginger, thyme and orange peel around the dish. Cover tightly with foil and bake for 2½ hours or until the meat is soft and coming away from the bone. Remove the duck from the oil and drain on paper towel. Just before serving, place the duck, skin side down, in a hot non-stick frypan to crisp up the skin.

4 For the sauce, heat the oil in a medium-sized saucepan. Sauté the garlic and onion until soft and translucent. Add the remaining sauce ingredients and bring to the boil, stirring constantly. Cook until the sauce has reached a syrupy consistency. Strain through a fine mesh sieve into a jug ready for serving.

Note: You can use duck fat for the confit instead – it is more expensive but the fat can be saved for other uses such as duck fat potatoes.

Duck breast with plum sauce

This dish is lovely served with steamed jasmine rice and Chinese broccoli.

Serves 4   Prep time: 5 minutes   Cooking time: 20 minutes

4 duck breast fillets (about 180 g
  each), skin on
½ teaspoon Chinese five-spice
½ teaspoon sea salt flakes
½ teaspoon freshly ground
  black pepper

⅓ cup Shaoxing wine
  (Chinese cooking wine)
¼ cup plum jam
6 teaspoons rice wine vinegar
3 teaspoons light soy sauce

1 Using a sharp knife, score the skin across the width of the duck breasts. Mix together the five-spice, salt and pepper and rub the duck skin with this mixture. Turn over and rub the other side of the meat as well.

2 Place the duck breasts, skin side down, in a cool, non-stick pan (with no oil) and place on the stovetop over a medium-low heat. After a minute or so, the fat will start to render out of the duck breast. Leave the duck alone for about 10 minutes, but check it regularly. If the skin is getting dark too quickly, reduce the heat. Be patient, this part of the process is really important so that

Roast duck with cherry port sauce, recipe page 89

you end up with crisp skin but also so that the thick layer of fat under the skin renders out. Note that if the breast fillets are small or thin, the cooking time may be less.

3 After 10 minutes the skin should be dark, golden and crisp. Remove the breasts from the pan and pour out most of the fat from the pan, leaving about a tablespoon, into a heat-proof container to save for another delicious recipe. Place the fillets, skin side up, back in the pan and cook for a further 5 minutes. There should be a little colour on the bottom but not much. Remove the fillets to a board to rest, uncovered, while you make the sauce.

4 Deglaze the pan by pouring the Shaoxing wine into it and allow half of it to evaporate. Mix the plum jam, rice wine vinegar and soy sauce in a jug and stir. Pour it into the pan and bring to the boil, stirring, until the sauce has reduced and thickened. There should be about ½ cup sauce.

5 To serve, slice the rested duck breasts 1 cm thick. Pour the sauce onto warmed plates and place the sliced duck on top of it. (Pouring the sauce over the duck will make the skin lose its crispness.)

Roast duck with cherry port sauce

The cherry port sauce is rich and sweet with a hint of peppery tang. It is perfect with duck meat. If you need to cook the duck ahead of time, the skin can be crisped back up under the grill.

Serves 8 as part of a Christmas banquet
Prep time: 10 minutes   Cooking time: 3 hours

1 whole duck (about 2 kg)
450 g fresh cherries
   (yields 400 g pitted)
1 tablespoon light soy sauce
½ cup port

¼ teaspoon ground
   black pepper
2 tablespoons sugar
1 tablespoon balsamic vinegar

1 Preheat the oven to 170°C.

2 Wash the duck and pat dry inside and out. Using a skewer, prick the skin of the breast, into the fat but not as deep as the meat. Make about 10 holes in each side. This will allow the fat to render out during cooking and will make the skin lovely and crispy. Place the duck on a rack in a baking tray and roast for 2½–3 hours.

3 While the duck is roasting, cut the cherries in half and remove the stalks

and pips. Put them in a small saucepan over medium heat along with the soy sauce, port, pepper, sugar, balsamic vinegar and ½ cup of water. Bring to the boil then reduce the heat and simmer for about 20 minutes until it becomes syrupy. The sauce will thicken a little more on cooling.

Turkey and quail

Christmas turkey with bacon and craisin stuffing

Serves 12   Prep time: 30 minutes   Cooking time: 3 hours

1 turkey – size 60

For the stuffing
6 rashers bacon, cut into
    5 mm strips
5 brown onions, roughly chopped
½ packet (85 g) craisins
2 bunches parsley, stalks discarded
    and leaves roughly chopped

1 loaf bread, crusts removed
½ cup pine nuts
1 teaspoon salt
½ teaspoon freshly
    cracked black pepper
100 g butter, melted

1 Preheat oven to 180°C.

2 In a frypan over medium heat, fry the bacon until it renders its fat and starts to turn golden brown. Add the onions and stir until they become translucent and fragrant. Add ½ cup of water and the craisins to the pan, along with the parsley. Continue to sauté until the water evaporates. Remove from the heat.

3 Process the bread to a very coarse crumb, about the size of a fingernail. Combine the bacon mixture with the breadcrumbs, pine nuts, salt and pepper. Add enough of the melted butter to bring the stuffing together.

4 Clean the cavity of the turkey with water and dry with paper towel. Place some of the stuffing in the cavity.

5 Place the turkey into a large baking tray and bake for 3 hours. As juices collect in the baking tray, baste the breast. Remove any excess juices and reserve. If the wing tips or ends of the drumsticks (or any other part of the turkey) start to colour too quickly, protect them with foil. The turkey is cooked when it is golden brown, the legs are loose in their joints and juices run clear when a skewer is inserted into the thickest part of the thigh meat.

6 About halfway through the turkey cooking time, pile the extra stuffing into

a shallow baking tray. Drizzle the stuffing with some melted butter and 1 cup reserved turkey juices. Bake for 1½ hours. If the stuffing starts to dry out, add more juices. The end result should be moist with a crunchy golden top.

7 Rest the turkey under foil for 30 minutes before serving with the extra stuffing.

Note: I recommend brining your turkey the night before cooking it. This causes some kind of wonderful chemical reaction that keeps the breast beautifully moist. To brine the turkey, mix 1 cup salt and 2 cups sugar in a tub of water large enough for the turkey to be submerged. Stir to dissolve the salt and sugar. Put the turkey into the tub. Chances are, the tub won't fit in the fridge so my trick is to use giant ice cubes made by freezing water in small ice cream or takeaway containers. The ice cubes take ages to defrost, but keeping them topped up is effectively keeping the turkey refrigerated. Remove the turkey from the brine water at least an hour before cooking – pat it dry, inside and out, and allow it to come to room temperature.

Turkey, pistachio and bacon terrine

Serves 4 as an entree   Prep time: 20 minutes   Cooking time: 1 hour

2 rashers bacon, rind removed,
  roughly chopped
1 brown onion, finely sliced
2 cloves garlic, crushed
250 g chicken thigh fillets
250 g cooked turkey breast or
  thigh meat, cut into 2 cm cubes
¼ cup pistachio kernels,
  roughly chopped

1 tablespoon fresh thyme leaves
½ teaspoon salt
¼ teaspoon ground white pepper
1 egg, lightly beaten
10–12 slices prosciutto
Sweet fruit relish or sweet chilli
  and ginger jam (see page 216),
  for serving

1 Preheat the oven to 180°C.

2 In a medium frypan over medium-high heat, sauté the bacon until it starts to brown. Add the onion and garlic and sauté until soft and translucent. Set aside to cool.

3 Mince the chicken thigh fillets. Place into a large mixing bowl with the diced turkey.

4 When the bacon mixture is cool, add it to the chicken, along with the pistachios, thyme, salt and pepper. Knead the mixture vigorously with your hands until well combined. Add the egg and mix through.

5 Line a medium loaf tin with foil, leaving some to overhang the sides. Lay the prosciutto into the tin, starting in the centre of the tin. Make sure that the pieces overlap in the base, with no gaps, and also that there is plenty of overhang. Fill the prosciutto-lined tin with the turkey mixture and press in, then fold overhanging prosciutto over the top. Cover with foil and seal tightly. Bake for 1 hour. The terrine should be firm to touch.

6 Place the loaf tin in the sink or on a tea towel. Place a second loaf tin on top and press down to release excess juice. Put a couple of tins in the top loaf tin (tinned tomatoes, for example) to weigh it down then refrigerate overnight.

7 To unmould the terrine, remove the top loaf tin and the foil off the top then turn the terrine tin upside down. There will be some jelly-like aspic on the outside of the terrine; this can be wiped off with a paper towel. Cut into slices and serve with a sweet fruit relish or sweet chilli and ginger jam.

Quail cacciatore

Serves 4   Prep time: 15 minutes   Cooking time: about 35 minutes

8 quail halves on the bone
½ cup flour
1 tablespoon olive oil
1 large brown onion, diced
2 cloves garlic, chopped
1 teaspoon dried oregano leaves
800 g tin crushed tomatoes
½ teaspoon salt

½ teaspoon freshly
  ground black pepper
½ cup red wine
About 20 pitted Kalamata olives
½ bunch flat-leaf parsley,
  roughly chopped
Cooked pasta or crusty
  bread, for serving

1 Toss the quail pieces in flour and shake off any excess.

2 In a large chef pan or enamel pot over medium-high heat, heat the oil. Place the floured quail pieces, skin side down, in the pan and leave for about 5 minutes until golden brown. Turn and brown on the other side for about 2 minutes. Remove from the pan and set aside.

3 Pour off most of the fat in the pan, leaving about a tablespoon. Sauté the onion, garlic and oregano leaves for 2 minutes until soft and fragrant. Add the tomatoes, salt, pepper and wine, stir through then simmer for about 5 minutes. Arrange the quail pieces, skin side down, in the pan and cover with a lid. Simmer for 15 minutes, then turn the quail over. Scatter the olives over and simmer for a further 10 minutes with the lid off.

4 Serve with parsley scattered on top, with pasta or crusty bread.

Quail cacciatore,
recipe page 92

Seafood

Introduction

There's nothing more delicious than truly fresh seafood. I have had to come to the sad realisation that I am an abject failure at fishing, so I rely on my local fishmongers to provide me with the fresh delicious things I need.

One of my favourite fish co-ops is under the bridge on the far south coast of New South Wales, at Narooma. They can tell me what's running, what the guys on the boats are catching. The boats pull right into the side of the store and offload their catch, where it's cleaned, filleted and put straight into my waiting hands. It's the next best thing to catching the fish myself.

Buying seafood

When you are looking for a fishmonger to frequent, look for somewhere busy, with high turnover. Ask them when they do their run to the market so you know when the seafood will be freshest. The fish store should smell fresh, like the sea, not fishy or off – this goes for your seafood as well.

When looking for whole fish, look for bright, clear eyes and a bit of a slimy feel to the skin – this indicates freshness. Fillets should be firm to touch.

When you are buying green prawns, note that they will have been frozen on the boat and thawed for your convenience. I prefer to ask for them straight from the freezer so that I can choose when the thawing process begins, ensuring the prawns are as fresh as they can possibly be when I use them.

Storing seafood

Transport your seafood in an esky or cooler bag with ice. Every hour your seafood spends out of the fridge is around a day off its shelf life. As soon as you get home, unwrap the fish from its paper, lay it on paper towel on a plate and cover with plastic wrap. Storage time will vary greatly depending on how fresh the produce was to begin with, so it's best not to buy too far in advance of using it.

The ethics of seafood can be quite confusing, especially when looking into fishing and how our oceans are being utilised for food. There are a few apps freely available that you can refer to when you're in the market or the store to see if a species is being overfished in your area. I tend to think, though, that the best thing to do is question the fishmonger and ask what might be local, what's best eating or running at any given time.

Shellfish

Prawn and serrano ham brochettes

This is a lovely simple Spanish tapas, great for entertaining. If you can't find Serrano ham, use prosciutto instead.

Makes 12   Prep time: 25 minutes   Cooking time: 5 minutes

6 slices Serrano ham, thinly
 sliced lengthways
12 large green (raw) prawns,
 peeled and deveined, tails intact

¼ cup olive oil, for brushing
A few grinds of black pepper
2 lemons, cut into wedges

1 Preheat a griddle plate or barbecue to a high heat.

2 Wrap the ham around the prawns. Use a metal skewer to secure them. Brush with olive oil and sprinkle with a little pepper.

3 Grill over a high heat for about 2 minutes per side, or until the ham is golden and the prawn just cooked through. Serve immediately with lemon wedges.

Grilled prawn satay

Makes 24 canapes   Prep time: 20 minutes   Cooking time: 10–15 minutes

½ bunch coriander
½ brown onion, quartered
2 cloves garlic
1 lime, zested and juiced
1 small red fresh chilli
1 tablespoon peanut oil
½ teaspoon ground turmeric
¼ teaspoon ground dried chillies
200 ml coconut cream

½ cup crunchy peanut butter
2 tablespoons fish sauce
2 tablespoons brown sugar
24 large green (raw) prawns,
 peeled, tails intact
24 iceberg lettuce leaves, cut
 into 10 cm circles with a
 cookie cutter

1 Wash the roots and stems of the coriander and place in a food processor along with the onion, garlic, lime zest and fresh chilli. (Reserve the coriander leaves for serving.) Process until very fine. Alternatively, crush in a mortar and pestle.

Grilled prawn satay,
recipe page 97

2 Heat half the oil in a large non-stick frypan over medium heat. Add the onion mixture and fry until soft and fragrant. Be careful not to let it 'catch' or start to burn. Add the turmeric and ground chilli and stir for a further minute or so.

3 Stir in half the coconut cream and the peanut butter, then bring to a simmer. Simmer for 5 minutes or so. The sauce will split – this is okay.

4 Reduce the heat to low and add the fish sauce, brown sugar and half the lime juice. Taste to see if the sauce needs any more of these three things. This is very dependent on personal taste. Stir in the rest of the coconut cream, taste again and adjust seasoning if need be. Remove from heat and set aside.

5 Heat a wok or frypan to a high heat and brush or drizzle in a little of the remaining oil. Stir-fry the prawns in 3 batches, ensuring that they cook quickly without stewing. After about 1 minute, remove the prawns and set aside on paper towel while you cook the next batch.

6 Serve each prawn on a lettuce leaf, topped with a little satay sauce.

Crab cocktail with avocado mousse

Serves 6 as an entree   Prep time: 20 minutes + setting time

3 avocados
Juice of 1 lemon
1 teaspoon gelatine
½ teaspoon salt
¼ teaspoon finely ground
   white pepper
450 g crab claw meat
1 red capsicum,
   very finely diced
½ bunch chives,
   very finely chopped

2 tablespoons very finely
   chopped coriander leaves,
   plus 6 reserved leaves,
   for garnish
1 small red chilli, seeded and
   very finely chopped (optional)
¼ cup whole egg mayonnaise
¼ teaspoon sea salt
¼ teaspoon finely ground
   white pepper

1 In a food processor, puree the avocados to a smooth paste. Warm the lemon juice in a microwave-safe jug until lukewarm, and stir in the gelatine. Add the gelatine mixture, salt and pepper to the avocado and stir to combine. Place evenly into the bases of 6 serving glasses and place in the fridge to set.

2 Combine the remaining ingredients in a bowl. When the avocado has set, spoon the crab salad carefully over the top and garnish with a coriander leaf.

Fresh lobster with dill mayonnaise

Serves 2   Prep time: 15 minutes

1 whole fresh lobster, about
   1 kg, cooked (see note)
Lemon wedges, for serving

Sea salt flakes, for serving

Dill mayonnaise
½ cup mayonnaise (see page 212)
1 bunch chives, finely chopped
½ bunch dill, leaves
   finely chopped

Zest and juice of ½ lemon

1 To prepare the lobster, twist the head and pull out the tail. Using kitchen scissors, cut the tail in half lengthways, top and bottom, and remove the flesh. Rinse out and reserve the shell and the head for presentation.

2 Cut the flesh into chunks. Arrange the head and the halves of the tail on a platter and place the chunks into the shell.

3 To make the dill mayonnaise, combine all the ingredients in a small bowl.

4 Serve the lobster with lemon wedges, a little dish of sea salt flakes and dill mayonnaise.

Note: There are three ways to approach the buying of a fresh whole lobster: you can purchase it already cooked; if you have a fishmonger in your area that sells live lobsters, you can select your lobster and have them cook it for you; or you can bring it home live, despatch of it humanely and cook it yourself. According to the RSPCA, the humane killing of a lobster involves desensitising the lobster, and destroying the nervous system before cooking. This is a process best done by professionals. Visit RSPCA.org.au for a detailed description of what to do.

If cooking a live lobster, once it has been desensitised and had the nerves destroyed, place it in rapidly boiling salted water and cook for 7 minutes per 500 g. Pull it from the pot and plunge into a large bowl with water and ice to stop the cooking process.

Lobster mornay

Makes 1   Prep time: 10 minutes   Cooking time: 10 minutes

1 cooked whole lobster (about 1 kg)
25 g butter
5 teaspoons plain flour
1 cup milk
2 teaspoons Dijon mustard
¾ cup grated tasty cheese
Salt and finely ground
   white pepper

4 shallots (spring onions),
   white and pale green
   parts only, finely sliced
½ teaspoon smoked paprika
Lemon wedges, for serving
2 cups of rock salt for stable
   cooking

1 Preheat the grill to 200°C.

2 In a small saucepan over medium heat, melt the butter and stir in the flour using a wooden spoon. Keep stirring until the mixture bubbles. Add a splash of milk, stirring all the time. The mixture will come together like a dough. When this happens, add a dash more milk and stir it in, then keep repeating until all the milk is incorporated. If the milk is added too quickly, it will form lumps. When all the milk has been added, allow the sauce to boil for 1–2 minutes then stir in the mustard and half of the grated cheese. Taste and add salt if necessary, and add a pinch of white pepper.

3 To prepare the lobster, slice in half lengthways. Remove the flesh from the tail of the lobster and rinse out the shell, including the head. Chop the lobster flesh into rough chunks and return to each half of the cleaned shells.

4 Place the lobster halves on a baking tray on mounds of rock salt to keep them stable and even. Scatter the shallots over the lobster and divide the sauce between the halves. Scatter the remaining cheese over the top and sprinkle the paprika over. Cook under the hot grill for 2 minutes or until the cheese is golden and bubbling. Serve with lemon wedges.

Soft shell crab tacos,
recipe page 103

Soft shell crab tacos

Makes 8 tacos   Prep time: 20 minutes   Cooking time: 15 minutes

¼ cup sea salt flakes
1 tablespoon ground dried chilli
1 teaspoon Chinese five-spice
2 teaspoons garlic powder
1 cup cornflour
2 tablespoons sesame seeds
Oil, for deep-frying
1 kg frozen soft shell crab, thawed
  and cut in half (or quarters if
  they are large)

3 eggwhites, lightly whisked
½ cup Kewpie (Japanese-style)
  mayonnaise
8 small soft flour tortillas
Asian coleslaw (see page 210)
1 avocado, cut into small dice
Limes wedges, for serving

1 Place the salt and chilli into a dry frypan over medium heat. Shake the pan for 1–2 minutes or until the chilli is fragrant and the salt begins to crackle. Remove from the pan and cool. Place into a mini food processor with the five-spice and garlic powder and blitz until some of the salt and chilli is powdered (but there is still some texture). Combine with the cornflour and sesame seeds in a large bowl and mix well.

2 Heat the oil in a deep-fryer to 180°C. Preheat the oven 150°C and line a baking tray with paper towel.

3 Dip the crab pieces into the eggwhites then gently lower into the chilli salt mixture and coat evenly. Cook the crab in batches for 4–5 minutes or until cooked through and the coating is crisp. Drain on paper towel and place in the oven to keep warm.

4 To assemble the tacos, spread some Kewpie mayonnaise on each tortilla. Top with ⅓ cup Asian slaw (make sure there's plenty of dressing on the coleslaw). Divide the diced avocado between the tacos and top evenly with the crab. Serve with lime wedges.

Note: Soft shell crabs are available frozen from your fishmonger.

Chermoula-marinated king prawns

Serves 4   Prep time: 10 minutes + marinating time
Cooking time: 5 minutes

½ cup fresh mint,
  finely chopped
½ cup fresh parsley,
  finely chopped
½ cup fresh coriander,
  finely chopped
2 cloves garlic, finely chopped
½ large brown onion,
  finely chopped

Finely grated zest of ½ lemon
1½ teaspoons ground cumin seed
¼ teaspoon ground black pepper
1 kg green (raw) king prawns,
  shelled and deveined, tails intact
1 tablespoon vegetable oil
Extra salt and pepper

1 Combine all the ingredients except for the prawns, oil and extra salt and pepper, making sure they are well mixed. Place in a snap-lock bag with the prawns and refrigerate for 15 minutes.

2 Remove the bag from the fridge and heat the flat plate of the barbecue to high. Drizzle the oil onto the hot plate and when it is smoking, put the prawns on. Turn carefully after a couple of minutes and cook for a further minute. Depending on the size of the prawns, they will take 2–3 minutes to cook through. Remove when still very slightly underdone as they will cook for a few moments after being removed.

Note: Overcooking, or a barbecue plate that is not hot enough, will result in tough prawns.

Thai-style salad of seared scallops

Serves 6 as an entree   Prep time: 20 minutes   Cooking time: 6 minutes

For the dressing
½ cup caster sugar
½ cup white vinegar
1 bird's eye (small red) chilli,
  seeded and sliced finely

1 clove garlic, finely chopped
2 tablespoons fish sauce

For the salad
1 telegraph cucumber,
  made into spaghetti
  with a spiralizer
1 carrot, made into spaghetti
  with a spiralizer
½ red capsicum,
  julienned very finely
1 red onion, sliced very finely
18 sea scallops

Peanut oil, for frying
1 cup bean sprouts
1 bunch coriander,
  leaves picked
⅓ cup toasted sesame seeds

1 To make the dressing, in a medium saucepan over medium-high heat, place the sugar and vinegar with ⅔ cup of water. Bring to the boil, stirring to dissolve the sugar. Boil for 5 minutes and remove from the heat. Allow to cool to lukewarm. Stir in the chilli, garlic and fish sauce. Allow to cool completely.

2 In a large bowl, combine the cucumber and carrot spaghetti with the capsicum and onion.

3 Pat the scallops dry with paper towel. In a large frypan over high heat, heat a splash of peanut oil and place 6 scallops in the pan. Cook for about 1 minute on one side (depending upon their thickness), or until they develop a lovely golden crust. Flip the scallops and cook very briefly on the other side. Remove from the pan to some fresh paper towel and cover while cooking the remaining scallops.

4 Just before serving, toss about half the dressing through the salad. Place a little mound of salad in the centre of each entree plate. Top with bean sprouts and coriander leaves. Place 3 scallops around the perimeter of the salad. Drizzle the remaining dressing over the scallops and salad, and top very generously with toasted sesame seeds.

Scallops with pea puree, speck and pangrattato

Serves 4   Prep time: 20 minutes   Cooking time: 15 minutes

2 cups frozen baby peas
2 cups chicken stock (see page 152)
50 g unsalted butter
Salt, to taste
100 g piece of smoked speck,
   cut into 5 mm thick batons
2 tablespoons olive oil

½ cup (20 g) very coarse
   fresh breadcrumbs
Zest of 1 lemon
2 tablespoons finely chopped
   flat-leaf parsley
1 tablespoon butter
12 fat scallops, roe removed

1 Place the peas in a medium saucepan with the chicken stock. Cover and bring to the boil. Boil rapidly for 3–4 minutes. Place the peas and stock in a food processor with the butter and a pinch of salt, and process until smooth.

2 Sauté the speck in a frypan over medium-high heat until golden and the fat has rendered out. Remove and drain on paper towel. To make the pangrattato, add 1 tablespoon olive oil to the fat in the pan, and add the breadcrumbs. Stir continually, until the breadcrumbs are golden and crunchy, then drain on paper towel. Toss the breadcrumbs with the lemon zest and parsley.

Vietnamese rice paper rolls,
recipe page 107

3 Heat the butter and remaining oil in the hot frypan. When it is foaming, add the scallops and cook for 1–2 minutes until golden brown and turning opaque. Turn and cook for a further 30 seconds to 1 minute.

4 Dollop roughly 3 tablespoons of pea puree onto the serving dishes. Settle 3 scallops on top of the puree. Place the speck batons around the scallops and finish with a generous sprinkle of the pangrattato.

Vietnamese rice paper rolls with dipping sauce

Serves 8   Prep time: 20 minutes   Cooking time: about 2 minutes

Dipping sauce
2 tablespoons sugar
1½ tablespoons lime juice
2 tablespoons fish sauce
1 teaspoon chopped garlic
½ teaspoon chopped bird's eye
  (small red) chilli

Rice paper rolls
1 teaspoon peanut or vegetable oil
100 g green (raw) prawn
  meat, chopped
½ teaspoon sugar
½ teaspoon salt
½ cup bean sprouts
½ cup grated cucumber, seeded
½ cup grated carrot
4 shallots (spring onions),
  sliced finely lengthways
2 teaspoons lime juice
1 pinch extra sugar and salt
8 sheets dry rice paper
½ cup shredded lettuce leaves
½ cup chopped mixed fresh herbs
  (coriander, Vietnamese mint,
  common mint, basil)

1 First make the dipping sauce. In a bowl, combine the sugar, lime juice and fish sauce. Stir to dissolve the sugar. Stir in the garlic and chilli. Taste and add more sugar or fish sauce if desired.

2 Heat the oil in a wok over medium heat. Add the prawns, sugar and salt and stir-fry for 1 minute or until cooked.

3 In a separate bowl, add the bean sprouts, cucumber, carrot, shallots, lime juice and an extra pinch each of sugar and salt. Toss together and set aside.

4 To make the rolls, dip 1 sheet of rice paper into warm water and rest on a damp cloth. Arrange one-eighth of the lettuce and herbs in a line along the top edge of the rice paper, followed by one-eighth of the salad mixture and

one-eighth of the prawn mixture. Roll the paper tightly, folding over the ends when you reach the halfway point. Place the roll on a damp cloth and cover to prevent drying out. Repeat for the remaining 7 rolls.

5 To serve, cut the rolls in half diagonally and place on a platter with a small dish of dipping sauce.

Note: Instead of prawns, you can use cooked chicken.

Coquilles St Jacques

Serves 4 as an entree   Prep time: 15 minutes   Cooking time: 15 minutes

Seafood

20 g butter
1 tablespoon olive oil
12 scallops in the half-shell
   (unattached)
8 small Swiss brown mushrooms
   (about 100 g), stalk removed,
   finely sliced
1 tablespoon flour

⅓ cup white wine
1 cup thickened cream
Salt and finely ground
   white pepper
40 g Gruyère cheese, grated
2 tablespoons chopped parsley
Lemon wedges, for serving

1 In a medium frypan over medium-high heat, add half the butter and half the oil until the butter is frothing and starting to brown. The pan must be hot. Place the scallops in the pan and sauté for a bare 15–20 seconds each side, enough for a small amount of gold to appear. Remove to paper towel and set aside. They will cook further in the sauce.

2 Add the remaining butter and oil to the pan. When the butter is frothing, add the mushrooms and sauté for about 5 minutes. The mushrooms will wilt and appear wet, then the moisture will evaporate and the mushrooms will brown. At this point, sprinkle the flour over the mushrooms in the pan. Add the wine and stir with a spatula to combine. Cook for about a minute. Add the cream and stir again to combine. Taste and season with salt and white pepper.

3 Preheat the grill to high. Wash and dry the scallop shells and put them on a baking tray. Place a spoonful of the mushroom cream sauce in each shell and top with a scallop. Top with another spoonful of sauce. Divide the Gruyère cheese between the shells. Place the tray under the hot grill for about 4 minutes, until the cheese is golden and bubbling. Top with the chopped parsley and serve 3 scallop shells to a plate with lemon wedges alongside.

Prawn and pasta salad

Serves 4   Prep time: 15 minutes   Cooking time: 15 minutes

375 g packet large pasta spirals
1 tablespoon olive oil
1 cup whole egg mayonnaise
  (see page 212) or store bought
½ cup sour cream
1 tablespoon Dijon mustard
¼ cup tomato sauce
6 shallots (spring onions),
  white and pale green parts
  only, finely sliced
1 small red capsicum,
  finely chopped

1 punnet cherry or grape
  tomatoes, halved
1 cucumber, halved, seeded and
  sliced into 5 mm thick slices
2 celery stalks, sliced finely
500 g cooked Crystal Bay or
  tiger prawns, peeled
  and deveined
Lemon wedges, for serving
Ground black pepper, for serving

1 Cook the pasta according to packet directions. Drain and toss through olive oil to prevent it from sticking.

2 In a large bowl, combine the mayonnaise, sour cream, mustard and tomato sauce. Toss through the shallots, capsicum, tomatoes, cucumber, celery, prawns and pasta. Serve with lemon wedges and ground black pepper.

Note: After refrigerating, the dressing in this salad will seize up. It can be refreshed by adding a little mayonnaise and possibly some lemon juice, and giving it a good stir.

Fish

Whole salt-crusted snapper

Serves 4   Prep time: 10 minutes   Cooking time: 45 minutes

6 eggwhites
2 kg cooking salt
1 whole snapper (about 1 kg),
   gutted but unscaled

¼ bunch parsley
2 cloves garlic, sliced
1 lemon, sliced

1 Preheat the oven to 180°C.

2 In a bowl, whisk the egg whites until frothy. Add the salt and whisk again to combine.

3 Place half the salt mixture on a baking tray and place the snapper on top. Cut the stalks off the parsley and place in the cavity of the fish along with the garlic and half the lemon slices. Cover the fish with the remaining salt mixture.

4 Bake for 45 minutes. The crust will harden.

5 To serve, crack the top of the crust open, lift off and discard. Carefully lift away the scaly skin and discard. Lay the remaining lemon slices on the fish and scatter with parsley. Serve whole to the table.

Tuna cauliflower gratin

Serves 4   Prep time: 15 minutes   Cooking time: 30 minutes

1 smallish head cauliflower,
   cut into 4 cm florets
425 g tin tuna in brine
25 g butter
25 g flour
1¾ cups milk

1 tablespoon Dijon mustard
1½ cups grated tasty cheese
Salt and pepper
½ cup fresh breadcrumbs
Green salad, for serving

1 Preheat the oven to 180°C.

2 Steam or microwave the cauliflower until tender. This will take about 6 minutes, covered, on high in the microwave. Make sure any excess moisture is drained off then arrange the florets into 4 individual gratin dishes. Try to keep the 'flower' side up where possible.

3 Drain the tuna and break it into chunks. Arrange the tuna around the cauliflower.

Whole salt-crusted snapper,
recipe page 110

4 To make cheese sauce, in a medium saucepan over medium heat melt the butter and add the flour. Stir constantly with a wooden spoon until it gathers into a dough. Continue to stir for another minute or so. This begins to cook the flour. Add a little milk – about ¼ cup – and stir. This will incorporate fairly quickly into the dough and will once again come away from the sides of the pan. Once this happens, you can stir in another ¼ cup milk, then repeat until all the milk has been added. Stir in the mustard, then add 1 cup cheese and stir until it melts. Taste, and season with salt and pepper if required.

5 Pour the cheese sauce over the tuna and cauliflower, making sure the sauce covers and surrounds it all and there are no gaps.

6 Mix the remaining cheese with the breadcrumbs and sprinkle over each gratin. Bake uncovered for 10–15 minutes or until golden brown on top. Serve with a simple green salad.

Sesame-crusted snapper with bok choi

Serves 4   Prep time: 15 minutes   Cooking time: 15 minutes

2 cups jasmine rice
2 tablespoons peanut or
  vegetable oil
¼ cup sesame seeds
4 boneless, skinless snapper
  fillets (about 150 g each)
3 cm knob ginger,
  peeled and chopped

2 cloves garlic, chopped
1 bunch bok choi, cut into
  5 cm lengths
1 bunch shallots (spring onions),
  cut into 5 cm lengths
2 cups fish or chicken stock
  (see page 152) or store bought
2 tablespoons soy sauce

1 Put the rice with 3 cups of water in a microwave rice cooker and put the lid on. Microwave on high for 18 minutes.

2 Heat a chef pan over medium-high heat and add 1 tablespoon oil.

3 Place the sesame seeds in a shallow dish. Dip the fish portions, one side only, into the sesame seeds. Place the fish, seed side down, in the hot pan and cook for 2–3 minutes or until the sesame seeds are golden and the fish is turning opaque. Flip carefully and cook for a further minute or two. The cooking time will depend on the thickness of the fish. Once cooked, remove the fish from the pan and put on a plate, seed side up, to rest.

4 Add the rest of the oil to the pan and reduce the heat to medium. Add the ginger and garlic and sauté for a minute or until soft and fragrant. Raise the heat and toss through the bok choi and shallots. Pour in a little chicken stock,

then add the soy sauce. Pour in the rest of the stock and bring back to the boil then remove from the heat.

5 Ladle the broth and divide the vegetables into 4 bowls. Top each bowl with a piece of fish. Remove the rice from the microwave and fluff with a fork. Serve alongside the fish.

Whole barbecued snapper stuffed with seafood

Serves 4   Prep time: 15 minutes   Cooking time: 45 minutes

2 limes, zested and cut into slices
8 large green (raw) prawns,
  shelled and deveined,
  cut into chunks
100 g crab meat
1 clove garlic, chopped
1 tablespoon grated ginger
2 tablespoons chopped
  coriander leaves

1 small red chilli, seeded and
  finely chopped
6 shallots (spring onions),
  sliced finely
1 whole snapper (about 1.8 kg)
1 tablespoon olive oil
A handful of loose coriander
  leaves, to serve

1 Preheat a barbecue with a hood to 180°C.

2 In a bowl, combine the lime zest, prawn, crab meat, garlic, ginger, chopped coriander, chilli, and half the shallots (reserving the rest for garnish). Mix well.

3 Score the fish deeply 3 or 4 times on each side. Drizzle with olive oil and rub thoroughly into the skin and the cuts.

4 Place the seafood mixture in the cavity of the snapper.

5 Tear some baking paper and heavy foil about 30 cm longer than the length of the fish. Place the foil with baking paper on top and lay the fish in the centre. Wrap the foil and baking paper around the fish, folding the seams over several times to ensure no juices can escape and keeping the main seam along the centre top of the fish.

6 Turn off the centre burners on the barbecue, leaving the outside burners on. Place the snapper in the centre of the barbecue and cook, with the hood down, for about 45 minutes. (Cooking time may vary with different barbecues and different thicknesses of the fish.)

7 Remove the fish from the barbecue and check that it is cooked. The eye

should be white and the flesh just underdone as it will continue to cook while resting. Do not remove the foil or baking paper; just tear a little hole near the head of the fish to check.

8 Place the fish on a serving platter and allow to rest for a few minutes. Neatly unwrap the foil and baking paper along the top seam. Peel back the skin to reveal the flesh. Scatter the flesh with the remaining lime slices, shallots and coriander leaves then take the platter to the table.

9 To serve, carve one side of the flesh into segments and carefully lift each slice with an egg lifter onto each plate. The seafood stuffing is served to the side. When the top half of the fish is served, remove the back bone and any other visible bones by lifting them away, exposing the bottom half of the flesh for carving.

Salmon fillet with lemon caper butter

Serves 4   Prep time: 5 minutes   Cooking time: 10 minutes

1 teaspoon olive oil
50 g butter
Sea salt and freshly
  ground black pepper
4 salmon fillets (about 180 g each),
  skin on

2 tablespoons baby
  capers, rinsed
1 tablespoon lemon juice

1 Heat a chef pan over medium-high heat. Add the olive oil and half the butter. When the butter is frothing, sprinkle some salt and pepper on the salmon skin and place the fillets skin side down in the pan. Cook for 3–4 minutes or until golden. Press gently with a spatula so that the skin retains contact with the pan. Turn the fish and cook for a further minute, seasoning the other side as well. Cooking time will depend on the thickness of the fish. Remove the fish from the pan and rest on a plate under foil for 3–4 minutes before serving.

2 Add the remaining butter to the pan and when it is starting to brown, add the capers and lemon juice and stir to combine. Serve 4 pieces of fish with the lemon caper butter over the top.

Crisp-skinned salmon with sweet soy glaze

Serves 4   Prep time: 10 minutes   Cooking time: 10 minutes

1 tablespoon peanut or olive oil
3 cm knob ginger, julienned finely
2 tablespoons light soy sauce
2 tablespoons honey

1 tablespoon white vinegar
4 salmon fillets (about 180 g each),
  skin on
Sea salt flakes, for serving

1 Preheat the barbecue flat plate to medium-high heat (or heat a large non-stick chef pan over medium-high heat).

2 In a small pot, place ½ teaspoon oil and add the ginger. Sauté for a minute until soft and fragrant. Add the soy sauce, honey and vinegar, and stir until combined. Bring to the boil then remove from the heat and set aside.

3 Place the remaining oil on the flat plate or in the pan and add the salmon, skin side down. Press down on the fish so the skin has full contact with the heat. Brush some glaze over the raw side of the fish while the skin side cooks. Cook for 3–4 minutes, then turn and cook for a further 1–2 minutes, or until done to your liking. Cooking time will depend on how thick the fillet is. Bear in mind that it will continue to cook for a minute or two after being removed from the heat. Put on a plate under foil to rest.

4 To serve, drizzle the fish with the remaining glaze and sprinkle with a few sea salt flakes.

Salmon croquettes

Please buy a good quality of salmon for this recipe. It's still a very cheap meal even when you use good salmon. It can be varied in any number of ways, by adding fresh herbs to the mixture if available, or using peas as well as corn.

Serves 4   Prep time: 10 minutes   Cooking time: 20 minutes

2 large or 3 medium potatoes,
  peeled
415 g tin pink salmon, drained,
  bones removed
½ bunch shallots (spring onions),
  white and pale green parts only,
  finely sliced
440 g tin corn kernels, drained

1 teaspoon salt
¼ teaspoon ground white pepper
1 egg, beaten
4 cups fresh breadcrumbs
Oil, for deep-frying
For serving: lemon wedges,
  whole egg mayonnaise
  (see page 212) and salad

1 In a pot of salted water, boil the potatoes until tender then drain well. Mash in a bowl.

2 Add the salmon, shallots, corn, salt and pepper to the potatoes, and stir through. Taste and adjust seasoning if necessary.

Vietnamese fish curry,
recipe page 117

3 Add the egg and mix well. Stir in up to 2 cups breadcrumbs, until the mixture is a good consistency for shaping into patties.

4 Place the remaining breadcrumbs in a shallow dish. Scoop out small amounts of the salmon mixture and form into balls about the size of golf balls. Roll the balls in the breadcrumbs and press firmly to coat. Flatten slightly so they are like mini patties.

5 Heat the oil in a deep-fryer to 190°C, or in a saucepan over medium-high heat. Deep-fry the croquettes in batches for 3–4 minutes or until a deep golden brown. Allow the oil to come back to temperature after each batch, before cooking the next. Drain on paper towel and serve piping hot with lemon wedges, whole egg mayonnaise and salad.

Vietnamese fish curry

Serves 4   Prep time: 15 minutes + marinating time
Cooking time: 15 minutes

1 brown onion, quartered
5 cm knob ginger, peeled and sliced
2 cloves garlic
2 tablespoons ground turmeric
1 tablespoon brown sugar
2 teaspoons fish sauce
4 white fish fillets (about 600 g total),
   cut into 3 cm pieces
1 tablespoon coconut or peanut oil

270 ml tin coconut cream
1 packet rice vermicelli,
   soaked and drained
½ bunch dill, very roughly
   chopped
½ bunch shallots, sliced finely
2 tablespoons lime juice
Lime wedges, to serve

1 Place the onion, ginger and garlic in the bowl of a mini processor and process to a paste. Combine the paste, turmeric, sugar and fish sauce in a bowl. Toss the fish pieces through the paste and refrigerate, covered, for an hour.

2 Heat a non-stick chef pan over medium-high heat and add the oil. Cook the marinated fish for about 2 minutes or until the marinade is golden. Turn the fish and cook for a further minute. Carefully remove the fish from the pan to a plate and set aside.

3 Add any remaining marinade to the pan and stir-fry for 1 minute. Add the coconut cream then the rice vermicelli and stir to mix. Remove from the heat and stir through half of the dill and half of the shallots. Add the lime juice and stir.

4 Place the noodle mixture in a serving dish and top with the fish pieces, then top with the remaining shallots and dill. Serve with lime wedges.

Poached side of salmon with herbed mayonnaise

Serves 6 as a main, 10–12 as part of a shared table   Prep time: 15 minutes
Cooking time: 20 minutes

Side of salmon, skinless
  and boneless
1 lemon, zested and sliced
1 small onion, quartered
2 bay leaves
½ teaspoon black peppercorns

½ bunch parsley, leaves
  finely chopped, stalks reserved
1 bunch chives, finely chopped
½ bunch dill, leaves
  finely chopped
⅔ cup whole egg mayonnaise

Seafood

1 Place the salmon in the base of a flame-proof baking dish which fits it comfortably. Add the lemon slices, onion, bay leaves, peppercorns and parsley stems and cover with water. Place on the stovetop over a low heat and bring to a gentle simmer. Cook for 10–15 minutes for a fillet that is about 3 cm thick at its thickest part. Err on the side of undercooking rather than overcooking, as the flesh will continue to cook for a few minutes after being removed from the poaching liquid. Using 2 slotted spoons or egg flips, very carefully lift the salmon out onto a platter and cover with foil.

2 For the herbed mayonnaise, stir the lemon zest, chopped parsley leaves, chives and dill into the mayonnaise.

3 Serve the salmon at room temperature with the mayonnaise on the side.

Coconut-crumbed fish fillets with tartare sauce

This is lovely with baby chat potatoes and a green salad.

Serves 4   Prep time: 20 minutes   Cooking time: 6–8 minutes per batch

Vegetable oil to fill pan to 5 mm
⅔ cup plain flour
½ teaspoon salt
¼ teaspoon ground white pepper
1 egg
½ cup desiccated coconut
1 cup homemade or
  panko-style breadcrumbs

Zest of 1 lemon
600 g boneless white
  fish fillets
1 lemon, cut into wedges
tartare sauce, to serve
  (see page 147)

1 In a wide frypan, heat the oil over a medium-high heat.

2 Combine the flour, salt and pepper in a shallow bowl. In another shallow bowl, beat the egg with 1 tablespoon water. In a third bowl, combine the coconut, breadcrumbs and lemon zest. Dip each piece of fish into the flour, then the egg, and finally the crumb mixture, pressing the crumbs gently so they stick. Lay each piece of fish in the frypan and cook for 3–4 minutes on each side or until golden brown and crunchy. It will depend on the size of your frypan whether you do the fish all at once or in batches – it's best not to overcrowd the pan. Keep the cooked fish warm in a 100°C oven.

3 Serve the fish with the tartare sauce and lemon wedges alongside.

Variation: Exchange the coconut for sesame seeds, or leave it out altogether and increase the amount of breadcrumbs.

Dukkah-crusted salmon

Serves 4   Prep time: 15 minutes   Cooking time: 10 minutes

¾ cup or 1 quantity dukkah
  (see page 167)
4 boneless salmon fillets
  (about 180 g each), skin on

1 tablespoon olive oil

1 Place the dukkah in a shallow dish. Press the salmon, skin side down, into the dukkah to coat.

2 Heat the olive oil in a chef pan over a medium-high heat and place the fish, skin side down, in the pan. Leave for 3–4 minutes, or until you can see the fish turning opaque from the bottom to about a quarter of the way up. Carefully turn the salmon over and cook for a further 2–3 minutes, or until the dukkah is golden and the fish has cooked through to your liking.

Note: Store-bought dukkah can be used if you prefer. This recipe needs about ¾ cup – whatever you don't use for the salmon can be stored in an airtight container and eaten with bread and olive oil.

Fish and leek pie

Serves 6   Prep time: 10 minutes   Cooking time: 35 minutes

50 g butter
2 leeks, white and pale green
   parts only, very finely sliced
¼ cup flour
3 cups milk
½ teaspoon salt
¼ teaspoon ground white pepper
500 g firm-fleshed, white fish,
   cut into 3 cm cubes

300 g green (raw) king prawns,
   shelled, deveined and halved
6 sheets puff pastry
   (or 2 quantities from
   the recipe on page 234)
1 egg, beaten

1 Preheat the oven to 220°C.

2 In a chef pan, heat the butter over a medium heat and sauté the leek until soft – about 5 minutes. Add the flour and stir until well combined. Add 2½ cups milk, a little at a time, stirring and ensuring that the flour cooks after each addition. Season with salt and pepper.

3 Fold through the fish pieces and prawns. The sauce will seem quite thick but the fish releases some juices while baking. Spread the fish mixture carefully into 6 individual gratin dishes or ramekins.

4 Over each dish, drape the puff pastry, rolled out to 3 mm thick, and press all around the edges of the dish so that it sticks. Use a small sharp knife to cut off the excess pastry. Pierce the pastry top in 3 places, then brush with beaten egg. Bake for 30 minutes or until the puff pastry is golden brown.

Barbecued baby snapper with chimichurri

Serves 4   Prep time: 10 minutes   Cooking time: 20 minutes

2 whole baby snappers
   (about 500 g each)
1 quantity chimichurri
   (see page 139)

1 lemon, thickly sliced, plus
   lemon wedges, for serving

1 Preheat a hooded barbecue – turn on the outside burners and leave the middle ones off. Alternatively, preheat the oven to 180°C.

2 For each fish, lay out 2 pieces of aluminium foil, joined in the middle.

Cover this with extra-wide baking paper (or 2 normal pieces folded to join in the middle). Lay the snapper in the middle of the paper and score deeply 3–4 times on each side. Work half of the chimichurri into the cuts and place some lemon slices in the cavity. Repeat with the second fish.

3 Gather the foil around each fish to form a parcel that is loose but has no gaps in the joins. Place on the middle plates of the barbecue (the ones with no direct heat under them) for 16–20 minutes. The cooking time will depend on a number of things – how many times you open the barbecue to check it, the thickness of the fish, the temperature of the outside air. To test if the fish is cooked, carefully open the foil at the top and, using a fork, check that a small piece of the flesh in its thickest part moves away from the bone.

4 Serve the fish with the other half of the chimichurri and some fresh lemon wedges on a platter and allow diners to help themselves. When the flesh on the top side of the fish has been served, the skeleton can be lifted off to allow access to the flesh underneath.

Salmon cannelloni

Serves 4–6   Prep time: 15 minutes   Cooking time: 50 minutes

50 g butter
2 brown onions, finely sliced
2 cloves garlic
1 leek, finely sliced
¼ cup flour
1½ cups milk
½ teaspoon salt
¼ teaspoon ground white pepper

600 g skinless Atlantic salmon,
    cubed into 3 cm pieces
½ bunch fresh dill leaves,
    roughly chopped
1 packet fresh lasagne sheets
1 cup grated tasty cheese
Lemon wedges, for serving

1 Preheat the oven to 200°C.

2 In a chef pan or large, heavy-based frypan, heat the butter over a medium heat and sauté the onion, garlic and leek until soft – about 5 minutes. Add the flour and stir until well combined. Add the milk a little at a time, stirring and ensuring that it is incorporated after each addition. Season with salt and pepper. Reserve 1 cup of this béchamel sauce.

3 Add the fish and dill to the sauce in the pan and fold through. The sauce will seem quite thick but the fish releases some juices while baking. Spread ⅓ cup fish mixture onto a lasagne sheet and roll up to enclose. Place in a baking dish. Repeat with remaining fish mixture and lasagne sheets. Cover the top of the cannelloni with the reserved sauce, then top with tasty cheese.

4 Bake for 40 minutes or until the top is golden. Serve with lemon wedges.

Squid and octopus

Barbecued squid stuffed with chorizo saffron risotto

Serves 4   Prep time: 30 minutes   Cooking time: 25 minutes

2 cups good-quality
   liquid chicken stock (see page 152)
   or store bought
½ teaspoon saffron threads
1 chorizo, cut into ½ cm cubes
25 g unsalted butter
1 brown onion, finely chopped
2 garlic cloves, crushed
¾ cup arborio rice
½ cup white wine

½ cup freshly grated parmesan
1 bunch flat-leaf parsley,
   roughly chopped
Salt and ground black pepper
   to taste
4 large prepared squid tubes
   (or whole fresh arrow squid,
   see note)
1 tablespoon olive oil
2 lemons, cut into wedges

1 Combine the stock and saffron in a medium saucepan over high heat. Bring just to the boil. Reduce heat and simmer gently.

2 Heat a large non-stick frypan over medium-high heat. Add the chorizo and sauté until the fat renders out and the chorizo is lightly golden. Add the butter, onion and garlic and cook, stirring, for 5 minutes or until soft and translucent.

3 Add the rice and stir for 1 minute or until grains appear slightly translucent. Add the wine and cook, stirring constantly, until the liquid is completely absorbed.

4 Add a ladleful (about ½ cup) of hot stock. Stir very gently, to distribute the rice evenly through the stock. Continue to add the stock, a ladleful at a time, stirring constantly and allowing the liquid to be absorbed before adding the next ladleful. Cook for 20 minutes or until the rice is tender yet firm to the bite, and the risotto is creamy.

5 Remove the pan from the heat. Stir in the grated parmesan and half the parsley. Taste and season with salt and pepper. When the risotto has cooled enough to handle (but is not cold), spoon it into the squid tubes and secure the openings with a bamboo skewer.

6 Heat a barbecue char grill to high. Brush the outsides of the squid with a little olive oil and place on the hot grill. Leave it, without turning, for about 1 minute or until char marks appear. Turn a quarter-turn, leave until char

123

Barbecued squid stuffed with chorizo
saffron risotto, recipe page 122

marks appear, and repeat twice more. The squid should be just cooked through with prominent char lines. (If you prepare your own squid, cook the tentacles and wings on the hot grill also.)

7 Serve the squid tubes scattered with the rest of the parsley and lemon wedges on the side.

Note: *To clean squid*
Grasp the tentacles firmly and pull from the body. Be careful not to burst the ink sac. Cut the head from the tentacles just below the eyes, and pop the hard beak out. Run your fingers along the tentacles and remove any little shell-like circles. Separate into single tentacles.

Pull the hard cartilage from the centre of the squid tube. Reach into the tube with a butter knife and scrape out any slime.

Grasp the wing and peel it to remove the skin. Continue to remove the skin from the whole tube, including the second wing.

The squid tube is now ready to stuff.

Crumbed calamari

Makes about 50 pieces   Prep time: 10 minutes
Cooking time: 2–3 minutes per batch

Vegetable oil, for deep-frying
3 large or 4 small squid tubes
½ cup plain flour
1 teaspoon salt
¼ teaspoon ground white pepper
1 teaspoon garlic powder
½ teaspoon Chinese five-spice

1 egg, beaten with a little water
3 cups homemade or
   panko breadcrumbs
1 quantity tartare sauce
  (see page 147)
1 lemon, cut into 8 wedges

1 Heat the oil in a deep-fryer to 190°C. If using a large pot, half fill with oil and heat until a piece of bread dropped in takes a minute to turn golden brown.

2 Cut the squid tubes down one side and lay them out flat. Scrape any membrane from inside the tubes. Lightly score in a diamond pattern using a sharp knife. Cut the tube in half lengthways and then cut across into 2 cm wide strips.

3 Combine the flour, salt, pepper, garlic powder and five-spice in a shallow bowl. Place the beaten egg and breadcrumbs into separate shallow bowls.

4 Dip the squid strips in the seasoned flour, then the egg, and allow excess egg to drain before coating in the breadcrumbs. Prepare 6–8 calamari pieces at a time and then fry in the 190°C oil for 2–3 minutes or until golden brown. It's important that the oil is the right temperature – if it's too cold the calamari will be tough and greasy; if it's too hot they will burn on the outside before cooking on the inside. Remove from the oil and place on a tray in a 100°C oven. Continue to prepare and cook the calamari in batches of 6–8 pieces at a time.

5 Serve hot, with tartare sauce and lemon wedges.

Combination

Seafood stew

Serves 4   Prep time: 30 minutes   Cooking time: 30 minutes

1 chorizo (about 100 g),
  diced quite small
12 green (raw) king prawns,
  body shell removed, head
  and tail intact
400 g tin crushed tomatoes
1 medium brown onion,
  peeled and cut into quarters
1 red capsicum, seeded and
  cut into large pieces
3 cloves garlic, peeled
2 tablespoons olive oil

2 teaspoons smoked paprika
1 cup white wine
1 litre chicken stock (see page 152)
  or store bought
¼ teaspoon saffron
1 kg pot-ready live mussels
  (see note)
A little extra olive oil
½ cup flat-leaf parsley,
  roughly chopped
2 lemons, cut into wedges

1 Heat a large, non-stick pot over medium-high heat. Cook the diced chorizo for about a minute or until golden brown. Remove to a bowl, leaving any oil released in the pot.

2 Sauté the prawns briefly until slightly golden and just cooked through. Remove to another bowl.

3 Place the tomatoes, onion, capsicum and garlic in a food processor and puree until smooth. Add the olive oil to the pot and then the capsicum mixture. Stir until most of the moisture has evaporated. This will take about 5 minutes. The mixture will start to crackle and become more paste-like when it is ready. Add the paprika and stir for a further minute.

4 Pour in the wine and stir for a minute. Add the chicken stock and saffron

Seafood stew,
recipe page 125

and bring to a simmer. Drop in the mussels and the chorizo. After 8 minutes, add the prawns and remove the pot from the heat.

5 Serve in bowls drizzled with a little olive oil and scattered with parsley, and the lemon wedges alongside.

Note: Pot-ready live mussels are available from your fishmonger and some supermarkets.

Seafood risotto

Serves 4   Prep time: 25 minutes   Cooking time: 25 minutes

2 tablespoons olive oil
12 large green (raw) king prawns,
  body shell removed, head
  and tail intact
150 g skinless salmon fillet,
  cut into 3 cm cubes
2 squid tubes, cut into rings
1 litre fish or chicken stock
  (see page 152) or store bought

¼ teaspoon saffron threads
25 g unsalted butter
1 brown onion, finely chopped
2 garlic cloves, crushed
1½ cups arborio rice
½ cup white wine
½ teaspoon salt
¼ teaspoon ground white pepper
½ bunch fresh dill leaves

1 In a large chef pan over medium-high heat, place 2 teaspoons olive oil. Sauté the prawns until light golden brown and just cooked through. Remove to a bowl and cover with foil.

2 Add another 2 teaspoons oil to the pan and sauté the salmon and squid rings until just undercooked. Remove to another bowl and cover with foil.

3 Combine the stock and saffron in a medium saucepan over high heat. Bring just to the boil. Reduce heat and simmer gently.

4 Heat the butter and remaining oil in a large non-stick frypan over medium heat. Add the onion and garlic and cook, stirring, for 5 minutes or until soft and translucent. Add the rice and stir for 2–3 minutes or until the grains appear slightly translucent. Add the wine and cook, stirring constantly, until it is completely absorbed.

5 Add a ladleful (about ½ cup) of hot stock. Stir gently, just enough to ensure the stock is evenly distributed through the rice. Continue to add the stock, a ladleful at a time, stirring constantly and allowing the liquid to be absorbed before adding the next ladleful. Cook for 20 minutes or until the rice is tender yet firm to the bite, and the risotto is creamy.

6 Remove the pan from the heat. Stir in the salt and pepper, then add the salmon and squid and stir gently through. Nestle the prawns into the rice, body-down so the heads and tails sit up for beautiful presentation. Scatter with dill leaf tips.

Creamy seafood chowder

Serves 6 as an entree, 4 as a main meal
Prep time: 20 minutes   Cooking time: 30 minutes

1 cup white wine
12 mussels, live pot-ready
2 tablespoons olive oil
4 tablespoons butter
200 g boneless, skinless white
  fish fillets, cut into 6 pieces
200 g boneless, skinless
  salmon fillet, cut into 6 pieces
12 green (raw) king prawns,
  shell removed, tails
  intact, deveined
12 sea scallops
2 brown shallots, sliced
2 cloves garlic, sliced

50 g butter
50 g plain flour
300 ml milk
300 ml cream
Sea salt and ground
  white pepper
2 tablespoons lemon juice
½ bunch fresh dill, leaf tips
  roughly chopped
4 shallots (spring onions),
  white and pale green parts only,
  finely sliced diagonally
Lemon wedges, to serve

1 In a pot, bring the white wine to the boil and add the mussels. Steam for 2–3 minutes or until opened. Set the mussels aside and reserve the liquid.

2 In a chef pan, heat ½ tablespoon olive oil and 1 tablespoon butter over medium-high heat. Sauté the white fish fillet pieces until white on the outside but still slightly underdone. Set aside with the mussels.

3 Repeat the process with the salmon, then prawns, then scallops. Each piece of seafood should be just slightly undercooked as it will cook further when the hot soup is added.

4 Using the same chef pan as the seafood has been cooked in, reduce the heat and sauté the shallots and garlic until they are translucent and soft. Do not brown.

5 Deglaze the pan using the reserved wine from cooking the mussels. Reduce the heat to a very gentle simmer while you make the béchamel.

6 In the pot which the mussels were cooked in, heat the butter and flour over a medium heat. Stir constantly until the mixture starts to bubble and come

together. Add a little of the milk and stir until it is incorporated. Repeat until all the milk has been added then simmer for a few minutes to ensure that the flour is well cooked.

7 Strain the shallots and garlic and return the liquid to the béchamel sauce. Stir in the cream and bring back up to a simmer.

8 Add the béchamel sauce to the chef pan, little by little, whisking well after each addition. Add enough so that the consistency is as thick as you like it. Taste and season with salt and pepper. Once the soup is simmering gently, turn the heat off and stir in the lemon juice, dill leaf tips and shallots.

9 Divide the seafood evenly and artistically among shallow soup bowls and pour the steaming hot soup over the top. Serve immediately with lemon wedges on the side.

Variation: Fry up some very thinly sliced bacon to sprinkle over the top before serving.

Note: Pot-ready live mussels are available from your fishmonger and some supermarkets.

Seafood lasagne

Serves 4–6   Prep time: 15 minutes   Cooking time: 50 minutes

50 g butter
2 leeks, white and pale green
  parts only, finely sliced
  on the diagonal
¼ cup flour
1½ cups milk
½ teaspoon salt
¼ teaspoon ground
  white pepper
200 g firm-fleshed white fish,
  cut into 3 cm cubes
200 g skinless Atlantic salmon,
  cut into 3 cm cubes

300 g green (raw) king prawns,
  shelled, deveined and halved
  crossways
½ bunch dill, leaves
  roughly chopped
100 g baby spinach leaves
Large packet dried lasagne sheets
1 cup grated tasty cheese
1 cup finely grated parmesan

1 Preheat the oven to 200°C.

2 In a chef pan, heat the butter over a medium heat and sauté the leek until soft – about 5 minutes. Add the flour and stir until well combined. Add the milk a little at a time, stirring and ensuring that the flour cooks after each addition. Season with salt and pepper. Reserve 1 cup of this béchamel sauce.

3 Add all the fish pieces, prawns and dill leaves to the chef pan and gently fold through. The sauce will seem quite thick but the fish releases some juices while baking. Spread one-third of the fish mixture carefully into a shallow baking dish with a 2-litre capacity. Top with a layer of baby spinach leaves, then a layer of lasagne sheets to fit the dish. Repeat twice more with remaining fish mixture, spinach leaves and lasagne sheets. Cover the top lasagne sheet with the reserved béchamel sauce, then top with tasty cheese and parmesan.

4 Bake for 40 minutes or until the pasta is cooked and the top golden.

Sauces, soups and dips

Introduction

This chapter covers three things that make life grand – sauces, soups and dips.

Having a range of sauces in your cooking repertoire means you can quickly and easily turn the plainest of meat-and-three-veg meals into a gourmet delight. Knowing how to make basic sauces, whether it's using the roasting pan juices or making from scratch, will increase your cooking range enormously.

Soup is the most comforting of comfort foods. I love to make it in big batches and keep it in the fridge, ready for an afternoon pick-me-up or as an easy midweek meal. This chapter contains a whole lot of the classics, along with some of my personal favourites.

And once you've made your own dip – vibrant, fresh, delicious and cheap – you'll never want to buy it in a tiny plastic tub again. There's a range of different dips in here to complete any cheese platter and make you the hit of the party.

Sauces – Savoury

Apple sauce

Makes about 1 cup   Prep time: 5 minutes   Cooking time: about 10 minutes

4 Granny Smith apples   Pinch of freshly grated nutmeg
Caster sugar, to taste

1 Peel and core the apples and place in a saucepan with ¼ cup of water over a medium heat. Simmer until softened. Taste and add sugar if the apples are too tart. At this point, if a smooth sauce is preferred, puree in a blender or food processor.

2 Serve in a dish with a sprinkle of freshly grated nutmeg on top.

Plum sauce

Makes about 1 cup   Prep time: 5 minutes   Cooking time: 7–8 minutes

1 tablespoon olive oil
3 cm knob ginger, peeled and
  finely chopped
3 garlic cloves, finely chopped
½ teaspoon Chinese five-spice

⅔ cup plum jam
2 tablespoons hot chilli sauce
2 tablespoons white vinegar
¼ cup light soy sauce

1 Heat the olive oil in a small saucepan over medium heat. Sauté the ginger and garlic until soft and fragrant. Add the five-spice and stir for another minute. Stir in the plum jam, chilli sauce, vinegar and soy sauce. Bring to the boil, stirring, and boil for 4–5 minutes or until fully combined and thickened.

Apricot sauce

Great for chicken, pork and duck.

Makes ⅔ cup   Prep time: 3 minutes   Cooking time: 20 minutes

3 sprigs thyme
1 cup apricot nectar
1 cup chicken stock

1 tablespoon brown sugar
2 tablespoons white wine vinegar

1 Combine all the ingredients in a small saucepan and simmer for 10 minutes.

2 Strain the sauce through a fine wire sieve and return it to the same pan. Simmer for a further 10 minutes or until the sauce has reduced to a slightly syrupy consistency. There will be about ⅔ cup left.

Pepper sauce

Makes about 1 cup   Prep time: 5 minutes   Cooking time: 5 minutes

1 tablespoon olive oil
3 cloves garlic, finely chopped
2 tablespoons brandy
⅓ cup beef stock
55 g tin green
  peppercorns, drained

1 tablespoon ground
  black pepper
½ cup thickened cream
1 teaspoon salt

1 Heat the oil in a large, non-stick frypan over medium heat. Sauté the garlic until soft and fragrant. Pour the brandy into the pan and stir in the stock, peppercorns and ground pepper, followed by the cream. Simmer for 5 minutes until thickened slightly. Taste and add salt if needed.

Simple gravy for lamb or beef

Makes about 2–3 cups   Prep time: 5 minutes   Cooking time: 10–15 minutes

⅓ cup plain flour   Salt and pepper, as required
3–4 cups beef stock

After the roast has rested, remove it to the carving board and leave it under foil. If the roast was very fatty, pour off some but not all of the fat from the pan. Stir the flour into the pan juices, ensuring there are no lumps. Place the pan over a medium heat and introduce the beef stock little by little. Bring to the boil, and boil until the gravy is the thickness you like it to be. Taste and season. Strain into a serving jug.

Simple gravy for pork and poultry

Makes about 2–3 cups   Prep time: 5 minutes   Cooking time: 10–15 minutes

1 cup white wine   ⅓ cup plain flour
2–3 cups chicken stock   Salt and pepper to taste

After the roast has rested, remove it to the carving board and leave it under foil. If the roast was very fatty, pour off some but not all of the fat from the pan. Stir the flour into the pan juices, ensuring there are no lumps. Place the pan over a medium heat and introduce the chicken stock little by little. Bring to the boil, and boil until the gravy is the thickness you like it to be. Taste and season. Strain into a serving jug.

Red wine gravy for red meats

Makes about 1–1½ cups   Prep time: 5 minutes   Cooking time: 10–15 minutes

2 tablespoons plain flour   1 cup red wine
1 cup beef stock   4 stalks thyme

Place the roasting pan on the stovetop over medium heat and stir the flour into the pan juices. Use a spatula to scrape up any tasty brown bits from the bottom of the pan. Add about ¼ cup red wine and stir until the flour is incorporated and thickened. Add another ¼ cup wine and keep repeating this process until the sauce is becoming looser. Add the beef stock and thyme stalks and boil for 5 minutes or until thickened. Strain the gravy into a jug for serving.

Creamy lemon sauce

Lovely for chicken or salmon.

Makes about 1 cup   Prep time: 10 minutes   Cooking time: 5 minutes

200 ml thickened cream
Zest of 2 lemons
Juice of 1 lemon
1 tablespoon butter

2 egg yolks
4 tablespoons chopped dill
  leaf tips
Cracked black pepper

1 In a medium saucepan, heat the cream and lemon zest over a low heat until warm. Add the lemon juice and butter and stir to combine. Add the egg yolks and whisk until the sauce thickens. Just before serving, stir through the dill. Season to taste with pepper.

Red wine jus

Makes about 1½ cups   Prep time: 10 minutes   Cooking time: 25 minutes

1 tablespoon olive oil
1 kg beef bones (see note)
3 cloves garlic, peeled
  and halved
1 brown onion, peeled and
  roughly chopped
1 carrot, diced
1 bunch thyme

1 cup red wine
1 cup beef stock
50 g butter, cubed,
  very cold
1 teaspoon sea salt flakes
½ teaspoon ground
  black pepper

1 Heat the oil in a large, non-stick chef pan over medium-high heat. Add the beef bones and cook for 5 minutes, turning, so that all sides are browned. Add the garlic, onion and carrot and continue to cook for 5 minutes until the vegetables are becoming golden. It's really important to get this colour on the bones and vegetables so that the jus has a lovely rich flavour.

2 Stir in the thyme, red wine and beef stock. Bring to a simmer and simmer for about 15 minutes or until the sauce has reduced and thickened.

3 Strain the sauce and return to the pan over low heat. Whisk the butter into the sauce one cube at a time. (This process is called 'monte'.) This will give the sauce a gloss and a bit of extra thickness.

Note: Beef bones can be purchased from your butcher. If you are making the jus to go with a beef roast or pan-fried steak, you can just use the pan juices instead of cooking beef bones.

Sauces, soups & dips

137

Béarnaise sauce

Makes about 1 cup   Prep time: 5 minutes   Cooking time: 15 minutes

12 white peppercorns
½ cup tarragon vinegar
  (or white or cider vinegar)
2 large shallots
  (spring onions), sliced
1 bunch tarragon, chopped
  (including stems)

3 egg yolks
125 g butter, at room
  temperature, cubed
Salt and ground
  white pepper, to taste

1 Place the peppercorns, vinegar, shallots and tarragon in a saucepan, reserving 1 tablespoon finely chopped tarragon leaves. Bring to the boil and reduce by half – you should have about ¼ cup. Strain and allow to cool.

2 Put the egg yolks in a bowl over a pot of barely simmering water. Add 2 tablespoons vinegar reduction and whisk. Add the butter one cube at a time, whisking thoroughly. The sauce should start to emulsify and thicken up. Be careful not to allow the egg mixture to get too hot or it will scramble.

3 When all the butter has been added and the sauce is thick and lovely, taste and season with salt and pepper. Stir through the reserved tarragon leaves and serve immediately.

Salsa verde

Makes about 1 cup   Prep time: 5 minutes

½ bunch (½ cup) fresh parsley
½ bunch (¼ cup) fresh mint
½ large bunch (½ cup) fresh basil
1 clove garlic
1 tablespoon capers

1 tablespoon Dijon mustard
¼ teaspoon ground black pepper
¼ teaspoon salt
Zest and juice of 1 lemon
¼ cup olive oil

1 Place all the ingredients except the olive oil into the bowl of a food processor and blitz while pouring in the oil in a stream.

Béchamel sauce

Makes over 1 litre   Prep time: 5 minutes   Cooking time: 15 minutes

50 g butter
50 g flour
3½ cups milk

1 tablespoon Dijon mustard
200 g tasty cheese, grated
Salt and pepper, to taste

1 In a large pot over medium heat, melt the butter and add the flour. Stir constantly with a wooden spoon until it gathers into a dough. Continue to stir for another minute or so. This begins to cook the flour.

2 Add a little milk, about ¼ cup, and stir. This will incorporate fairly quickly into the dough which will again come away from the sides of the pan. Once this happens, you can stir in another ¼ cup milk, then repeat until all the milk has been added. Stir in the mustard, then add the cheese and stir until it melts. Taste, and season with salt and pepper if required.

Chimichurri

An all-round condiment that works well with beef, chicken and seafood.

Makes about 1 cup   Prep time: 10 minutes   Cooking time: 20 minutes

½ cup olive oil
1 bunch parsley, chopped
  (about 1 cup)
4 cloves garlic, finely chopped
2 tablespoons red wine vinegar

¼ teaspoon chilli flakes
1 teaspoon sea salt flakes
Plenty of freshly cracked
  black pepper

1 Combine all the ingredients in a non-reactive bowl and allow the flavours to infuse for about 20 minutes.

Creamy garlic prawn sauce

Makes about 1½ cups   Prep time: 15 minutes   Cooking time: 5 minutes

2 teaspoons olive oil
16 green (raw) king prawns,
  shelled, deveined, tails intact
20 g butter
3 cloves garlic, crushed
¼ cup white wine (or ¼ cup
  beef stock)

1 cup cream
¼ teaspoon ground
  white pepper
1 tablespoon cornflour
Salt, to taste

1 Heat the oil in a non-stick frypan over medium-high heat and sauté the prawns until just cooked – about 2 minutes. Remove from the pan and reduce the heat to medium.

2 Put the butter and garlic in the pan and sauté gently until soft. Stir in the wine and cook for a further minute. Pour in the cream and add the pepper.

3 Dissolve the cornflour in a little water and stir into the sauce to thicken. Cook for 3–4 minutes until thickened and the cornflour has cooked out. Taste and add salt.

4 Toss the prawns through the sauce to reheat them before serving.

Garlic and chilli dipping sauce

Makes about 1 cup   Prep time: 10 minutes
Cooking time: 6–7 minutes + cooling time

½ cup caster sugar
½ cup white vinegar
2 bird's eye (small red) chillies,
    sliced finely

2 cloves garlic, finely chopped
⅓ cup fish sauce

1 In a medium saucepan over medium-high heat, place the sugar and vinegar. Bring to the boil, stirring to dissolve the sugar. Boil for 5 minutes and remove from the heat. Allow to cool to lukewarm. Add the chilli, garlic and fish sauce. These sauces taste better after a little bit of time. It will keep in the fridge for a week.

Parsley sauce

Lovely over poached fish or corned beef.

Makes about 1½ cups   Prep time: 5 minutes   Cooking time: 10 minutes

10 g butter
1 tablespoon flour
1 cup milk
1 teaspoon Dijon mustard

½ teaspoon salt
¼ teaspoon ground white pepper
½ bunch parsley,
    leaves finely chopped

1 Melt the butter in a small saucepan over medium heat and add the flour. Stir to combine. Add the milk a little at a time, stirring constantly, until all incorporated. Stir in the mustard, then taste and season with salt and pepper. Stir through the parsley.

Note: The sauce can be varied with the addition of dill and a little lemon juice or lemon zest.

Garlic sauce (Toum) with mint

Makes about 1½ cups   Prep time: 5 minutes

4 cloves garlic, peeled and halved
1 bunch mint, leaves only
Pinch of salt
Juice of 1 lemon

1 eggwhite
1 cup neutral oil
  (such as rice bran, canola
  or vegetable oil)

1 Place all the ingredients in a tall, narrow jug or cup. (The ones that come with most hand-held stick blenders are perfect.) Place the stick blender in the very bottom of the jug and turn it on. Leave the stick blender going at the bottom of the cup until the mixture starts to turn white and fluffy. Slowly draw the blender upwards. By the time the blender reaches the top of the mixture, it will be fully emulsified and fluffy. If you want more of a pouring consistency, add iced water a little at a time and blend until you achieve the result you want.

Ginger and shallot oil

This is a lovely condiment with poached chicken breast or grilled fish. To spice it up a bit, add a very finely chopped small red chilli.

Makes about ¾ cup   Prep time: 5 minutes   Cooking time: 10 minutes

3 or 4 shallots (spring onions),
  very finely chopped
6 cm knob ginger, peeled and
  finely grated

2 teaspoons salt
½ cup peanut oil

1 Stir together the shallots, ginger and salt in a heat-proof bowl.

2 Heat the oil in a saucepan over medium heat for a few minutes, until it is shimmering on the bottom and very hot but not smoking.

3 Carefully pour the oil into the bowl with the shallots and ginger mixture. Wait for the sizzling to stop before stirring. Allow to cool down before serving. This will keep for about a week in the fridge.

Hoisin peanut dipping sauce

This is great with rice paper rolls, dumplings and chicken wings.

Makes about 1 cup   Prep time: 5 minutes

½ cup hoisin sauce   1 tablespoon rice wine vinegar
¼ cup crunchy peanut butter

1 Combine all the ingredients in a bowl.

Note: If you're making this sauce for a dinner party, top it with some chopped shallots (spring onions), finely sliced chilli and a few crushed peanuts to make it look nice.

Hollandaise sauce

Makes about 2 cups   Prep time: 5 minutes   Cooking time: 10 minutes

¼ cup white wine vinegar   2 tablespoons lemon juice
3 egg yolks   ½ teaspoon salt
175 g butter, melted then   ¼ teaspoon ground white pepper
    cooled to room temperature

1 In a small saucepan, simmer the vinegar until reduced to 2 tablespoons.

2 Place a glass bowl over a pot of barely simmering water. The bowl should not touch the water. Put the vinegar reduction in the bowl and add the egg yolks, whisking until they are thick and pale.

3 Ladle in the butter a little bit at a time, whisking as you go. The sauce will be thin at first, then start to thicken. Continue this process until all the butter has been added.

4 Remove the bowl from the heat and whisk in the lemon juice a little at a time, tasting as you go and stopping when it has the right amount of zing. Season with salt and pepper.

Note: If the sauce splits, or looks grainy, remove the bowl immediately from the heat and sit it in cold water. In a fresh bowl, put 1 tablespoon lemon juice and whisk in a little bit of the split sauce until they combine. Then add the remaining sauce to the fresh bowl a bit at a time until it's all incorporated.

Napoletana sauce

Serves 4   Prep time: 5 minutes   Cooking time: 15 minutes

1 tablespoon olive oil
2 onions, finely diced
4 cloves garlic, chopped
1 tablespoon dried oregano leaves

800 g tin chopped tomatoes
2 teaspoons salt
2 tablespoons sugar

1 Heat the oil over medium heat in a non-stick chef pan or large saucepan. Sauté the onion and garlic until soft and translucent. Add the oregano and cook for a further minute.

2 Add the tomatoes, salt and sugar and bring to the boil. Reduce to a simmer and cook, stirring occasionally, for about 15 minutes or until the sauce is thick, rich and fragrant.

Mushroom sauce

Serves 4   Prep time: 10 minutes   Cooking time: 10 minutes

40 g dried porcini mushrooms
1 tablespoon butter
1 tablespoon olive oil
2 cloves garlic, crushed
400 g button mushrooms, sliced
1 tablespoon plain flour

½ cup white wine
½ cup thickened cream
2 teaspoons Dijon mustard
½ teaspoon salt
¼ teaspoon ground white pepper

1 Place the porcini mushrooms in a bowl and cover with 1½ cups of boiling water. Allow to soak. When plump and reconstituted, remove the mushrooms from the water. Reserve ½ cup of the soaking water, being careful not to get any grit or sediment from the bottom of the bowl. Rinse the mushrooms to remove any last traces of grit, and chop roughly.

2 Place the butter and olive oil in a chef pan over medium-high heat. Add the garlic and button mushrooms. Sauté until the mushrooms are browned – this will take several minutes. First, the mushrooms will release some liquid, then the liquid will evaporate. Only after this will the mushrooms brown.

3 Add the chopped porcini mushrooms. Sprinkle the contents of the pan with the flour. Add the wine and stir until the mixture thickens. Stir in the reserved mushroom water, cream and mustard and simmer until the sauce is thick and the flour has cooked. Season with the salt and pepper.

Burnt butter sauce

Serves 4   Prep time: 5 minutes   Cooking time: 5 minutes

125 g butter
½ bunch sage, leaves picked

Juice and zest of 1 lemon
½ teaspoon sea salt flakes

1 Place the butter in a frypan over medium heat and add the sage leaves. Cook until the milk solids turn brown and the sage leaves crisp up.

2 Just before serving, stir in the lemon zest, juice and salt.

Note: This sauce is beautiful on chicken or fish, or on filled pasta.

Beurre blanc

This sauce goes well with fish and other seafood, or on vegetables like asparagus.

Serves 4   Prep time: 5 minutes   Cooking time: 10 minutes

2 brown shallots, very finely diced
½ cup white wine
¼ cup white wine vinegar
200 g unsalted butter, cubed,
   very cold

½ teaspoon salt
¼ teaspoon ground white pepper

1 Place the shallots, wine and vinegar in a frypan over medium-high heat and bring to a simmer. Simmer until the shallots are soft and the liquid has reduced to about 2 tablespoons. Remove from the heat.

2 Add the butter to the pan one cube at a time and whisk vigorously. The sauce will thicken. When all the butter is incorporated, add the salt and pepper.

Note: Lemon juice can be used in place of the vinegar.

Harissa (Tunisian chilli paste)

This paste can be added to yoghurt to make a sauce, added to dips or curries, or just used as a condiment on its own.

Makes about ¾ cup   Prep time: 10 minutes + soaking time
Cooking time: 5 minutes

100 g dried chillies (see notes)
6 long red fresh chillies
1 teaspoon coriander seeds
1 teaspoon cumin seeds

6 cloves garlic
¼ cup olive oil, plus oil for storing
1 teaspoon salt flakes

1 Place the dried chillies in a bowl and cover with boiling water. Soak until soft. Cut the stems off the long red chillies and halve them. Use a teaspoon to scrape out the seeds and chop roughly.

2 Place the coriander and cumin seeds in a small frypan over medium heat, and toast until they are fragrant.

3 Place all the chillies, spices and garlic in the bowl of a food processor and blitz. With the motor running, add the oil in a steady stream. Stop the processor to scrape down the sides of the bowl occasionally. Stir in the salt. Store in an airtight jar in the fridge covered with a thin layer of oil. Refresh the oil on top each time you use the harissa.

Notes: You can use whatever dried chillies you like. Vary the heat – for a milder paste, use roasted capsicums instead of chillies; or remove the seeds from the dried chillies.

For a hotter paste, use bird's eye (small red) chillies instead of long red; and for extra-hot, use habaneros or similar. Leaving the seeds in the fresh chillies will also dial up the heat.

Onion gravy

This gravy is lovely with grilled sausages, rissoles or meat loaf.

Serves 4   Prep time: 10 minutes   Cooking time: 10 minutes

1 tablespoon vegetable oil
20 g butter
3 large brown onions, sliced
¼ cup flour
600 ml beef stock

2 tablespoons
  Worcestershire sauce
¼ cup tomato sauce
½ teaspoon salt
¼ teaspoon white pepper

1 Place the oil and butter in a non-stick chef pan over medium-high heat and sauté the onion for 7–8 minutes or until golden brown. Take care not to have the heat too high; if the onion burns, it will have a bitter flavour.

2 Add the flour to the pan and stir. Add the stock a little at a time, stirring to incorporate, until all the stock is added. Stir in the Worcestershire sauce, tomato sauce, salt and pepper.

Satay sauce

Lovely as a dipping sauce or served over grilled meat or seafood skewers, or use as a sauce for stir-fried meat and vegetables.

Makes about 3 cups   Prep time: 10 minutes   Cooking time: 15 minutes

½ bunch coriander
1 brown onion, peeled and
   quartered
4 cloves garlic
2 limes, zested and juiced
2 long red chillies,
   halved and seeded

1 tablespoon peanut oil
1 teaspoon ground turmeric
400 ml tin coconut cream
1 cup crunchy peanut butter
¼ cup fish sauce
¼ cup brown sugar

1 Wash the roots and stems of the coriander and place in a food processor along with the onion, garlic, lime zest and chillies. Process until very fine. Alternatively, crush in a mortar and pestle.

2 Heat the oil in a large non-stick frypan over medium heat. Add the onion mixture and stir-fry until soft and fragrant. Be careful not to let it 'catch' or start to burn. Add the turmeric and stir for a further minute or so.

3 Stir in half the coconut cream and the peanut butter and bring to a simmer. Simmer for about 5 minutes. The sauce will split – this is ok.

4 Reduce the heat to low and stir in the fish sauce, brown sugar and half the lime juice. Taste to see if the sauce needs any more of these three things. This is very dependent on personal taste. Stir in the remaining coconut cream, taste again and adjust seasoning if needed. Remove from heat and serve. This recipe makes quite a large quantity and can be stored in the fridge in an airtight container.

Compound butter

Makes about 16 pats of butter   Prep time: 10 minutes + chilling time

250 g butter, at room temperature
4 cloves garlic, very finely chopped
2 tablespoons chopped
   fresh dill leaves
2 tablespoons chopped chives
1 tablespoon Worcestershire sauce

1 tablespoon Dijon mustard
2 teaspoons sweet paprika
2 teaspoons salt
1 teaspoon freshly ground
   black pepper

1 Place all the ingredients in a bowl and mix well.

2 Lay a long piece (about 60 cm) of plastic wrap vertically on the bench top. Place the butter mixture across the bottom of the plastic wrap, leaving enough room either side to twist together. Roll the butter away from you, enclosing it in the plastic, until you have formed a cylinder. Continue to the end of the plastic wrap and twist each end to seal. The result will be the shape of a bonbon. Place the roll in the freezer.

3 Remove the butter roll from the freezer 10 minutes before you need to use it. Unwrap plastic wrap. Heat a sharp knife by pouring boiling water over the blade, and slice as many pieces as you need – no thicker than 1 cm to put on steak.

4 To use, place a 1 cm thick disc onto hot steak; soften and place under the skin of whole or flattened chicken; or cook in a frypan on the stove for a quick sauce for fish.

Variations per 250 g butter:

Herb – Zest of 2 lemons, 4 cloves garlic, ½ cup fresh herbs (your preference), salt and pepper

Moroccan – Zest of 1 orange, 2 tablespoons cumin seeds, 1 tablespoon ground coriander seed, ½ cup parsley, 4 cloves garlic, salt and pepper

Lebanese – 1 tablespoon dried oregano, 2 tablespoons sumac, zest of 1 lemon, 4 cloves garlic, salt and pepper

Especially for seafood – 2 tablespoons baby capers, zest of 2 lemons, 1 bunch chives and 1 bunch dill, salt and pepper

Tartare sauce

Makes about 2 cups   Prep time: 10 minutes

1 cup mayonnaise
2 teaspoons Dijon mustard
¼ cup capers, finely chopped
¼ cup gherkins or dill pickles,
   finely chopped

2 tablespoons finely chopped
   fresh dill

1 Combine all ingredients in a bowl and store in the fridge for up to a week.

Fresh tomato salsa

Place spoonfuls on toasted baguette slices; a fresh addition to nachos and tacos; serve as a dip with fresh bread or corn chips.

Makes about 2 cups   Prep time: 10 minutes

6 very ripe, red tomatoes,
   seeded and diced
1 small red onion, finely chopped
½ bunch basil, leaves picked and
   finely shredded (see note)

1 teaspoon salt
1 teaspoon sugar
¼ teaspoon black pepper
Juice of 1 lemon

1 Combine all the ingredients in a bowl, preferably at least 30 minutes before serving. Serve at room temperature for best flavour.

Note: To cut the basil, roll the leaves up into a tight log and slice as finely as possible. This is called 'chiffonade'.

Pineapple mint salsa

Serve with chicken breast, pork or white fish.

Makes about 2 cups   Prep time: 10 minutes

½ fresh ripe pineapple, peeled,
   cored and finely diced
3 small red chillies, seeded and
   finely sliced
½ small red onion, finely diced
½ bunch coriander, leaves
   finely chopped

1 bunch mint,
   leaves finely chopped
Finely grated zest and
   juice of 1 lime
1 tablespoon caster sugar

1 In a medium bowl, combine the pineapple, chilli, onion, coriander, mint and lime zest. In a separate bowl, combine the lime juice and sugar and stir until dissolved. Toss the dressing through the salsa.

Variations: Leave out the chilli, onion and coriander for this to be a fresh addition to summer desserts. Freeze in cubes for use in cocktails or punch instead of ice cubes.

Mango salsa

Makes about 2 cups   Prep time: 10 minutes

2 mangoes, diced into
   1 cm cubes (see note)
2 small red chillies,
   seeded and finely sliced
2 shallots (spring onions),
   finely sliced

½ red capsicum, seeded and
   finely diced
Freshly ground black pepper
Juice and zest of 1 lime

1 Combine all the ingredients in a bowl. Store in an airtight container in the fridge for 3–4 days.

Note: To remove the mango flesh, slice the two 'cheeks' off using a sharp knife. Use a small drinking glass to scoop the flesh out of the skin. Peel the remaining centre of the mango and remove what flesh you can from the seed.

Sauces – Sweet

Baileys and white chocolate dipping sauce

Makes about 1½ cups   Prep time: 5 minutes   Cooking time: 2 minutes

125 g white chocolate melts
½ cup Baileys liqueur

½ cup thickened cream

1 Place the chocolate in the bowl of a food processor. Heat the Baileys and cream in a microwave-safe jug for 1 minute 40 seconds on high. Start the food processor and pour the Baileys and cream in as it runs. When everything is combined, remove from the bowl of the food processor and set aside to cool.

Note: Serve with strawberries, churros or sponge finger biscuits.

Butterscotch sauce

Makes about 2 cups   Prep time: 5 minutes   Cooking time: 5 minutes

300 ml thickened cream   ½ cup brown sugar
120 g butter   ½ cup golden syrup

1 Place all the ingredients in a medium-sized saucepan and bring to the boil. Boil for 5 minutes – watching carefully so that it does not boil over – then place in a serving jug. This sauce will solidify on cooling but will liquefy again on reheating. It can be stored in the fridge for a week.

Caramel sauce

Makes about 1½ cups   Prep time: 5 minutes   Cooking time: 5 minutes

1 cup caster sugar   1 cup thickened cream

1 Place the sugar in a medium saucepan over medium-high heat, along with ½ cup of water. Stir gently until the sugar dissolves then stop stirring and allow it to come to the boil. Watch carefully – it takes some time for the sugar syrup to start to turn golden, but once it happens it is very fast.

2 When the syrup has turned the colour of golden syrup, remove the pot from the heat and stir in the cream. The sauce will bubble up so be careful. Return the pot to a low heat and stir until the cream is incorporated.

Chocolate sauce

Use as an ice cream topping or poured over warm chocolate cake.

Makes about 1½ cups   Prep time: 5 minutes   Cooking time: 5 minutes

250 g choc bits or buttons,   1 cup thickened cream
  or grated cooking chocolate –
  dark, milk or white, whichever
  you prefer

1 Place the chocolate in a heat-proof bowl. Place the cream in a small saucepan on the stove and bring to scalding point (almost, but not quite boiling). Pour the cream over the chocolate and stir rapidly until all the chocolate has melted.

Sauces, soups & dips

Butterscotch sauce,
recipe page 150

Baileys and white chocolate dipping
sauce, recipe page 149

Passionfruit syrup

Makes about 1 cup   Prep time: 5 minutes   Cooking time: 5 minutes

Pulp of 8 passionfruit   ¾ cup sugar

1 Place the passionfruit pulp in a saucepan with the sugar and ½ cup of water. Bring to the boil, stirring occasionally, skimming the yellow froth off the top. Boil for 5 minutes then remove from the heat.

Soups

Basic chicken stock

Any recipe calling for chicken stock can use a good-quality packaged liquid stock. However, making your own is simple and can reduce waste. Chicken offcuts from other dishes can be frozen and used when convenient to make stock. For example, the wingtips from the chicken wing recipe (see page 74), or the carcass that remains if you use a whole chicken to cut pieces from.

This recipe yields about 3 cups of a richly flavoured glaze, which sets to a jelly in the fridge. It can be frozen in ice-cube trays and used as required. To reconstitute it to a normal stock, simply add an equal quantity of water.

I do not season the stock with salt, I season whatever dish I am using the stock for.

Makes 3 cups   Prep time: 15 minutes   Cooking time: 3 hours

2 tablespoons olive oil
1 kg chicken carcass or chicken
   pieces with bones, cut into
   small pieces
2 celery stalks, sliced thickly
2 carrots, diced

1 brown onion, diced
2 cloves garlic, halved
2 thyme sprigs
20 peppercorns
1½ litres water

1 Place the olive oil in a large pot over medium-high heat. When the oil is hot, add the chicken pieces and brown, turning occasionally.

2 When the chicken is beginning to brown, add the celery and carrot and allow to brown. Add the onion, garlic, thyme and peppercorns and stir until the onion is starting to brown.

3 Add the water. The water should cover the ingredients. Bring to a simmer, and simmer, uncovered, very gently for about 3 hours.

4 Remove the larger pieces of chicken with tongs. Strain the stock into a bowl and store in the fridge or freezer.

Master stock

Makes about 5 litres   Prep time: 15 minutes   Cooking time: 1 hour

5 star anise
2 cinnamon sticks
10 peppercorns
5 cardamom pods
1 teaspoon dried chilli flakes
6 cm knob ginger, sliced
⅔ cup white or raw sugar

3 strips orange peel, made
  using a vegetable peeler
½ cup dried sliced
  shiitake mushrooms
½ cup light soy sauce
8 litres water

1 Heat a large, heavy-based pot over medium heat. Toast the star anise, cinnamon, peppercorns and cardamom pods for a minute, stirring, until fragrant. Add the other ingredients and bring to the boil. Reduce heat and simmer gently, uncovered, for an hour. Strain stock and store in the freezer.

2 The stock can be re-used over and over, for many years. Just bring it to the boil each time then gently poach meat in it – pork, beef, whole chicken, whatever you like. Each time you cook with the stock, it will take on the flavours of what you poach. Each time you use it, taste and see if it needs more of the original ingredients simmered in it to refresh the flavours.

Chicken and leek soup

Serves 6   Prep time: 15 minutes   Cooking time: 30 minutes

1 tablespoon olive oil
1 kg chicken thigh fillets, sliced
2 large or 3 medium leeks, white
  and pale green parts only,
  sliced thinly on the diagonal
2 brown onions, diced

2 cloves garlic, chopped
¼ cup plain flour
2 litres chicken stock
  (see page 152) or store bought
Salt and pepper, to taste

1 In a large heavy-based pot, heat the olive oil over medium-high heat. Add the chicken and sauté for 2 minutes. Add the leeks, onion and garlic and stir for 2–3 minutes until starting to soften.

2 Add the flour and stir to coat the contents of the pot.

Spanish potato and chorizo
soup, recipe page 155

3 Add the stock, ½ cup at a time, until all flour is incorporated, then add the rest. Simmer for 20 minutes, then taste and season.

Chicken, corn and bacon soup

Serves 4   Prep time: 15 minutes   Cooking time: 15 minutes

1 tablespoon olive oil
4 rashers bacon, cut into 1 cm pieces
4 chicken thigh fillets,
   cut into 3 cm cubes
400 g tin corn kernels, drained
¼ cup plain flour
2 litres chicken stock (see page 152)
   or store bought

½ teaspoon salt
¼ teaspoon ground white pepper
½ bunch shallots (spring onions),
   white and pale green parts only,
   finely sliced

1 Heat a large, non-stick soup pot over medium-high heat. Place the oil in the pan, add the bacon and sauté for 3–4 minutes or until golden. Add the chicken and sauté for a further 2 minutes, until it is slightly golden.

2 Add the drained corn, then add the flour and stir to coat the contents of the pot. Add the stock, ½ cup at a time, until all flour is incorporated, then add the rest. When all the stock has been added, boil rapidly for 6–8 minutes or until the chicken is cooked through. Taste and season with salt and pepper. At the last moment, stir through the shallots and serve with some good bread.

Spanish potato and chorizo soup

Serves 4   Prep time: 10 minutes   Cooking time: 30 minutes

3 chorizo sausages, quartered
   lengthways and cut into
   1 cm pieces
2 brown onions, diced
2 cloves garlic, chopped
1 tablespoon smoked paprika
¼ teaspoon ground chilli

3 Sebago potatoes, peeled and
   cut into 1 cm cubes
700 g jar tomato passata
3 cups beef stock
Salt and pepper
¼ cup chopped parsley

1 In an enamel pot over medium-high heat, place the chorizo and stir for 2 minutes or until it starts to release its oil and turn golden. Add the onion and garlic and stir for a further 2 minutes. Add the paprika and chilli, and stir through.

2 Add the potato, tomato passata and beef stock. Bring to the boil and cook, stirring occasionally, for 25 minutes or until the potatoes are tender. Season with salt and pepper to taste. Serve topped with chopped parsley and with crusty bread.

Cauliflower soup with croutons

Serves 8   Prep time: 10 minutes   Cooking time: 20 minutes

1 litre milk
1 large head cauliflower
  (about 1.4 kg), broken up
  into florets
80 g butter

2 teaspoons salt
½ teaspoon finely ground
  white pepper
Croutons (see below)

1 In a large soup pot, heat the milk. While the milk is heating, process the cauliflower in batches in a food processor to the consistency of large breadcrumbs. This allows the cauliflower to cook quickly while maintaining all its lovely flavour.

2 When the milk is almost at boiling point, add the cauliflower to the pot. Bring back to a simmer and simmer, stirring frequently, for about 15 minutes. To test if the cauliflower is cooked, crush a little piece between your thumb and forefinger. It should disintegrate. If it is still a bit hard, continue cooking. Add the butter, salt and pepper.

3 Use a hand-held stick blender to blend the soup very thoroughly, until it is velvety smooth. Serve the soup topped with croutons.

Croutons for soup and salad

Serves 4   Prep time: 2 minutes   Cooking time: about 5 minutes

2 tablespoons olive oil

2 slices bread, crusts removed
  and cut into 1 cm cubes

1 Heat the oil over a medium heat in a large non-stick frypan. Toss the bread through the oil and cook, stirring, until the bread is golden and crunchy. Store the cooled croutons in an airtight container.

Bacon crumble

This is a lovely topping to many salads and creamy, smooth soups.

Serves 4   Prep time: 5 minutes   Cooking time: about 8 minutes

3 rashers bacon, rind removed,
  cut into a very fine dice
3 slices bread, processed to a
  very coarse crumb

Salt to taste (optional)

1 In a frypan over medium-high heat, sauté the finely diced bacon. (The bacon pieces should not be more than 2 mm in size.) When the bacon is starting to cook and release its fat, add the breadcrumbs. Stir continually, until the breadcrumbs are golden and the bacon pieces are crunchy. Taste and season with salt if required – this will depend on how salty the bacon is. Drain on paper towel. Store in an airtight container in the fridge.

French onion soup with damper

Serves 4   Prep time: 15 minutes   Cooking time: 1 hour

100 g butter
2 kg brown onions, very finely sliced
1 litre chicken stock (see page 152)
  or store bought
4 thyme sprigs
4 parsley stalks
1 bay leaf

1 teaspoon salt
¼ teaspoon ground white pepper
2 cups self-raising flour
1 cup tasty cheese, grated
½ cup parmesan, grated
1 cup milk, plus extra for glazing

1 Preheat the oven to 200°C.

2 In a large, heavy-based pot over medium heat, melt half the butter. When it starts to brown, add the onions to the pot and reduce the heat to low. Stir occasionally with a wooden spoon until the onions collapse and release their fluids. This will take about 20 minutes.

3 Add the stock a little at a time, stirring, until all mixed in. Tie together the thyme, parsley and bay leaf with kitchen twine and put into the pot. Simmer, stirring occasionally, until the onion has become very soft and viscous and the soup has thickened. Taste and season with half the salt and the ground white pepper. Remove the thyme, parsley and bay leaf.

4 For the damper, mix the flour, remaining salt and cheeses in a bowl. Chop the remaining butter and rub through the flour until it resembles breadcrumbs.

Gradually add the milk and stir to form a dough. Turn the dough out onto a floured board and knead a couple of times to just bring it together. Divide into 8 pieces and shape into small, fairly flat loaves (similar to rissoles).

5 Place on a lined or greased baking tray and brush the tops with a little milk. Bake for 15 minutes or until golden brown and hollow-sounding when tapped.

Freezer notes: Wrap the individual portions of damper dough in plastic wrap and freeze. Defrost fully to room temperature and bake the day you want to eat it. The soup can be frozen after cooking for up to 3 months.

Simple roast pumpkin soup

Makes about 2 litres   Prep time: 10 minutes   Cooking time: 35 minutes

1 kg butternut pumpkin, cut into
  quarters lengthways
2 carrots, peeled and cut into
  4 cm lengths

2 tablespoons olive oil
500 ml chicken or vegetable stock
1 teaspoon salt
½ teaspoon ground white pepper

1 Preheat the oven to 200°C.

2 Place the pumpkin and carrot on a lined baking tray. Drizzle with the oil and bake for 30–35 minutes or until golden and soft. Using a spoon, scoop the pumpkin flesh out of its skin and place in a large pot with the carrot and stock.

3 Using a hand-held stick blender, blend the soup until smooth and season with salt and pepper. Bring to a simmer to reheat just before serving.

Slow-cooker pea and ham soup

This soup is filling enough to be a main meal on its own, and it's very straightforward to make. Yet another family favourite for the cooler months, it's also a great standby in the fridge for afternoon tea for hungry teenagers.

Makes about 3 litres   Prep time: 15 minutes   Cooking time: 3 hours

1 tablespoon olive oil
1 brown onion, roughly chopped
1 clove garlic, chopped
1 carrot, diced

1.2 kg ham hocks (see notes)
500 g green split peas
2 cups frozen peas
Ground black pepper

French onion soup with damper,
recipe page 157

1 Heat the oil in a frypan over medium-high heat. Sauté the onion, garlic and carrot for 2 minutes or until starting to soften. Place in the bowl of the slow cooker with the ham hocks and cover with water. Add the split peas to the pot.

2 Cook, covered, on high for about 4 hours. (You may need to top the water up to keep the ham hocks covered, but try not to add any more than necessary or it will just need to be reduced at the end.) The split peas should be completely soft. Remove the ham hocks and set aside to cool.

3 Add the frozen peas to the slow cooker. These provide a brighter green colour and fresh flavour. Using a hand-held stick blender, blend the soup in the pot until all the ingredients are completely pureed and smooth. If you don't have a hand-held stick blender, transfer the soup in batches to a blender.

4 If the soup is too thin for your liking, cook on high, uncovered, until it has reduced to the consistency you like.

5 Remove the skin, bone and fatty bits from the hocks. Shred or slice the meat – the consistency is up to you. I like it quite fine so each mouthful of soup has some ham in. Return the ham to the soup and serve with black pepper.

Notes: Instead of ham hocks you can use a similar amount of bacon bones – I prefer the hock as I feel you get more meat from them and there is less chance of small bones ending up in the soup.

When the soup is chilled in the fridge, it will solidify. Don't worry – on reheating it becomes liquid again.

Variation: Minted pea and ham soup – add ½ cup firmly packed mint leaves to the soup with the frozen peas.

Sweet potato and coconut soup

Serves 4   Prep time: 10 minutes   Cooking time: 25 minutes

1 tablespoon vegetable oil
1 brown onion, chopped
4 cloves garlic, minced
2.5 cm knob ginger, peeled and
  finely chopped
2 red chillies, seeded and
  finely chopped
1 teaspoon ground coriander seeds
1 teaspoon ground cumin seeds
½ teaspoon ground cardamom
½ teaspoon ground cinnamon

750 g sweet potato,
  roughly chopped
2 cups salt-reduced chicken
  stock (or vegetable for a
  vegetarian dish)
2 tins coconut cream
1 teaspoon salt
½ teaspoon freshly
  ground black pepper
¼ cup coriander leaves (optional)

1 Heat the oil in a large, heavy-based saucepan with a lid. Add the onion, garlic, ginger, chilli and spices. Cook, stirring constantly, until the onion is soft and the spices fragrant, about 10 minutes.

2 Add the sweet potato, stock and coconut cream and bring to the boil. Put the lid on the saucepan and simmer for 15 minutes, stirring occasionally.

3 Using a hand-held stick blender or in a food processor, blend the soup until smooth. Season with salt and pepper. If you like, sprinkle with coriander leaves before serving.

Vietnamese chicken pho

Serves 4   Prep time: 15 minutes   Cooking time: 25 minutes

2 chicken breast fillets
2 litres chicken stock, cold
  (see page 152)
2 cm knob ginger, sliced
2 cloves garlic, halved
1 bunch coriander, roots and
  stems washed, leaves reserved
1 long green chilli,
  cut into 3 pieces

6 shallots (spring onions),
  finely sliced
2 tablespoons fish sauce
400 g shelf-fresh rice noodles
1 bunch choy sum
½ bunch mint leaves
2 cups bean sprouts
4 small red chillies, sliced

1 In a large pot over medium-high heat, place the chicken breasts and cover with stock. While it is coming up to the simmer, add the ginger, garlic, coriander roots and stems, chilli and the white parts of 2 shallots. Simmer for 15 minutes or until the chicken is cooked through. Remove the chicken and slice very finely or shred. Simmer the soup for another few minutes then strain into a clean pot. Discard the contents of the strainer and bring the stock back to the boil. Remove from the heat and add the fish sauce.

2 Boil the kettle. Place the noodles in a heat-proof bowl and pour the boiling water over. Soak for a few minutes until soft then strain through a colander and divide between 4 serving bowls. Divide the choy sum between the bowls, placing on top of the noodles. Divide the chicken between the bowls. Pour the stock into the bowls.

3 Serve to the table with the reserved coriander leaves, shallots, mint leaves, bean sprouts and chillies in the centre so that diners can help themselves to whatever they want to add to their bowl.

Mushroom soup, recipe
page 163

Mushroom soup

Serves 4   Prep time: 10 minutes   Cooking time: 15 minutes

25 g unsalted butter
2 tablespoons olive oil
2 cloves garlic, crushed
1 kg button mushrooms,
  stalks removed, finely sliced
¼ cup plain flour

1 litre chicken stock (or vegetable
  stock for vegetarian option)
¼ teaspoon finely
  ground white pepper
½ teaspoon salt
¼ cup thickened cream

1 In a large, heavy-based pot, heat the butter and oil over a medium heat. Add the garlic and gently sauté until translucent, soft and fragrant.

2 Add the mushrooms and stir through. Increase the heat and sauté until the mushrooms are soft and brown. This will take about 10 minutes – the mushrooms firstly will take up all the moisture from the oil, then they will exude their own juices, and eventually those will evaporate and the mushrooms will start to brown. This is the point that you want to reach before proceeding.

3 Add the flour and stir well. Add the stock, about ½ cup at a time, stirring continuously. When all the stock is added, bring to the simmer and cook for 2–3 minutes. Remove from the heat, season with pepper and salt, and finish with the cream.

Roast tomato soup

Serves 4   Prep time: 10 minutes   Cooking time: 60 minutes

3 kg ripe, red tomatoes, halved
  and stalk end removed
¼ cup olive oil
2 teaspoons salt

1 teaspoon ground black pepper
1 tablespoon dried oregano leaves
1 tablespoon sugar

1 Preheat the oven to 180°C.

2 Place the tomato halves on a baking tray, cut side up. Drizzle olive oil over the tomato and sprinkle with salt, pepper and oregano. Roast in the oven for about 45 minutes, until soft and collapsing.

3 When the tomatoes are cool enough to go into the food processor or blender, process until smooth. Place into a pot and add water until the soup is the consistency you like. Taste and see if you would like to add any more salt, pepper or sugar.

Laksa

Serves 4   Prep time: 15 minutes   Cooking time: 15 minutes

200 g packet rice vermicelli noodles
½ bunch coriander, roots scraped
  and washed, leaves reserved
1 stalk lemongrass, white part only,
  finely chopped
2 small red chillies, seeded
  and chopped
2 cloves garlic
5 cm knob galangal or ginger,
  peeled and roughly chopped
2 teaspoons shrimp paste
2 teaspoons ground cumin seeds
2 teaspoons ground turmeric
¼ cup peanut oil
1 small red onion, sliced very finely

2 kaffir lime leaves, sliced as
  finely as possible into threads
2 x 400 ml tins coconut cream
1 cup chicken stock (see page 152)
  or store bought
1 small zucchini, sliced
  into matchsticks
400 g white, boneless fish fillets,
  cut into 3 cm pieces
400 g green prawns, peeled,
  tails intact
1 tablespoon brown sugar
2 teaspoons fish sauce
2 tablespoons lime juice
½ cup bean sprouts

1 Place the noodles in a heat-proof bowl and cover with boiling water. Soak until soft then strain and set aside.

2 To make the laksa curry paste, place the coriander roots and stems in the bowl of a food processor with the lemongrass, chilli, garlic, galangal or ginger, shrimp paste, cumin, turmeric and oil. Blitz until it becomes a fine paste. This will take a few minutes and you will need to scrape down the sides of the bowl with a spatula several times.

3 Put the curry paste in a non-stick chef pan over medium-high heat and fry for 2 minutes or until fragrant. Add the onion and stir for a further minute. Add kaffir lime leaves, coconut cream and stock. Simmer for 7–8 minutes then drop in the zucchini, fish and prawns. Simmer for a further minute then remove the pan from the heat. Add the brown sugar, fish sauce and lime juice. Taste and add more of any of these things as your taste dictates.

4 Serve in bowls scattered with the reserved coriander leaves and bean sprouts.

Crab and sweet corn soup

Serves 4   Prep time: 10 minutes   Cooking time: about 12 minutes

4 cobs corn, husk and silk removed
1 tablespoon peanut oil
2 cloves garlic, chopped
3 cm knob ginger, peeled and
  finely chopped or grated
1.5 litres chicken stock
  (see page 152) or store bought
¼ cup light soy sauce
1 tablespoon cornflour

¼ cup water
2 eggwhites
225 g crab claw meat, chopped
  (see note)
4 shallots (spring onions),
  finely sliced
1 teaspoon ground white pepper

1 Run a sharp knife down the length of the corn cobs to remove the kernels.

2 Heat the oil in a large pot over medium heat and sauté the garlic and ginger until soft and translucent. Add the stock and corn kernels and simmer until the corn is soft.

3 In a small bowl, whisk together the soy sauce, cornflour and 1 tablespoon water. Add it into the pot, whisking the whole time.

4 Using the same small bowl, whisk the eggwhite with the remaining water. Keep stirring the soup while pouring in the egg mixture in a steady stream. Add the crab, shallots and pepper and stir through.

Note: Crab claw meat is available from fishmongers, ready cooked and shelled, in the tub. If you prefer, you can buy and cook the crab and shell it yourself.

Baked camembert with pear and candied walnuts, recipe page 167

Flatbread, recipe page 227

Roast beetroot dip, recipe page 169

Cannellini bean dip, recipe page 174

Dips

Dukkah

Makes about ¾ cup   Prep time: 5 minutes   Cooking time: 5 minutes

⅓ cup roasted unsalted almonds
⅓ cup sesame seeds
2 tablespoons coriander seeds
2 tablespoons cumin seeds

12 white peppercorns
½ teaspoon sea salt flakes
¼ teaspoon ground
   hot chillies (optional)

1 Place the almonds in the bowl of a food processor and process until mostly about the size of sesame seeds. There will be some bigger pieces and some powder – this is ok.

2 Heat a large non-stick frypan or chef pan over medium-high heat and dry-roast the almonds until golden and aromatic. Remove to a bowl.

3 Add the sesame seeds to the hot pan and toast until golden, then remove to the bowl with the almonds.

4 Place the coriander seeds, cumin seeds and peppercorns into the pan and toast until starting to colour and aromatic. Transfer to the bowl of the food processor with the sea salt and process to a coarse powder.

5 Place the coriander mix in the bowl with the almonds and sesame seeds, and add the chilli if using. Mix well and allow to cool before storing in an airtight container.

Baked camembert with pear and candied walnuts

Serves 4 as an entree   Prep time: 10 minutes   Cooking time: 20 minutes

1 x 200 g camembert
1 teaspoon fresh thyme leaves
½ crusty baguette, torn into chunks
2 tablespoons garlic-infused olive oil
1 cup walnuts

1 cup icing sugar
1 ripe Corella pear, cored and
   cut into wedges
1 tablespoon honey

1 Preheat the oven to 180°C.

2 Remove all wrapping from the camembert and place into a snug-fitting ovenproof dish. (Terracotta or crockery work well.) Prick the top of the cheese in several places using a sharp knife and poke the thyme leaves into it. Place the dish on a baking tray and bake for 15–20 minutes or until soft and gooey.

3 Place the bread on another baking tray, drizzle with the olive oil and bake until light golden.

4 Place the walnuts in a medium frypan over medium-high heat. Toast, stirring, for a couple of minutes until fragrant. Sift the icing sugar over the walnuts and stir with a spoon until the sugar becomes liquid and turns golden. Tip onto a tray lined with baking paper and use the spoon to separate the nuts so they are not in a big clump. Allow to cool then break into pieces.

5 Serve the camembert in its dish on a board alongside the pear wedges drizzled with honey and the walnuts and toasted bread.

Basil and pine nut pesto

Serves 4   Prep time: 10 minutes

200 g pine nuts
3 cups basil leaves, loosely
    packed (about 2 large bunches)
3 cloves garlic

150 g parmesan, grated
1 cup olive oil
Salt and ground white pepper,
    to taste

1 Place the pine nuts in a frypan over medium heat and toss or stir them until they are light golden brown. Remove to the bowl of a food processor.

2 Add the basil, garlic and parmesan and process to a paste. With the motor running, add the oil in a stream. When everything is combined, season with salt and pepper and stir through.

3 To store, place the pesto in a sealed glass jar and keep in the fridge.

Broccoli pesto

This pesto is lovely as a dip on its own and is also great as a pasta sauce, loosened with a little of the water the pasta cooks in.

Makes 4 cups   Prep time: 10 minutes   Cooking time: about 5 minutes

500 g broccoli (2 small heads),
   cut into florets
100 g block parmesan
2 cloves garlic
100 g pine nuts, toasted
1 cup basil leaves
   (about 1 large bunch)

1 cup baby spinach leaves
1 teaspoon sea salt flakes
1 cup olive oil, plus extra
   for storing

1 Place the broccoli in a microwave-safe container and cook on high for 5 minutes. Remove, take the lid off and allow to cool.

2 Break the parmesan up into a few pieces and place in the bowl of the food processor. Blitz until it is finely chopped. Add the garlic, pine nuts, basil, spinach and salt and blitz again. Scrape down the sides of the bowl and blitz again, pouring in the olive oil in a steady stream as you go.

3 Place in a lidded container and cover the surface of the pesto with a thin film of oil to prevent discolouration. Store in the fridge for 2–3 days.

Roast beetroot dip

Serves 4   Prep time: 10 minutes   Cooking time: 45 minutes

4 medium-sized beetroots
1 head garlic
2 teaspoons olive oil
200 g walnut pieces

200 g feta
½ teaspoon salt
½ teaspoon ground white pepper

1 Preheat the oven to 180°C. Remove the leaves and trim the roots from the beetroot. Trim the top off the head of garlic. Place the garlic and beetroot on a baking tray and sprinkle with oil.

2 Bake for 30 minutes, then remove the garlic. It should be soft. Bake the beetroot for a further 30 minutes, or until a skewer goes easily through them. In the last 10 minutes of cooking, add the walnuts to the tray.

3 Remove the tray from the oven and allow everything to cool down. Peel the beetroot – the skin should come off quite easily. (I wear latex gloves for this procedure so I don't end up with bright pink hands.) Cut the beetroot into a few pieces and put in the bowl of a food processor.

4 Squeeze the flesh from the garlic cloves and add to the food processor along with the feta and toasted walnuts. Blitz until everything is combined. It's up to you how smooth you like your dip to be. Taste and season with salt and pepper.

Nut-crusted labne balls

Use as a spread on crusty bread or flatbread, or as an addition to a cheese platter.

Makes 8 balls   Prep time: 10 minutes + 24 hours straining time
Cooking time: 5 minutes

1½ teaspoons salt
1 kg plain Greek yoghurt
¼ cup roasted smoked almonds
¼ cup sesame seeds
1 tablespoon cumin seeds
¼ teaspoon freshly
  ground black pepper

¼ teaspoon sea salt flakes
Oil, for storing (use rice bran,
  vegetable or canola oil – olive
  oil will solidify in the fridge)

1 Place a fine wire strainer over a larger bowl so that the strainer sits well above the bottom of the bowl. Line the strainer with muslin cloth or new Chux cleaning cloth. Stir the salt through the yoghurt and place into the lined strainer. Place in the fridge for 24 hours.

2 Place the almonds in the bowl of a food processor and process until mostly about the size of sesame seeds. There will be some bigger pieces and some powder – this is ok. Heat a large non-stick frypan or chef pan over medium-high heat and dry-roast the almonds until golden and aromatic. Remove to a bowl.

3 Place the sesame seeds in the hot pan and toast until golden, then remove to the bowl. Repeat with the cumin seeds. Add the salt and pepper to the bowl and mix well.

4 Remove the now solid yoghurt from the fridge and discard the liquid. Roll the yoghurt into balls about the size of a golf ball. Place the nut crust mixture in a shallow dish. Dip the balls in the nut mixture to coat and place into a clean lidded glass jar. Pour in enough oil to cover the labne. Store with the lid on the jar. This will keep in the fridge for several weeks.

Sundried tomato hommous

Use as a dip, or a sauce for kebabs or lamb burgers.

Makes about 2½ cups   Prep time: 5 minutes

400 g tin chickpeas, drained
100 g sundried tomatoes
1 clove garlic
¼ cup tahini

Juice of 1 lemon
1 tablespoon iced water
1 teaspoon sea salt flakes
½ teaspoon ground white pepper

1 Place all the ingredients in the bowl of a food processor. Blitz, scraping down the sides occasionally, until smooth.

Blue cheese and almond dip

Makes about 2½ cups   Prep time: 10 minutes

½ cup sour cream
250 g cream cheese,
   at room temperature
200 g soft blue cheese, such as
   Castello Creamy Blue
½ cup smoked roasted almonds,
   roughly chopped

1 bunch dill, leaves chopped
1 teaspoon salt
½ teaspoon finely ground
   white pepper

1 Place the sour cream, cream cheese and blue cheese in a bowl and stir to thoroughly combine. Stir through the almonds, dill, salt and pepper. Store, covered, in the fridge for up to a week. If you would like the dip to last longer, leave out the dill leaves and it will last for several weeks.

Smoky eggplant and capsicum dip

Makes about 2½ cups   Prep time: 10 minutes + cooling time
Cooking time: 5 minutes

3 small or 2 medium eggplants
2 capsicums
¼ cup tahini
3 cloves garlic, peeled

Juice of 1 lemon
1 teaspoon salt
Olive oil and paprika, to garnish

1 To get the smoky flavour into the eggplant and capsicum, sit them directly onto the gas burner on your stovetop. (If you don't have a gas stovetop, place them under a hot grill or on the grill plate of a barbecue.) Turn regularly, until all the skin is charred, the eggplant is soft through and the skin of the capsicum is blackened and blistering. Place the eggplant in a bowl to cool, and put the capsicum into a plastic bag. This will help the skin to peel. Once cooled, peel the eggplant and capsicum with your hands. The skin will peel away easily from the flesh. Cut the capsicum in half and remove the seeds and pith.

2 Place the eggplant and capsicum in the bowl of a food processor with the tahini, garlic, lemon juice and salt. Blend thoroughly, scraping down the sides of the bowl occasionally. The end result will be smooth, creamy and incredibly flavourful.

3 Place in a serving dish and garnish with olive oil and paprika. Store, covered, in the fridge for up to a week but allow the dip to return to room temperature before serving as it solidifies when cold.

Pumpkin, carrot and cumin dip

Makes about 3 cups   Prep time: 10 minutes   Cooking time: 45 minutes

½ butternut pumpkin, unpeeled, cut into quarters
3 large carrots, peeled and cut into 2 cm pieces
2 teaspoons cumin seeds
2 tablespoons olive oil
½ cup plain Greek yoghurt, plus 1 tablespoon to garnish

Juice of 1 lemon
1 clove garlic, finely chopped
½ teaspoon sea salt flakes
½ bunch coriander leaves, roughly chopped (a few reserved for garnish)
½ cup pine nuts, toasted

1 Preheat the oven to 180°C and line a large baking tray with baking paper.

2 Place the pumpkin, carrots and cumin seeds on the tray and drizzle with the olive oil. Bake for 45 minutes or until the pumpkin is completely soft and a knife or skewer goes easily through it. Allow the vegetables to cool, then scoop the flesh out of the pumpkin skin. Place the pumpkin, carrots and cumin seeds in the bowl of a food processor and blitz, scraping down the sides occasionally, until smooth.

3 Stir through the yoghurt, lemon juice, salt, coriander leaves and pine nuts. Place in a serving dish and garnish with extra yoghurt and reserved coriander leaves.

Tzatziki

Use as a dip or a sauce on kebabs, chicken wraps or lamb burgers.

Makes about 1½ cups   Prep time: 10 minutes + standing time

1 Lebanese cucumber, seeded
  and grated
½ teaspoon salt
1 cup plain Greek style
  natural yoghurt
1 bunch mint, leaves
  finely chopped

1 bunch dill, leaves very
  finely chopped
1 clove garlic, finely chopped
Juice and zest of 1 lemon

1 Place the cucumber in a bowl and mix with the salt. Allow to stand for 15 minutes then place into a clean tea towel. Wring the moisture out of the cucumber.

2 In a bowl, place the cucumber, yoghurt, mint, dill, garlic and lemon juice and zest. Mix well and refrigerate until serving time.

Avocado and corn dip

Enjoy on its own as a dip with corn chips or flatbread, with nachos or tacos, or as an accompaniment to grilled chicken.

Makes about 3 cups   Prep time: 10 minutes   Cooking time: 5 minutes

3 cobs corn, with husks
3 ripe avocados
Juice of 1 small or ½ large lemon
2 very ripe tomatoes,
  seeded and chopped

4 shallots (spring onions),
  cut in half lengthways
  then finely chopped
1 teaspoon sea salt flakes
½ teaspoon ground white pepper

1 Place the corn, in its husk, in the microwave and cook on high for 5 minutes. Remove from the microwave and place in the fridge to cool. When cool, remove the husk and run a sharp knife down the length of the cobs to remove the kernels.

2 Scoop the flesh out of the avocados into a bowl and add the lemon juice. This not only adds flavour but prevents the avocado from oxidising (going brown). Mash well. Stir through the tomatoes, shallots, corn kernels, salt and pepper. Store in an airtight container in the fridge for up to 3 days.

Olive tapenade

Use as a dip, a spread, or dolloped onto a Greek salad.

Makes about 2 cups   Prep time: 20 minutes   Cooking time: 15 minutes

400 g pitted Kalamata
  olives, drained
2 tablespoons capers
6 small anchovies

1 clove garlic
¼ cup olive oil
200 g feta

1 Place the olives, capers, anchovies, garlic and olive oil in the bowl of a food processor and process to a chunky paste. Crumble the feta into the olive mixture and stir through with a spoon.

Cannellini bean dip

Makes about 3 cups   Prep time: 5 minutes

2 x 400 g tins cannellini beans,
  drained and rinsed
1 clove garlic
1 tablespoon olive oil

Zest and juice of 1 lemon
½ cup water
½ teaspoon salt

1 Place all the ingredients in the bowl of a food processor and blitz to a smooth paste. You will need to scrape down the sides of the food processor once or twice.

Spinach dip in cob loaf

Serves a crowd   Prep time: 15 minutes   Cooking time: 20 minutes

1 tablespoon olive oil, plus extra
  for drizzling
4 brown onions, finely sliced
4 cloves garlic, finely chopped
¼ cup balsamic glaze
500 g sour cream
500 g spreadable cream cheese

100 g baby spinach
2 teaspoons garlic powder
1 teaspoon salt
½ teaspoon ground black pepper
1 round cob loaf

1 Preheat the oven to 200°C.

2 Place the olive oil in a large frypan over medium heat. Sauté the onion and garlic for 5 minutes or until soft and fragrant. Add the balsamic glaze

and cook for a further 5 minutes. Add the spinach to the pan and sauté for a minute until wilted.

3 In a large bowl, mix together the sour cream, cream cheese, garlic powder, salt and pepper. Stir through the onion and spinach mixture.

4 Cut the top off the cob loaf. Using your hands, tear out the bread in the middle of the loaf to create a 'bowl' of bread. Tear up the extra bread, and cut the 'lid' into pieces. Place the pieces onto a lined tray and drizzle with extra olive oil. Place the dip mixture into the cob loaf and place on same tray. Bake for 10–15 minutes until the bread is hot and crunchy.

5 Serve with the extra bread alongside, and encourage diners to tear down the sides of the cob loaf bowl as they eat the dip.

Roasted onion and bacon dip

Makes about 3 cups   Prep time: 20 minutes
Cooking time: 1 hour 45 minutes

1 head garlic
4 brown onions, diced
2 tablespoons olive oil
4 rashers bacon, cut into 5 mm dice
1 cup sour cream

250 g cream cheese
1 tablespoon balsamic vinegar
1 teaspoon salt
¼ teaspoon finely ground
   white pepper

1 Preheat the oven to 140°C.

2 Slice the top off the head of garlic and place on a baking tray with the diced onion. Drizzle the lot with olive oil and roast for 1 hour, stirring the onions every 20 minutes or so. Remove the garlic after 30 minutes or when the flesh is very soft. When cool, squeeze the flesh out of the cloves of garlic. It should come easily.

3 While the onions cook, heat a frypan over medium-high heat and sauté the bacon until it is golden and starting to crisp up. Remove from the pan and allow to cool on paper towel.

4 The onions are ready when they are soft, deeply golden and fragrant. If any of the pieces on the edges have hardened or gone black, discard them. Set aside to cool.

5 In a bowl, combine the sour cream, cream cheese, balsamic vinegar, salt, pepper, garlic flesh and cooled onions and bacon. Mix well.

Vegetables and preserves

Introduction

One of my favourite things to do when I am cooking at home is to wander out into the backyard and gather some of the ingredients from my garden. There's something tremendously satisfying about growing something that ends up on your own dinner table.

Mick and I are not the world's greatest gardeners but each year we're getting better and able to harvest more. The vegetable patch is the highest maintenance part of the edible garden, but there's quite a lot that has very little upkeep, which is great in a busy life. Besides a range of fruit trees, the easiest things we grow are kaffir lime, lemongrass, bay leaves, and hard herbs like rosemary and thyme. Soft herbs are easy, too, and can grow in pots.

We don't grow enough to sustain us, so the next best option is the local growers' markets. Look for the truly local growers. These have produce that is in season, and fresh, with a small carbon footprint.

If you don't have access to growers' markets, roadside stalls or small independent local grocers, it's important to know what's in season when you're shopping at the supermarket. Chain stores will often stock fruit and vegetables that are out of season, to meet consumer demand. This could mean the produce has been imported or stored.

Produce that is in season is abundant and cheap – when things are in season they grow easily. They are at their peak in flavour and nutrition. When produce looks old, or is very expensive, it indicates short supply, which suggests it's not in season.

Fruit and vegetables at their peak are an absolute joy to cook with and to eat. And with every piece of scientific and medical advice urging us to increase our intake of plants, why wouldn't you?

Mains

Vegetarian moussaka

If I am serving a vegetarian meal to my family, it needs to be filling and very tasty. This eggplant moussaka fits the bill at our place.

Serves 4   Prep time: 20 minutes + standing time
Cooking time: 40 minutes

1 eggplant, sliced into 1 cm rounds
Cooking salt
1 teaspoon olive oil
1 brown onion
2 cloves garlic
2 tablespoons tomato paste
600 g (1½ tins) chopped tomatoes

¼ teaspoon dried ground oregano
2 teaspoons sugar
500 g ricotta
¼ teaspoon ground white pepper
¼ teaspoon salt
¼ teaspoon ground nutmeg
1 cup grated tasty cheese

1 Preheat the oven to 180°C.

2 Lay the eggplant slices on paper towel and sprinkle with salt. After 15 minutes turn the slices over and repeat with the other side. Pat dry with a paper towel.

3 Heat the oil in a chef pan or large frypan over medium-high heat. Sauté the onions and garlic for 2 minutes, then add the tomato paste and stir for a further minute. Add the tomatoes, oregano and sugar. Simmer for about 10 minutes, until the sauce thickens and reduces by about a quarter. The time this takes will depend on the pan being used.

4 In a bowl, combine the ricotta, pepper, salt and nutmeg.

5 Heat a char grill or grill pan to a high heat. Spray or brush the eggplant slices with oil and char grill for 2 minutes on each side.

6 In a 20 cm square baking dish, layer half the tomato sauce, followed by half the eggplant slices, followed by half the ricotta mixture. Sprinkle half the tasty cheese over the top. Repeat the layers a second time.

7 Bake for 20 minutes or until the cheese on top is golden brown.

Bacon and corn croquettes

Makes 12   Prep time: 25 minutes   Cooking time: 15 minutes

6 rashers bacon, cut into
  5 mm pieces
4 cobs corn, blanched,
  kernels removed
125 g butter
½ cup plain flour
2 cups milk
1 tablespoon Dijon mustard

½ teaspoon salt
¼ teaspoon finely ground
  white pepper
1 cup grated tasty cheese
3 cups homemade or
  panko breadcrumbs
3 eggs, beaten
Oil, for deep-frying

1 In a medium frypan over medium-high heat, sauté the bacon until golden.

2 Remove from the pan, drain on paper towel and place into a bowl with the corn kernels.

3 In a medium saucepan over medium-high heat, melt the butter. Add the flour and stir, until the mixture starts to froth. Add a little splash of milk and stir until it comes together in a dough. Add a little more milk and stir in, then repeat until all the milk has been added. Add the mustard, salt and pepper and stir. Stir through the bacon and corn. Place the mixture into a tray and set in the fridge for several hours or until firm enough to work with.

4 Preheat a deep-fryer to 180°C. Using damp hands, form the mixture into 12 cylindrical patties. Place the breadcrumbs and beaten egg in separate shallow bowls. Dip the croquettes into the breadcrumbs, then into the beaten egg, and back into the breadcrumbs. When all the mixture has been made into croquettes, deep-fry in batches until golden brown.

Freestyle mushroom lasagne

Serves 4   Prep time: 15 minutes   Cooking time: 25 minutes

1 tablespoon olive oil
25 g butter
800 g cup mushrooms, sliced finely
3 cloves garlic, chopped
¼ cup tomato paste

2 tablespoons plain flour
1½ cups beef stock
Salt and black pepper to taste
4 fresh lasagne sheets, cut in half
20 g freshly shaved parmesan

1 In a large chef pan, heat the oil and butter over medium-high heat until the butter is frothing. Add the mushrooms and garlic. This is a large quantity of mushrooms and they'll take a while to cook – about 15 minutes. They will release a lot of liquid, which will eventually evaporate, and the mushrooms will start to turn golden.

2 When the mushrooms are at this point, add the tomato paste to the pan and stir for a minute. Sprinkle the flour over the mixture and stir for another minute. Add the stock a little bit at a time, allowing the sauce to come to the boil after each addition. Add the salt and pepper to taste.

3 Bring a large pot of well-salted water to the boil and cook the lasagne sheets 2 at a time. Remove from the water and drape onto a plate. Cover with foil.

4 To assemble the lasagne, place a spoonful of mushroom sauce on each plate, top with a lasagne square, repeat, and finish off with another spoonful of sauce and shaved parmesan.

Note: To make this recipe even easier, you can cut the lasagne sheets into wide pappardelle ribbons, cook them then toss through the sauce.

Handmade gnocchi with pesto

Serves 4   Prep time: 20 minutes   Cooking time: 20 minutes

1 kg Sebago potatoes
½ cup plain flour
1 egg, lightly beaten
1 quantity basil and pine nut
   pesto (see page 168)

40 g parmesan, freshly grated
Drizzle of olive oil, for serving

1 Peel the potatoes and cut in half if they are large. Try to have them all a similar size so they will cook at the same time. Place in a large pot of salted water and bring to the boil. Boil for 10–15 minutes, depending on the size of the potatoes, or until a skewer easily goes into them. Drain the potatoes. Make sure they are very dry. Put the potatoes through a potato ricer – it is important that they are mashed very finely. Scatter the flour over the potatoes, add the egg, and stir with a wooden spoon until it comes together in a dough.

2 Flour a work surface and turn the dough out. If it is very sticky, add a little more flour. Gently knead the dough for only as long as is necessary to bring it together in a smooth mass. Roll the dough into a large sausage and cut it into 8 pieces. Roll 1 piece into a sausage about the thickness of your thumb and cut into 2 cm lengths. Place the gnocchi onto a heavily floured tray. Repeat this process with the remaining pieces of dough.

3 Bring a large pot of well-salted water to a rolling boil. Drop a batch of the gnocchi in. They will start to bob to the surface in a couple of minutes. Once they are floating, they are cooked. Lift very gently out of the water with a slotted spoon and drain. Place into a large bowl containing the pesto and when the gnocchi are all cooked, toss to coat. Serve into warmed bowls and top with a sprinkle of parmesan.

Note: A potato ricer is similar to a big garlic crusher. It gives the best results for mashed potato. If you don't have one, use a potato masher, but be very thorough.

Lemon, pea and ricotta cannelloni

Serves 4   Prep time: 30 minutes   Cooking time: 30 minutes

2 x 400 g tins crushed tomatoes
¼ teaspoon dried oregano
1 tablespoon sugar
1 teaspoon salt
Ground black pepper
1 teaspoon olive oil
1 brown onion, finely chopped
1 garlic clove, crushed

500 g ricotta
200 g frozen baby peas, defrosted
⅓ cup pine nuts, toasted
Juice and zest of 2 lemons
¼ cup freshly grated parmesan
4 fresh lasagne sheets
2 cups grated mozzarella
⅓ cup grated parmesan, extra

1 Preheat the oven to 180°C.

2 In a medium saucepan, combine tomatoes, oregano, sugar and ¼ teaspoon salt and a pinch of pepper. Simmer for 10 minutes or until thickened. The tomatoes can be used as they are, or for a smoother result puree with a stick mixer. Pour half the mixture into the base of a medium baking dish.

3 Heat the olive oil over medium-low heat in a small frypan. Sauté the onion and garlic until translucent.

4 Combine the ricotta, peas, cooked onion and garlic, pine nuts, lemon juice and zest, parmesan, remaining salt and pepper to taste in a large bowl.

5 Cut each lasagne sheet into thirds. Place ¼ cup ricotta mixture along the length of each sheet and roll up to form a tube. Do not overlap the ends too much. Lay the tubes in 2 rows of 6 on the tomato sauce in the baking dish, making sure the joined part is at the bottom. Top with extra tomato sauce and cover with mozzarella, then parmesan. Bake for 25 minutes or until golden and bubbling.

Mushroom risotto

Serves 4   Prep time: 10 minutes   Cooking time: about 30 minutes

3 cups chicken stock (see page 152) or store bought
40 g dried porcini mushrooms
25 g unsalted butter
1 tablespoon olive oil
1 brown onion, finely chopped

2 garlic cloves, chopped
200 g button mushrooms, sliced
1½ cups arborio rice
½ cup white wine
½ cup freshly grated parmesan
Salt and ground white pepper

183

Mushroom risotto, recipe
page 182

1 Place the stock in a medium saucepan over high heat. Bring just to the boil. Reduce the heat and simmer gently. Place the porcini mushrooms in a bowl and cover with 1½ cups boiling water. Allow to soak. When plump and reconstituted, remove the mushrooms from the water. Carefully pour 1 cup of the soaking water into the pan with the stock, being careful not to pour in any grit or sediment at the bottom of the bowl. Rinse the mushrooms to remove any last traces of grit, and chop roughly.

2 Heat the butter and oil in a large non-stick frypan over medium heat. Add the onion, garlic, button mushrooms and porcini mushrooms and cook, stirring, for 5 minutes or until the onions are soft and translucent.

3 Add the rice and stir for 1 minute or until grains appear slightly translucent. Add the wine and cook, stirring constantly, until it is completely absorbed.

4 Add a ladleful (about ½ cup) of hot stock. Stir very gently, being careful not to break the grains of rice. Continue to add the stock, a ladleful at a time, stirring constantly and allowing the liquid to be absorbed before adding the next ladleful. Cook for 20 minutes or until the rice is tender yet firm to the bite, and the risotto is creamy.

5 Remove the pan from the heat. Stir in the grated parmesan. Taste and season with salt and pepper.

Milanese risotto

Serves 4   Prep time: 10 minutes   Cooking time: 25 minutes

1 litre good-quality chicken stock
½ teaspoon saffron threads
25 g unsalted butter
1 tablespoon olive oil
1 brown onion, finely chopped
2 garlic cloves, crushed

1½ cups arborio rice
½ cup white wine
½ cup freshly grated parmesan
Salt and ground black pepper
  to taste

1 Combine the stock and saffron in a medium saucepan over high heat. Bring just to the boil then reduce heat and simmer gently.

2 Heat the butter and oil in a large non-stick frypan over medium heat. Add the onion and garlic and cook, stirring, for 5 minutes or until soft and translucent.

3 Add the rice and stir for 1 minute or until the grains appear slightly translucent. Add the wine and cook, stirring constantly, until it is completely absorbed.

4 Add a ladleful (about ½ cup) of hot stock. Stir very gently, being careful not to break the grains of rice. Continue to add the stock, a ladleful at a time, stirring constantly and allowing the liquid to be absorbed before adding the next ladleful. Cook for 20 minutes or until the rice is tender yet firm to the bite, and the risotto is creamy.

5 Remove the pan from the heat. Stir in the grated parmesan. Taste and season with salt and pepper.

Veggie lasagne

Serves 4   Prep time: 15 minutes   Cooking time: 1 hour 20 minutes

1 tablespoon olive oil
1 large brown onion, finely chopped
2 cloves garlic, crushed
2 medium carrots, grated
2 zucchini, grated
1 eggplant, peeled and
  cut into 1 cm dice
2 x 400 g tins chopped tomatoes

3 teaspoons salt
1 tablespoon sugar
40 g butter
2 tablespoons flour
2 cups milk
3 cups grated tasty cheese
1 cup grated mozzarella
1 packet dried lasagne sheets

1 Preheat the oven to 180°C.

2 In a large chef pan over medium-high heat, heat the olive oil and sauté the onion and garlic until soft and translucent. Add the carrot, zucchini and eggplant and stir to combine. Stir in the tomatoes, 2 teaspoons salt and the sugar and reduce the heat to a simmer. Simmer for about 40 minutes, or until the sauce is thickened and the eggplant and zucchini are very soft. Top up the pan with a little bit of water if it is drying out too much before the flavours are rich. The sauce should be fairly thick and not too wet. Be patient, this is an important part of getting a lot of flavour into the lasagne.

3 In a medium saucepan over medium heat, stir the butter and flour together until it forms a dough-like substance. Add the milk a little bit at a time, stirring and ensuring that the flour cooks after each addition. When all the milk is added, bring to the boil then take the pan off the heat. Add 2 cups tasty cheese, taste and season with salt.

4 In a baking dish approx. 25 x 30 cm, spread half the vegetable mixture. Top with a third of the cheese sauce, then a layer of lasagne sheets. Repeat this process. On top of the final layer of lasagne sheets, pour the rest of the cheese sauce. Scatter with the remaining tasty cheese and mozzarella, and bake for 40 minutes or until the top is golden and the pasta soft.

Note: This recipe can be frozen before the baking stage.

Winter vegetable crumble

I have used mainly orange vegetables in this recipe, but any hard winter veg can be substituted, such as celeriac, parsnip or potato.

Serves 4–6   Prep time: 20 minutes   Cooking time: 1 hour

3 carrots (about 250 g), peeled and
  cut into 3 cm pieces
1 small sweet potato (about 400 g),
  peeled and cut into 3 cm pieces
¼ butternut pumpkin (about 400 g),
  peeled and cut into 3 cm pieces
2 onions, peeled, base intact,
  cut into 6 wedges
1 tablespoon olive oil

½ teaspoon nutmeg
Ground white pepper, to taste
½ teaspoon salt
50 g butter
¼ cup flour
1½ cups milk
2 cups grated tasty cheese
1 cup homemade or
  panko breadcrumbs

1 Preheat the oven to 200°C.

2 Place the vegetables into a baking dish approx. 25 x 35 cm. Drizzle with olive oil, sprinkle with nutmeg and season with pepper and ½ teaspoon salt. Bake for 45 minutes or until soft and golden brown. Remove from the oven.

3 In a medium saucepan on medium heat, melt the butter and add the flour. Stir until well combined. Add the milk a little at a time, stirring and ensuring that the flour cooks after each addition. Stir 1 cup cheese through the sauce. Taste and season with salt and pepper.

4 Pour the cheese sauce over the vegetables in the baking dish. Combine the breadcrumbs and remaining cheese, and sprinkle all over the top. Return the baking dish to the oven and cook for 25 minutes or until golden brown and bubbling.

Eggplant parmigiana

Serves 4   Prep time: 20 minutes   Cooking time: about 25 minutes

2 large or 4 small eggplants
Cooking salt
2 teaspoons olive oil
1 brown onion, chopped
2 cloves garlic, crushed
800 g tin chopped tomatoes
1 tablespoon sugar
¼ teaspoon ground dried oregano
½ cup plain flour

¼ teaspoon ground white pepper
2 eggs, beaten with
  1 tablespoon water
3 cups fresh breadcrumbs
Vegetable oil, for frying
½ cup grated tasty cheese
½ bunch parsley,
  roughly chopped
1 lemon, cut into wedges

1 Slice the eggplant into 1 cm thick slices. Place the slices on a clean tea towel and sprinkle generously with salt. After 15 minutes, wipe the salt off, turn the slices over and repeat the process. Thoroughly wipe the salt from the eggplant slices.

2 Heat the olive oil in a medium saucepan over medium heat and gently sauté the onion and garlic until soft and fragrant but not brown. Stir in the tomatoes, sugar, ½ teaspoon salt and oregano and simmer for 15 minutes or until it has reduced and thickened slightly.

3 Meanwhile, combine the flour, ¼ teaspoon salt and white pepper in a shallow dish. Place the beaten egg and breadcrumbs in separate shallow dishes. Dip each slice of eggplant into the flour, then the egg and then into the breadcrumbs. Place on a plate and repeat until all the eggplant is crumbed.

4 Heat the vegetable oil in a large chef pan or frypan over a medium-high heat and fry the eggplant for 2–3 minutes each side or until golden brown. Only fry a couple of pieces at a time to avoid overcrowding the pan.

5 Preheat the griller to a high heat.

6 Arrange the fried eggplant on a lined baking tray and top each piece with a couple of generous spoonfuls of tomato sauce and a good handful of the tasty cheese. Grill for about a minute, or until the cheese begins to turn golden. Remove from the griller, top with parsley and serve with lemon wedges.

Sides

Autumn vegetable tray bake

Serves 4–6 as a side dish   Prep time: 15 minutes
Cooking time: about 45 minutes

2 tablespoons balsamic vinegar
Zest and juice of ½ orange
2 tablespoons brown sugar
2 tablespoons olive oil
1 tablespoon thyme
Ground black pepper
6 small beetroots, scrubbed and
  cut into quarters
4 small red onions, peeled,
  base intact, cut into quarters

3 large carrots, peeled and
  cut into 4 cm long pieces
¼ butternut pumpkin, peeled
  and cut into 3 cm cubes
½ cup hazelnuts, toasted
100 g goat's cheese, crumbled
Sea salt flakes

Autumn vegetable tray bake,
recipe page 187

1 Preheat the oven to 180°C.

2 Combine the vinegar, orange juice and zest, brown sugar, olive oil, thyme and pepper in a bowl.

3 Arrange the vegetables on 2 baking trays. Pour half the vinegar mixture over each tray and toss to coat the vegetables. Bake for 45 minutes.

4 When the vegetables are tender and browning, remove from the oven and arrange on a serving platter. Scatter with the hazelnuts and goat's cheese and season with salt.

Colcannon mash

This is a hearty Irish dish that goes well with roast pork. Be sure to cook the potatoes all the way through or the mash will be lumpy.

Serves 4   Prep time: 10 minutes   Cooking time: about 10 minutes

3–4 Sebago or Dutch cream
  potatoes (about 700 g), peeled
Salt
80 g unsalted butter, cubed,
  at room temperature

¾ cup milk
¼ small green cabbage,
  very finely sliced or shredded
4 shallots (spring onions), sliced

1 Cut the potatoes in half and place in a large pot of cold salted water. Bring to the boil and cook until tender – about 10 minutes. Strain the potatoes well, empty the pan and dry it. Reserve 1 teaspoon butter, and place the rest of the butter in the base of the still-warm pot. Place the potatoes in a bowl.

2 While the potatoes are still hot, use a potato ricer to mash the potatoes as quickly as possible, then put back into the pot with the butter. Using a wooden spoon, stir in the milk a little at a time. Taste and add salt. Be aware that potato does tend to take quite a lot of salt in order to not taste bland. Keep stirring until the puree is completely smooth and lump free. Add milk until the puree is the consistency you want.

3 In a frypan over medium heat, melt the reserved 1 teaspoon butter and add the cabbage and shallots. Sauté until the cabbage 'collapses', or becomes soft and bright green, but still retains some crunch. Mix through the mashed potato and serve immediately.

Note: As the potato cools it will thicken up. To reheat, stir in a little extra milk over a gentle heat.

Cauliflower puree

Serves 6   Prep time: 10 minutes   Cooking time: 20 minutes

1 litre milk
1 large head cauliflower
 (about 1.4 kg), broken up
 into florets

100 g butter
2 teaspoons salt
½ teaspoon finely ground
 white pepper

1 In a large soup pot, heat the milk over medium-high heat.

2 While the milk is heating, process the cauliflower in batches in a food processor to the consistency of large breadcrumbs. This allows the cauliflower to cook quickly while maintaining all its lovely flavour.

3 When the milk is almost at boiling point, add the cauliflower to the pot. Bring back to a simmer and simmer, stirring frequently, for about 20 minutes. To test if the cauliflower is cooked, crush a little piece between your thumb and forefinger. It should disintegrate. If it is still a bit hard, continue cooking.

4 When the cauliflower is cooked, stir in the butter, salt and pepper. Taste for seasoning. Process the puree in a blender to a velvet smooth consistency.

Paris mash

This mash is very rich and best for special occasions. For an everyday mashed potato, use the same method but reduce the butter to 20–50 g and increase the milk if needed.

Serves 6–8 as an accompaniment
Prep time: 15 minutes   Cooking time: 10 minutes

600 g Sebago or Dutch cream
 potatoes, peeled and cut
 roughly into 5-cm cubes
125 g good quality unsalted
 butter, cubed

1 (250 ml) cup milk
Salt, to taste

1 In a large pot of cold salted water, bring the potatoes to the boil. Boil until tender – about 10 minutes. Strain the potatoes well, empty the pot and dry it.

2 Place the butter into the pot. Using a potato ricer (see note), rice the potatoes back into the pot. Using a sturdy whisk, whisk in the milk a little at a time until the potatoes are the required consistency.

3 Taste and add salt. Be aware that potato does tend to take quite a lot of salt in order to not taste bland.

4 To reheat, stir in a little extra milk over a gentle heat.

Note: A potato ricer is similar to a big garlic crusher. It gives the best results for mashed potato. If you don't have one, use a potato masher, but be very thorough.

Sweet potato mash

Serves 4   Prep time: 15 minutes   Cooking time: 20 minutes

2 sweet potatoes (about 400 g), peeled and cut into chunks
20 g butter

Salt and pepper to taste
Warm milk, optional

1 In a medium saucepan, cover the sweet potato with water and boil until tender.

2 Drain the sweet potato and mash with the butter and season with salt and pepper. For a smoother, looser puree, add warm milk and blitz with a hand-held stick blender.

Patatas bravas

Serves 6   Prep time: 15 minutes   Cooking time: 45 minutes

4 large or 6 medium Desiree or Pontiac potatoes, peeled, cut into 3 cm cubes
½ cup vegetable or rice bran oil
1 teaspoon sea salt
½ teaspoon ground black pepper
1 tablespoon olive oil

1 brown onion, finely diced
3 cloves garlic, finely diced
1 tablespoon smoky paprika
1 tablespoon Tabasco sauce
½ cup mayonnaise
½ cup tomato sauce

1 Preheat the oven to 180°C. Place the potatoes on a lined baking tray and toss through with the vegetable oil. Sprinkle with salt and pepper and bake for 45 minutes or until golden and crunchy.

2 In a medium pan over medium heat, heat the olive oil. Sauté the onions and garlic until translucent and fragrant, about 3 minutes. Add the paprika and stir for a further minute. Remove the mixture from the pan and allow to cool.

In a small bowl, combine the Tabasco, mayonnaise and tomato sauce. Stir through the onion mixture.

3 Serve the potatoes piping hot, drizzled with the sauce.

Loaded potato skins

Serves 4   Prep time: 15 minutes   Cooking time: 50 minutes

4 large Pontiac or Desiree potatoes
  (the ones with deep pink skins),
  unpeeled
¼ cup olive oil
1 teaspoon sea salt flakes
½ teaspoon freshly
  ground black pepper
4 rashers bacon, cut into strips

2 avocados, diced
½ cup grated tasty cheese
½ cup sour cream
½ cup tomato salsa (see page 148)
  or store bought (whatever heat
  you prefer)
4 shallots (spring onions),
  sliced finely on the diagonal

1 Preheat the oven to 200°C and line a baking tray with baking paper.

2 Cut the potatoes in half lengthways, place on the baking tray and drizzle with a little oil. Bake for 30 minutes or until soft enough to scoop. Scoop the flesh out of the potato, leaving about a 1 cm thick shell inside the skin. (Reserve the scooped out flesh for mashed potato or salmon patties another night.) Drizzle the potato shells with more oil, salt and pepper and bake, cut side up, for 15 minutes or until brown and crispy on the cut surface.

3 While the potatoes are in the oven, in a medium frypan over medium-high heat, fry the bacon until golden and starting to crisp up. Remove from the pan and drain on paper towel.

4 Change the oven to the griller setting. Divide the diced avocado and the bacon between the potato 'bowls'. Top with cheese. Grill for 1–2 minutes or until the cheese is golden and bubbling.

5 Top the potatoes with a dollop of sour cream and salsa, and scatter with shallots.

Hasselback potatoes

Serves 4 as a side dish   Prep time: 10 minutes   Cooking time: 45–60 minutes

4 large or 8 small Desiree or
  Pontiac potatoes, unpeeled
50 g butter, melted

2 tablespoons olive oil
1 teaspoon sea salt flakes

Brussels sprouts with lemon burnt butter
& almonds, recipe page 199

Hasselback potatoes, recipe
page 192

1 Preheat the oven to 200°C (180°C fan-forced).

2 Working with one at a time, place a potato in between the 2 chopping boards aligned vertically on the bench. The idea is to cut through the potato almost, but not all the way, to the bottom. Take your time and cut each potato vertically at 2 mm intervals. Place the potatoes together in a small baking tray.

3 Mix together the melted butter and oil, and pour over the potatoes. Make sure some of the butter and oil gets down into the cuts. Bake for 45 minutes (small potatoes) or 1 hour (large potatoes) or until golden, slightly fanned out and crisp. Sprinkle with sea salt while still hot, and serve.

Variations: Place finely chopped garlic, smoked paprika, black pepper or other spices into the melted butter. These potatoes are also lovely served with chives and sour cream.

Roast lemon herb potatoes

Serves 8   Prep time: 15 minutes   Cooking time: 1 hour 15 minutes

2 kg Sebago or Dutch cream
  potatoes, peeled
Vegetable oil, for baking
½ bunch flat-leaf parsley,
  finely chopped

1 bunch chives, finely chopped
½ bunch basil, finely chopped
Zest of 2 lemons
2 teaspoons sea salt flakes

1 Preheat the oven to 220°C.

2 Place the potatoes in a large pot of cold salted water and bring to the boil. Boil for about 15 minutes or until the cut edges are just starting to soften, and a knife or skewer goes easily into the potato. Don't cook any further than this or the potatoes will fall apart. Drain the potatoes very well. It is critical that they are dry.

3 While the potatoes are draining, put about 3 mm vegetable oil into a roasting pan. Place the pan in the oven until the oil is hot.

4 Very carefully lower the potatoes into the hot oil. Gently turn them, so that the whole surface area of each potato has a coating of oil. Place the pan back in the oven and cook for about 30 minutes, turning the potatoes once or twice, until they are crisp and golden brown.

5 While the potatoes cook, combine the parsley, chives, basil, lemon zest and salt in a large bowl.

6 Remove the potatoes from the oven and drain briefly on paper towel. Place the potatoes in the bowl with the herb mixture, and toss lightly to combine. Transfer to a serving dish and serve hot.

Cheesy potato bake

Serves 8–10 as an accompaniment   Prep time: 15 minutes
Cooking time: 1 hour 30 minutes

2 kg washed potatoes, unpeeled,
  sliced 2 mm thick using
  a mandolin
600 ml sour cream
1 tablespoon Dijon mustard
1 teaspoon garlic powder
1½ cups grated tasty cheese

1 bunch shallots (spring onions),
  white and pale green parts only,
  finely sliced
1 teaspoon salt
½ teaspoon finely ground
  white pepper

1 Preheat the oven to 180°C.

2 Place the sour cream, mustard, garlic powder, 1 cup cheese, shallots, salt and pepper in a large bowl. Stir to combine well.

3 Place a layer of potatoes in a large baking dish. Ladle some of the sour cream mixture evenly over the potatoes. Repeat layering with the remaining potatoes and cream. Arrange the top layer of potatoes neatly, pour the last of the cream mixture on top, then press down into the dish. Cover with aluminium foil and press down again, so that the foil is touching the top layer. Seal tightly on all sides. Bake for 1 hour.

4 Remove the foil and scatter the remaining cheese over the top. Bake for a further 30 minutes or until the top is golden and bubbling. Test that the potatoes are fully cooked by inserting a skewer or small knife into the dish – it should go through easily.

Carrot cumin salad,
recipe page 197

Celeriac puree

Serves 4   Prep time: 15 minutes   Cooking time: 15 minutes

1 medium sized celeriac bulb,
  peeled and grated or processed
  into small pieces

1 cup milk
50 g butter
Salt

1 Into a medium saucepan over medium heat, place the celeriac and add enough milk to cover. Simmer for about 10 minutes or until tender enough to squash between your fingers.

2 Add the butter and a pinch of salt and puree to a smooth consistency. Taste and add more salt if required. Keep warm.

Carrot cumin salad

Delicious and versatile, this salad can be served warm, or completely cooled.

Serves 6   Prep time: 10 minutes   Cooking time: 8–10 minutes

2 teaspoons cumin seeds
1 kg carrots, peeled and
  cut into 2 cm pieces
¼ cup plain Greek yoghurt
Juice of 1 lemon

1 clove garlic, crushed
¼ teaspoon sea salt flakes
½ bunch coriander leaves,
  roughly chopped

1 In a small frypan over medium heat, toast the cumin seeds until they are fragrant. Remove to a mortar and pestle and crush lightly. (Alternatively, place in a mini food processor and blitz very briefly.)

2 In a large saucepan over high heat, cook the carrots in plenty of salted boiling water, for 3–4 minutes or until tender. Remove from the pot, drain and set aside.

3 In a large bowl, place the yoghurt, lemon juice, garlic, cumin seeds and salt and stir to combine. Toss through the carrots and coriander leaves.

Honeyed Dutch carrots

Serves 4 as an accompaniment   Prep time: 5 minutes
Cooking time: 6–8 minutes

2 bunches baby Dutch carrots,
    peeled and tops trimmed to 2 cm
1 tablespoon sesame seeds

20 g butter
2 tablespoons honey
Salt and ground black pepper

1 Steam or microwave the carrots for about 3 minutes, until tender but not soggy. The time will depend on how big the carrots are – very little ones may need even less time than this.

2 In a medium frypan over medium-high heat, place the sesame seeds and toast until pale gold. Remove from the pan. Place the butter in the pan. When it is starting to froth, add the carrots and honey. Toss in the pan for 2 minutes or until the honey becomes a lovely dark brown. Season with salt and pepper and serve straight away.

Roast beetroot and onions

Serves 4–6 as a side dish   Prep time: 15 minutes
Cooking time: about 45 minutes

2 tablespoons balsamic vinegar
2 tablespoons brown sugar
2 tablespoons olive oil
Ground black pepper
8 small beetroots, scrubbed
    and cut into quarters
6 small red onions, peeled,
    base intact, cut into quarters

½ cup walnuts, toasted
100 g Persian feta
½ cup roughly chopped
    continental parsley
Sea salt flakes

1 Preheat the oven to 180°C. Combine the vinegar, sugar, oil and pepper in a large bowl. Arrange the beetroot and onions on a large baking tray. Pour half the vinegar mixture over the tray and toss to coat the vegetables. Bake for 45 minutes.

2 When the beetroot and onions are cooked through, arrange on a serving platter. Top with the remaining dressing, walnuts, feta, parsley and salt.

Vegetables & preserves

Brussels sprouts with lemon burnt butter and almonds

Serves 4 as part of a shared meal   Prep time: 5 minutes
Cooking time: 6–8 minutes

400 g Brussels sprouts
 – as small as possible
¼ cup slivered almonds

40 g butter
Juice and zest of 1 lemon
Salt and ground black pepper

1 Steam or microwave the Brussels sprouts until they are just tender. Check every couple of minutes. They should be bright green. Cut in half.

2 In a medium frypan over medium-high heat, dry-fry the almonds until golden. Watch carefully as they burn easily. Remove from pan and set aside.

3 Add the butter to the pan. It will start to foam up. Use a spatula to stir the butter around and keep an eye on the colour. When this becomes a good deep golden brown, add the lemon zest and juice to the pan. It will spit a bit. Toss the Brussels sprouts through the butter. Season with salt and pepper. Serve with any remaining butter from the pan drizzled over the top and scatter with the toasted almonds.

Green beans and peas with yoghurt dressing

Serves 6 as an accompaniment   Prep time: 5 minutes
Cooking time: 7 minutes

1 cup frozen baby peas
400 g green beans, tops removed
1 tablespoon plain Greek yoghurt

1 teaspoon tahini
1 teaspoon lemon juice
½ teaspoon sea salt flakes

1 Place the peas in a lidded microwave-safe container and cook on high for 2 minutes. Remove and set aside, still covered.

2 Place the beans in another lidded microwave-safe container and cook on high for 4 minutes. Remove and set aside, still covered.

3 In a small bowl, place the yoghurt, tahini, lemon juice and salt and stir to combine. Combine the beans and peas in a serving bowl and drizzle with the dressing.

Hash browns

Makes 12   Prep time: 15 minutes   Cooking time: 15 minutes

8 large potatoes (about 1.8–2 kg)
  – Desiree, Coliban or a similar
  waxy variety

Vegetable or canola oil, for
  shallow-frying
Salt and pepper, to taste

1 Peel the potatoes and grate into a tea towel. Gather up the edges of the tea towel to form a bundle, and twist the top of the bundle to squeeze as much moisture out of the potatoes as possible.

2 Pour the oil about 5 mm deep in a large frypan and heat over a medium heat. The oil should be hot enough to produce a crisp golden shell without burning, while allowing the inside to cook.

3 Divide the grated potato into 12 equal portions. Place 4 portions into the oil. Use a spatula or egg flipper to flatten each portion into a disc about 6–7 cm round. Fry for 3–4 minutes each side until golden brown and crispy. Drain on paper towels and season with salt and pepper immediately, while hot. Repeat twice more to cook remaining potato portions and serve immediately.

Note: If you are making more than one batch, I recommend placing the hash browns, uncovered, on a tray in a 100°C oven to keep warm. Covering will produce steam and they will go soggy.

Cauliflower and feta fritters

Makes about 12   Prep time: 10 minutes + cooling time
Cooking time: about 30 minutes

½ head cauliflower, cut into florets
1 bunch shallots (spring onions),
  finely sliced
150 g feta, crumbled
1 cup grated tasty cheese
1 cup flour

3 eggs
2 cups milk
½ teaspoon salt
¼ teaspoon ground black pepper
2 tablespoons olive oil

1 Cook the cauliflower in a large pot of rapidly boiling salted water. It should be tender but not disintegrating. When cooked, remove from the pot and place in a colander to drain and cool.

2 When cooled, place the cauliflower in a large bowl and mix with the shallots, feta and tasty cheese. Sprinkle the flour over and stir to combine. In a jug, whisk the eggs, milk, salt and pepper together. Pour into the cauliflower mixture and stir to combine well.

3 Place a tablespoon of olive oil in a large, non-stick chef pan over medium-high heat. When the oil is hot, dollop large spoonfuls of the fritter mixture into the pan. You should be able to fit 6 in the pan, using about half the mixture. Cook for 2 minutes or until golden underneath. Flip and cook for a further 1–2 minutes. Remove from the pan and put under foil. Repeat with the remaining mixture.

Corn fritters

Makes 12   Prep time: 15 minutes   Cooking time: 20 minutes + resting time

3 cobs fresh corn, silk and
  husk removed
½ teaspoon salt
¼ teaspoon ground white pepper
2 eggs, whisked
⅓ cup milk

¾ cup self-raising flour
4 shallots (spring onions),
  white and pale green parts only,
  finely sliced
Olive oil, for frying

1 Cook the corn cobs either by boiling or microwaving until the kernels are tender but still al dente. Boiling will take about 5 minutes; microwave time will depend on your machine but give it 1½ minutes per cob and then longer if required.

2 When the corn has cooled enough to handle, run a sharp knife down the length of the cobs to remove the kernels. Season with salt and pepper. For mini fritters, the kernels should then be chopped very roughly.

3 Meanwhile, mix the eggs and milk together. Place the flour in a bowl and add the milk mixture gradually, stirring to ensure there are no lumps. Stir in the corn kernels and shallots. Set aside for 15 minutes to rest.

4 Heat 1 tablespoon olive oil in a chef pan over medium heat. Drop small spoonfuls of the fritter mix in the pan. Give the fritters space to spread and yourself space to flip them. After about 2 minutes, they should start setting on the edges of the upper surface, and be golden brown underneath. Flip and cook for another minute. Remove from heat and drain on paper towel while cooking the remaining fritters.

Corn pudding

Light, creamy, fluffy and delicious, this is also an easy addition to the Christmas table. Because space in the oven can be at a premium when getting ready for a Christmas feast, the corn pudding can be done ahead of time and gently reheated.

Serves 8 as an accompaniment   Prep time: 10 minutes
Cooking time: 25 minutes

6 cobs fresh corn, silk and
  husk removed
300 ml thickened cream
⅓ cup self-raising flour
½ teaspoon salt

¼ teaspoon finely ground
  white pepper
5 eggs, lightly beaten
400 ml milk

1 Preheat the oven to 180°C. Lightly grease a glass or ceramic baking dish about 30 x 20 cm in size.

2 Microwave or boil the corn until the kernels are tender but still al dente. When the corn has cooled enough to handle, run a sharp knife down the length of the cob to remove the kernels. Place half the kernels in the bowl of a food processor with half the cream and process until mostly smooth.

3 In a large bowl, combine the pureed corn with the remaining kernels then stir through the flour, salt and pepper. Add the eggs, milk and remaining cream and mix well.

4 Place the mixture in the baking dish and bake for 25 minutes or until the top is golden and the mixture set.

Note: You can substitute the fresh steamed corn with tinned corn (well drained), if you like.

Cider-braised cabbage with bacon

Serves 4   Prep time: 10 minutes   Cooking time: 25 minutes

4 rashers bacon, rind removed,
  cut into 5 mm wide strips
¼ green cabbage, finely sliced
1 cup apple cider

2 tablespoons cider vinegar
½ teaspoon salt
½ teaspoon ground
  white pepper

1 In a large non-stick chef pan over medium-high heat, sauté the bacon until it starts to turn golden. Add the cabbage and stir for 5 minutes until the cabbage starts to collapse and become soft. Stir in the cider and vinegar and simmer for about 15 minutes or until almost all the liquid has evaporated and the cabbage is very soft. Taste, and stir through the salt and pepper.

Salads

Caesar salad

Makes a giant platter   Prep time: 20 minutes
Cooking time: about 10 minutes

1 large cos lettuce
4 rashers bacon, rind
  removed, cut into thin strips
6 slices bread, crusts removed,
  pulsed in a food processor to a
  very coarse crumb
Olive oil, to drizzle
Salt, to taste

1 quantity Caesar dressing
  (see page 211)
1 red onion, very finely sliced
4 eggs, boiled and sliced
  (I like it when the yolk is still
  a little bit soft in the middle)
100 g fresh parmesan, shaved
  using a vegetable peeler

1 Remove any shabby outer leaves from the lettuce and any leathery leaf tips. Cut the lettuce across into 3–4 cm wide strips.

2 Heat a non-stick frypan over high heat and fry the bacon until it begins to crisp up. Remove and drain on paper towel.

3 Reduce the heat to medium-low, then add the breadcrumbs to the same pan. Drizzle with olive oil and toss around the pan to coat with the combined oil and bacon fat. Season lightly with salt. Cook, tossing occasionally, until the breadcrumbs are brown and crisp. Remove and drain on paper towel.

4 This salad should not be assembled until it is just about to be served. When it's time to serve, toss most of the dressing through the red onion and lettuce. Arrange on a large, flat platter. Top with the egg, bacon, breadcrumbs and parmesan, and drizzle over the remainder of the dressing.

Basic potato salad

These are the building blocks of my potato salad. Once you have the basics, feel free to ad lib with anything you'd like – some suggestions are overleaf. The key to this salad is to cook the potatoes so that they are tender but not overdone, and then add plenty of dressing.

Potato and poached salmon
salad, recipe page 205

Serves 6 as an accompaniment   Prep time: 20 minutes
Cooking time: about 15 minutes

600 g Pontiac, Desiree or
    chat potatoes, unpeeled
½ cup sour cream
½ cup good-quality whole
    egg mayonnaise
2 tablespoons whole
    grain mustard

4 shallots (spring onions),
    finely sliced
Salt and ground white
    pepper, to taste

1 Place the potatoes in a saucepan of cold water and bring to the boil. Cook for about 15 minutes for chat potatoes, longer for the others, until tender (the time will depend on the size). Drain and set aside to cool.

2 In a fairly large bowl, combine the sour cream, mayonnaise and mustard. Fold through the shallots. Taste and season with salt and pepper.

3 Cut the warm potatoes into quarters if small, sixths if medium, and stir into the dressing.

Note: Choose potatoes of an even size, so they cook at the same time.

Variations:
Add chopped gherkins and baby capers.
Add hard-boiled egg.
Add a couple of rashers of chopped cooked bacon.
Add fresh herbs such as mint, parsley, basil, dill.
Stir through strips of smoked salmon and chopped dill.

Potato and poached salmon salad

Serves 8 as an accompaniment   Prep time: 10 minutes
Cooking time: about 15 minutes

12 small or 8 medium chat potatoes
    (about 600 g), unpeeled
2 eggs
2 skinless salmon fillets
    (about 180 g each)
⅔ cup sour cream
⅔ cup good-quality
    mayonnaise
2 tablespoons whole grain mustard

Juice and zest from ½ lemon
2 tablespoons dill, chopped
¼ cup shallots (spring onions),
    finely sliced
2 large dill pickles (gherkins),
    finely chopped
2 tablespoons baby capers,
    rinsed
1 lemon, cut into 8 wedges

1 In a large pot of salted water, boil the potatoes until tender, then drain. (Time will depend on size.) While the potatoes are boiling, cook the eggs for 4 minutes in the same water. Remove and allow to cool before peeling and chopping roughly.

2 Reduce the temperature of the water to a gentle simmer and poach the salmon fillets for 8–10 minutes. Remove and allow to cool before gently flaking the fish apart.

3 In a large bowl, combine the sour cream, mayonnaise, mustard, lemon juice and zest. Fold through the dill, shallots, dill pickles, capers and boiled egg.

4 Cut the cooled potatoes into quarters if small, sixths if medium sized, and stir into the dressing. Stir through the flaked salmon and serve with lemon wedges.

Note: If not serving immediately, keep the salad in the fridge. It will seize up a bit and needs to be brought back to room temperature before serving.

Waldorf salad

Serves 6 as an accompaniment   Prep time: 15 minutes

½ cup mayonnaise
¼ cup sour cream
2 tablespoons whole
  grain mustard
1 lemon, juiced
6 shallots (spring onions)

3 Granny Smith apples
3 celery stalks
100 g baby spinach leaves
¾ cup walnut pieces
Salt and ground white pepper

1 In a large mixing bowl, combine the mayonnaise, sour cream and mustard. Squeeze the lemon in and stir to combine.

2 Peel the shallots and slice ½ cm thick. Using a mandolin, julienne the unpeeled apples. Slice the celery in half lengthways and cut into 1 cm pieces. Right before serving, place the shallots, apples and celery into the mixing bowl with the dressing, along with the baby spinach and walnuts. Toss, season to taste with salt and pepper, and serve.

Warm brown rice salad

Serves 4   Prep time: 20 minutes   Cooking time: 35 minutes

1 cup brown rice
3 cups beef stock
1 teaspoon olive oil
2 brown onions, chopped
2 cloves garlic, chopped
2 long green chillies, seeded
  and finely sliced
1 bunch coriander, roots and
  stems cleaned and chopped,
  leaves reserved

2 teaspoons smoked paprika
2 teaspoons ground cumin seeds
400 g tin crushed tomatoes
1 teaspoon salt
400 g tin red kidney beans,
  drained and rinsed
¼ cup olive oil
2 tablespoons red
  wine vinegar

1 Rinse the brown rice and place it in a tightly covered microwave-safe container with the beef stock. Cook, covered, on high for 10 minutes or until the stock is at a rapid boil. Remove the lid and cook, uncovered, for a further 25 minutes. Remove from the microwave and place the lid back on while the rice rests.

2 In a large non-stick chef pan over medium heat, heat the olive oil and sauté the onion, garlic, chilli and coriander until soft and fragrant. Add the paprika and cumin and stir for a further minute. Stir in the tomatoes and salt, and increase the heat. Bring to a simmer and simmer for 5 minutes or until rich and fragrant. Stir through the kidney beans and the rice, along with any liquid still left in the rice.

3 Combine the oil and vinegar in a small bowl, then stir through the rice along with the reserved coriander leaves. Serve warm.

Winter Greek salad

Serves 4   Prep time: 15 minutes   Cooking time: 5 minutes

¼ cup lemon-infused olive oil
1 tablespoon dried oregano leaves
Juice and zest of 1 lemon
2 cloves garlic, finely chopped
½ teaspoon sea salt flakes
¼ teaspoon ground black pepper
3 zucchini, sliced 5 mm
  thick lengthways

4 ripe Roma tomatoes, halved
2 red onions, peeled, bases intact,
  cut into wedges
100 g baby rocket
200 g feta, crumbled
12 Kalamata olives

1 Place half the oil, oregano, lemon juice and zest, salt and pepper in a large glass bowl and mix well.

2 Heat a char-grill pan over high heat. Drizzle a little oil over the zucchini, tomato and onion and place on the char grill. Leave to cook for 2 minutes to achieve good char marks, then turn and finish cooking.

3 Toss the rocket with half the dressing and arrange on a serving platter. Arrange the char-grilled vegetables on top of the rocket. Scatter with the crumbled feta and olives, then pour over the rest of the dressing.

Note: Lemon-infused olive oil can be found in supermarkets. Good quality olive oil can be used if it is not available.

Chorizo and haloumi salad

Serves 4   Prep time: 15 minutes   Cooking time: 10 minutes

100 g Californian walnuts
2 fresh chorizo sausages,
   sliced ½ cm thick on the diagonal
2 zucchini, cut into
   3 mm slices lengthways
¼ cup olive oil
200 g haloumi cheese,
   cut into ½ cm thick slices

2 tablespoons red wine vinegar
¼ teaspoon sea salt flakes
¼ teaspoon freshly
   ground black pepper
100 g rocket

1 Preheat the barbecue to a medium-high heat – both the flat plate and the grill plate.

2 Place the walnuts on the flat plate and watch them carefully until they start to brown. Remove and set aside.

3 Brush the chorizo and zucchini slices with just a little oil to prevent them sticking and place on the grill for a minute on each side until there are char-marks. Remove and set aside on paper towel to drain.

4 Brush the haloumi with a little oil and grill for about a minute on each side. This should be done just before serving.

5 To assemble the salad, place the remaining oil with the vinegar, salt and pepper in a small bowl and whisk with a fork. Toss half of the dressing through the rocket and arrange on a serving platter. Top with the zucchini, chorizo, haloumi and walnuts and drizzle the rest of the dressing over the top.

209

Chorizo and haloumi salad,
recipe page 208

Asian coleslaw

Serves 6–8 as a side dish   Prep time: 10 minutes

4 cups finely sliced green
   and/or red cabbage (about ½ head)
½ cup grated carrot
¼ cup very finely sliced onion
2 long red chillies, seeded
   and finely chopped

½ bunch coriander, leaves only
1 quantity garlic and chilli
   dipping sauce (see page 140),
   for dressing

1 Combine the cabbage, carrot, onion, chilli and coriander leaves in a large bowl. About 15 minutes before serving, toss through the garlic and chilli dressing.

Vietnamese chicken salad

Serves 4   Prep time: 20 minutes   Cooking time: 15 minutes

1 large single chicken
   breast fillet (about 400 g)
½ cup roasted salted peanuts,
   roughly chopped
½ cup white vinegar
½ cup white sugar
1 tablespoon fish sauce
   (more to taste if necessary)
1 teaspoon sesame oil
1 small red chilli, sliced
2 cloves garlic, sliced
1 baby cos lettuce, outer leaves
   removed, cut into 1 cm strips

2 Lebanese cucumbers,
   seeded and sliced very finely on
   the diagonal
2 carrots, julienned
   using a mandolin
1 red onion, very finely
   sliced using a mandolin
½ bunch mint leaves,
   roughly chopped
½ bunch coriander, leaves only
2 tablespoons crispy
   fried garlic (see note)

1 Place the whole chicken fillet in a medium pot. Cover with cold water. Place the pot over low heat and bring up to a gentle simmer. Simmer for 10 minutes then turn the heat off. Allow the chicken to cool in the water before slicing very thinly or shredding with a fork.

2 In a frypan over medium-high heat, toast the peanuts until golden with some little blackened bits. Remove from the pan.

3 In a small saucepan over high heat, place the vinegar and sugar with ¼ cup of water. Bring to the boil and boil for about 3 minutes until starting to thicken. Remove from the pot to a bowl, and add the fish sauce, sesame oil, chilli and garlic. Leave to cool.

4 In a bowl, mix the lettuce, cucumber, carrot, onion, and most of the mint and coriander leaves. Toss with a little of the fish sauce dressing. Place the salad in a serving bowl and top with the chicken, fried garlic and peanuts. Drizzle a little more dressing over and top with some extra coriander and mint leaves. Serve immediately.

Note: If you can't find crispy fried garlic in your supermarket, it will be available at your local Asian grocer.

Dressings

Caesar salad dressing

Makes 1 cup   Prep time: 10 minutes

1 tablespoon white wine vinegar
1 clove garlic, crushed
1 tablespoon Dijon mustard
6 anchovy fillets, finely chopped
1 tablespoon Worcestershire sauce

1 egg yolk
1 cup light olive oil
Lemon juice, to taste
Salt and white pepper, to taste

1 Place the vinegar, garlic, mustard, anchovies, Worcestershire sauce and egg yolk in a large mixing bowl.

2 Using electric beaters, beat the ingredients until they are well combined and the egg is pale and fluffy. Add the olive oil a few drops at a time until the dressing starts to thicken. The oil can then be added in a stream.

3 When the dressing is thick and smooth, add the lemon juice and salt and pepper to taste and mix well.

Note: Quick cheat: Add the vinegar, garlic, mustard, anchovies and Worcestershire sauce to a good-quality store-bought mayonnaise. Taste and stir in the lemon juice, salt and pepper to taste.

Basic vinaigrette

Prep time: 2 minutes

1 Use 1 part of an acidic ingredient, such as vinegar or lemon juice, to 2 parts of oil – a good-quality Australian olive oil is a good choice.

2 Add any number of flavours to this – seeded mustard, honey, orange or lemon zest, chopped thyme, finely chopped onion or crushed garlic.

Whole egg mayonnaise

Makes 1 cup   Prep time: 5 minutes

1 egg
1 tablespoon Dijon mustard
1 cup rice bran oil
  (or canola or vegetable oil)
1 teaspoon salt

¼ teaspoon ground
  white pepper
Juice of 1 lemon, or 1 tablespoon
  white wine vinegar

1 Place all the ingredients in a tall, narrow jug or cup. The ones that come with most hand-held stick blenders are perfect. Place the stick blender in the very bottom of the jug and turn it on. Leave the stick blender going at the bottom of the cup until the mixture starts to emulsify, or thicken and turn white. Slowly draw the blender upwards. By the time the blender reaches the top of the mixture, the mayonnaise will be fully emulsified and ready to use.

Variation: For garlic aioli, place 3 cloves garlic, halved, in the base of the jug. Make sure they are under the head of the stick blender when you turn it on.

Blue cheese dressing

Makes 1 cup   Prep time: 5 minutes

½ cup whole egg mayonnaise
  (see above)
75 g blue cheese (choose a mild
  creamy blue)
1 tablespoon Dijon mustard

1 tablespoon white vinegar
¼ teaspoon finely ground
  white pepper
1 clove garlic, peeled

1 Place all the ingredients in a food processor and process until smooth. Scrape down the sides of the bowl occasionally. Store in the fridge, but serve at room temperature.

Lime aioli

Perfect for a seafood dipping sauce.

Makes 2 cups   Prep time: 10 minutes

3 tablespoons lime juice
3 tablespoons Dijon mustard
2 cloves garlic, crushed

3 egg yolks
300 ml olive oil
Salt, to taste

1 Place the lime juice, mustard, garlic and egg yolks into a blender or food processor and blend.

2 Add the olive oil a couple of drops at a time and blend well after each addition. The mixture will begin to thicken or emulsify. When this happens, the oil can be added a little more quickly until it is all incorporated. Taste and season with salt.

Ranch dressing

Makes 1½ cups   Prep time: 10 minutes

1 cup whole egg mayonnaise
  (see page 212)
½ cup sour cream
Juice of 1 lemon
1 clove garlic, finely chopped
1 tablespoon finely
  chopped chives

1 tablespoon finely
  chopped parsley
1 tablespoon finely
  chopped dill
1 teaspoon salt
½ teaspoon freshly
  ground black pepper

1 Place all the ingredients in a bowl and stir to combine.

Yoghurt tahini dressing

Makes ⅓ cup   Prep time: 5 minutes

¼ cup plain Greek yoghurt
2 tablespoons tahini

1 tablespoon lemon juice

1 Place all the ingredients in a small bowl and stir to combine.

Pickles and preserves

To sterilise jars, place them on a tray in the oven at 100°C for 10 minutes. Boil the lids for 5 minutes. Place hot ingredients into hot jars to maintain sterilisation. Jars can be stored unopened in the pantry for 12 months or open in the fridge for about 6 weeks. If not storing in a sterile jar, store in an airtight container in the fridge for up to 2 weeks.

Caramelised onion jam

This savoury jam is delicious served on a cheese platter, with sausages or as a chutney on cold meat sandwiches.

Makes 2 cups   Prep time: 15 minutes   Cooking time: 40 minutes

1 tablespoon olive oil
1 kg brown onions, sliced very finely

1 cup balsamic vinegar
½ cup caster sugar

1 In a large chef pan, heat the olive oil over medium-low heat. Add the onions and sauté gently until they are soft, translucent and golden brown. This will take about 20 minutes.

2 Add the vinegar and sugar. Simmer, stirring, for about 20 minutes or until the liquid reduces and the onions have the consistency of a jam or chutney.

Sweet chilli and ginger jam

Makes 2 cups   Prep time: 15 minutes   Cooking time: 1½ hours

20 long red chillies, seeded
  and coarsely chopped
12 cloves garlic, chopped
10 cm knob ginger, peeled
  and chopped

¾ cup brown sugar
¾ cup white sugar
1 cup white vinegar
¼ cup fish sauce

1 Place the chilli, garlic and ginger into the bowl of a food processor and add ¼ cup of water. Process until smooth.

2 Pour the chilli mixture into a large saucepan and stir in the sugar and vinegar. Bring to the boil, and as the jam cooks, skim off any foamy scum that rises to the surface. Reduce the heat to low and simmer for an hour, stirring occasionally. Stir in the fish sauce and continue to cook for a further 30 minutes. As the jam thickens, stir continuously to prevent it from sticking.

3 The jam is ready when the spoon you are using starts to leave a trail and the bottom of the pan can be seen briefly. Turn off the heat and pour into sterilised jars.

Confit garlic

Makes 2 jars   Prep time: 30 minutes   Cooking time: 1 hour

This delicious garlic can be used as a milder, nuttier alternative to raw garlic. The oil is beautiful for cooking, or dipping bread into. It is also divine mashed into some real butter with sea salt for the ultimate garlic bread.

12 heads garlic, cloves separated and peeled

3 sprigs thyme
750 ml rice bran oil

1 Preheat the oven to 90°C. Place the garlic and thyme in an oven-proof casserole dish. Cover with the oil and bake uncovered for an hour. The garlic should be pale golden and aromatic. This will keep in an airtight container in the fridge for weeks. To store for longer, use 2 sterilised glass jars (see page 213). Place the garlic and oil into the jars as soon as they are removed from the oven. Seal with the lids. This can be stored unopened in the cupboard for 6 months. Refrigerate after opening.

Pickled onions

These tasty pickles are lovely on a cheeseburger or salad sandwich.

Makes 3 cups   Prep time: 5 minutes   Cooking time: 5 minutes

6 red onions, very finely sliced
2 cups white vinegar
2 tablespoons salt
2 tablespoons white sugar

1 teaspoon black peppercorns
4 whole cloves
1 bay leaf

1 Place the onion in a heat-proof bowl.

2 In a small saucepan over medium-high heat, stir together the vinegar, salt and sugar until the sugar dissolves. Add the peppercorns, cloves and bay leaf and bring to the boil then remove from the heat. Pour the hot pickling liquid over the onion and leave to stand for 30 minutes before eating. Refrigerate in an airtight container for several weeks.

Notes: You can use this recipe to make whole pickled onions. Choose small onions and follow the above procedure, but they will need to be sealed in sterilised jars (see page 213) and kept unopened for at least a month for the pickling process to be complete.

You can experiment with the pickling spices, adding whole coriander seeds, cardamom, cinnamon sticks, bay leaves or rosemary.

Eggplant mustard pickle

This is sour, spicy and delicious – perfect with Sri Lankan or Indian food.

Makes 4 cups   Prep time: 20 minutes + 1 hour standing
Cooking time: about 20 minutes

¼ cup mustard seeds
2 tablespoons white vinegar
2 garlic cloves
3 cm knob ginger, peeled and sliced
1 tablespoon ground dried chilli
2 teaspoons salt, plus 1 tablespoon
  extra, for salting eggplant

3 large eggplants (about 1.2 kg)
1 tablespoon ground turmeric
1 tablespoon salt
Olive oil, for frying
2 tablespoons white vinegar, extra
1 tablespoon sugar

1 Place the mustard seeds, vinegar, garlic, ginger, chilli and 2 teaspoons salt into a food processor and blend or process until smooth.

2 Cut the eggplant into 1.5 cm cubes, then place in a bowl with the turmeric and 1 tablespoon salt, and toss through until the cubes are coated. Cover the eggplant with cold water then put a plate over it to keep it submerged. Leave to stand for an hour, then drain and pat dry with paper towels.

3 Pour 2–3 cm olive oil into a deep frypan or wok and cook the eggplant in batches until golden in colour. Make sure you don't overcrowd the pan while frying. Remove the eggplant with a slotted spoon and drain on paper towels.

4 Heat 1 tablespoon oil in a large frypan and fry the mustard mixture. Add the extra 2 tablespoons of vinegar then stir in the sugar. Add the eggplant and stir gently until it is thoroughly coated with the mustard mixture. Ladle into hot sterilised jars (see page 213).

Quince paste

I love a bit of quince paste on a cheese platter. If you've never tried cooking with these hard, pear-like fruits before, this is a nice simple recipe to try.

Makes 16 pieces   Prep time: 5 minutes   Cooking time: 6 hours + 45 minutes

4 quinces, unpeeled, cored and
  cut into 3 cm pieces

White sugar – equal weight to the
  cooked quince

1 Place the chopped quinces in a pot and just cover with water. Simmer for 45 minutes or until soft. Using a hand-held stick blender, puree the quince until

Vegetables & preserves

completely smooth. Measure the puree (it will be about 5 cups) and measure out an equal amount of white sugar.

2 Place the puree and the sugar in the bowl of a slow cooker and cook on the high setting for 6 hours. The quince will become a beautiful ruby colour and be quite stretchy and thick. Pour into a square baking dish lined with plastic wrap and set in the fridge overnight. Cut into squares and store in the fridge wrapped in plastic wrap.

Strawberry jam

Makes 1 cup   Prep time: 5 minutes   Cooking time: 20 minutes

2 x 250 g punnets strawberries,
  hulled and quartered lengthways

500 g caster sugar
2 tablespoons lemon juice

1 In a large pot over medium-high heat, stir the ingredients together to combine. Bring the mixture to the boil, stirring to ensure the sugar dissolves. Allow the mixture to boil for a further 15–20 minutes, ensuring it does not boil over. Test to see if the jam will set (see note).

2 Remove from the heat and allow to cool a little. While the jam is still warm, pour into warm sterilised jars (see page 213) and seal.

Note: To tell whether the jam has cooked enough to set, place a saucer in the freezer until the saucer chills. Place a small amount of jam, about the size of a 5 cent piece, on the cold saucer and allow it to cool for a moment. When you push your finger through the little puddle of jam, it will 'wrinkle', and the trail through the jam will stay intact.

Peach, ginger and thyme jam

Makes 2 cups   Prep time: 20 minutes   Cooking time: 45 minutes

1.5 kg just under-ripe yellow
  peaches (about 10 peaches),
  peeled, stone removed and
  coarsely chopped

3 cups white sugar
5 cm knob fresh ginger, peeled
  and cut into thin strips
1 teaspoon fresh thyme leaves

1 Place all the ingredients into a large non-stick pot over high heat and bring to the boil. Stir constantly until the sugar has dissolved, while skimming off any scum that rises to the surface. Reduce the heat to low and continue to boil until the jam thickens. Spoon into sterilised jars (see page 213), seal and cool.

Passionfruit and lime curd

Makes 1 cup   Prep time: 5 minutes
Cooking time: 25 minutes + cooling time

125 g butter
250 g caster sugar
Pulp of 6 passionfruit

Juice and zest of 2 limes
3 eggs, lightly beaten

1 Place the butter and sugar in a large saucepan and stir over medium heat until the butter has melted and the mixture is combined. Add the passionfruit pulp, lime zest and lime juice and stir to dissolve the sugar. Remove from the heat and cool for 10 minutes.

2 Place the pan back on the stovetop over a very low heat and quickly whisk in the eggs. Stir continuously with a whisk for about 15 minutes, until the mixture thickens. Be careful not to overheat the mixture or it will curdle.

3 Pour the warm mixture into sterilised jars (see page 213) and seal. Keep in the fridge for up to a week.

Orange marmalade

Makes 2 cups   Prep time: 15 minutes
Cooking time: 25 minutes + overnight standing

500 g oranges
1.2 litres water

1 kg caster sugar
Juice of 1 lemon

1 Zest the oranges using a fine grater. Cut away the pith and finely chop the orange flesh, removing and reserving the pips. Tie the pips into a piece of muslin (or empty out a teabag and tie them up in there).

2 In a large pot with a lid, soak the orange zest, flesh and bag of pips overnight in the water.

3 The next day, bring the mixture to a slow simmer until the orange zest is very soft. This will take about 1½ hours.

4 Remove the bag of pips and stir in the sugar and lemon juice. Bring to the boil, and boil rapidly, uncovered, until setting point is reached. This should take about 20 minutes. To test, spread a teaspoonful onto a cold saucer. It should set to the correct consistency. Spoon the warm mixture into sterilised jars (see page 213), seal and cool.

Quick vegetable pickle

Makes 3 cups   Prep time: 15 minutes   Cooking time: 5 minutes

3 red onions, very finely sliced
6 carrots, cut into matchsticks
2 bunches radishes,
  cut into matchsticks
¼ small green cabbage,
  very finely sliced

2 cups white vinegar
2 tablespoons salt
2 tablespoons white sugar
1 teaspoon black peppercorns

1 Toss the vegetables together in a heat-proof bowl.

2 In a small saucepan over medium-high heat, stir together the vinegar, salt and sugar until the sugar dissolves. Add the peppercorns, bring to the boil then remove from the heat.

3 Pack the vegetables into 3 sterilised jars (see page 213). Pack them tightly as the vegetables will shrink when the hot liquid goes over them. Pour the hot pickling liquid over the vegetables and put the lids on. The pickles are ready to eat once cooled. These can be stored unopened in the cupboard for a year, or for several weeks in the fridge after opening.

Note: You can vary the vegetables, just make sure they are of a similar thickness.

Sweet and sour spicy pickled cucumbers

These are beautiful on burgers and in salads.

Makes about 1 cup   Prep time: 5 minutes
Cooking time: 7 minutes

3 Lebanese cucumbers, seeded
  and very finely sliced on
  the diagonal
3 garlic cloves, finely sliced
3 bird's eye (small red) chillies,
  stalks removed but seeds
  intact, sliced

½ cup white vinegar
½ cup white sugar

1 Place the cucumber, garlic and chilli in a heat-proof bowl.

2 In a small saucepan over medium-high heat, stir together the vinegar and sugar until the sugar dissolves. Bring to the boil and boil for 5 minutes or until the syrup thickens a little. Allow the syrup to cool for 10 minutes before pouring over the cucumber mixture. Refrigerate in an airtight container before eating. These will keep for several weeks.

Corn and capsicum relish

Makes 1 litre   Prep time: 15 minutes
Cooking time: 1 hour + 2 hours standing time

2 tablespoons olive oil
2 tablespoons brown mustard seeds
2 tablespoons ground turmeric
2 brown onions, diced
6 corn cobs, kernels cut off
2 red capsicums, seeded and
  very finely diced

2 cups white vinegar
2 cups white sugar
1 tablespoon salt
1 tablespoon cornflour

1 In a large, non-stick pot over medium-high heat, place the olive oil and mustard seeds. When the mustard seeds start to pop and crackle, add the turmeric and onion and stir for 3–4 minutes or until the onion is soft.

2 Place the corn kernels, capsicum, vinegar, sugar and salt into the pot and stir to combine. Bring to the boil and boil for 45 minutes. Combine the cornflour with 2 tablespoons of water and stir until there are no lumps. Pour into the bubbling corn mixture and stir quickly. Allow to boil for a further 5 minutes, stirring continuously. Pour into hot sterilised jars (see page 213).

Old-fashioned mustard pickle

Makes 3 litres   Prep time: 20 minutes
Cooking time: 1 hour + overnight standing time

4 telegraph cucumbers,
  peeled, halved and seeded
1 head cauliflower, chopped into
  2 cm pieces
6 large brown onions, diced
2 green capsicums, finely diced
½ cup cooking salt
3 cups white vinegar

3 cups white sugar
100 g mustard powder
2 tablespoons ground turmeric
1 tablespoon ground celery seed
1 tablespoon curry powder
1 tablespoon ground ginger
⅓ cup cornflour

1 Cut the cucumbers into 2 cm pieces. Place in a large bowl with the cauliflower, onion and capsicum. Add the salt and cover with water. Stand for 8 hours or overnight. Drain, rinse and drain again.

2 Place the vegetables into a pot with the vinegar, sugar and all the spices and stir to combine. Bring to the boil then reduce the heat and simmer for an hour.

3 In a small bowl, mix the cornflour with enough water to make a thin slurry. Pour into the pot, stirring. Simmer the mixture for a further 15 minutes or until the flour has cooked out and the mixture has thickened. Pour into hot sterilised jars (see page 213).

Note: These pickles will taste even better after a month or so. They will last for up to 2 years unopened. Refrigerate after opening.

Curried mango chutney

As well as being a great accompaniment to curries and rice, this chutney is delicious on sandwiches, burgers and cold meats.

Makes 4 cups   Prep time: 15 minutes   Cooking time: 25 minutes

2 bird's eye (small red) chillies,
  stalks removed
¼ cup peeled and sliced fresh ginger
3 cloves garlic
1 brown onion, quartered
1 red capsicum, seeded and
  cut into chunks
3 tablespoons olive oil

1 kg ripe mango flesh,
  roughly chopped
150 ml pineapple juice
200 ml white wine vinegar
¾ cup brown sugar
2 tablespoons curry powder
⅔ cup raisins

1 Place the chilli, ginger, garlic, onion and capsicum in the bowl of a mini food processor and process until finely chopped.

2 Place this mixture in a chef pan with the olive oil over medium-high heat. Stir for about 3 minutes or until soft and fragrant. Add the mango, pineapple juice, vinegar, sugar, curry powder and raisins. Stir well and bring the mixture to the boil. Reduce the heat to a simmer and simmer for about 20 minutes or until the chutney is reduced and the required consistency is reached. Spoon into sterilised jars (see page 213).

Baking

Introduction

My sons have wonderful bakers on both sides of their family. On my side, my mum, who was the strawberry shortcake, scone and lamington queen; my nan, who made rock cakes that I used to love slathered with butter, and Great-Aunty Joyce, who was responsible every year for the gigantic, brandy-soaked penny-filled Christmas pudding. On Mick's side, his mum and aunts are wonderful bakers and it's no surprise as his grandma was by far the best and most prolific baker I have ever met in my life. Every special occasion included one of Grandma's mammoth sponge cakes, but it didn't have to be a special occasion for us to enjoy her beautiful baking. Her cupboards were always full of containers of biscuits, cakes and treats.

Baking something fresh and delicious is always well received in this house. Not only does it give my boys something nice to eat, it creates a memory for them and connects them, and me, to the generations of cooks before us who showed their love through the act of baking.

Bread

Focaccia

Serves up to 12   Prep time: 20 minutes + rising time
Cooking time: 20 minutes

5 ⅓ cups plain flour
2 x 7 g sachets dried yeast
1 teaspoon salt
1 teaspoon sugar
¼ cup olive oil, plus extra
   for brushing

2 cups warm water
1 tablespoon poppy seeds
1 tablespoon sea salt flakes

1 In a bowl, combine the flour, yeast, salt and sugar. In a separate bowl, combine ¼ cup oil and the warm water then mix into the flour mixture. (The water needs to be a little cooler than water from the hot tap. Too hot and it will kill the yeast, not hot enough and it won't activate.)

2 Turn the dough out onto a floured work surface and knead for 10 minutes. (Alternatively, knead in an electric mixer using the dough hook for 5 minutes.) When it's ready, the dough will feel smooth and elastic.

3 Oil the inside of a large bowl. Place the dough in the bowl and cover with

plastic wrap. Put the bowl in a warm place. This is really important – find a spot in the sun, or sit it under the heat lamps in your bathroom. Leave for 30 minutes to 1 hour, or until the dough doubles in size.

4 Turn the dough back out onto a board and knock it down to its original size. Knead for 2–3 minutes.

5 Preheat the oven to 200°C. Roll the dough out to a rectangle about 20 x 30 cm and place on a large flat baking tray. Leave in your nice warm place for another 30 minutes and the dough will double in size again.

6 Pierce the surface of the dough every 5 cm. Brush with extra olive oil and sprinkle with the poppy seeds and sea salt.

7 Bake for 25–30 minutes in the middle shelf of the oven, or until the bread is golden and sounds hollow when tapped. Allow to cool.

Flatbread

Makes 12 pieces   Prep time: 10 minutes   Cooking time: 20 minutes

4 cups self-raising flour
1 teaspoon salt
100 g butter

375 ml milk
Olive oil, for frying

1 Combine the flour and salt in a bowl. Heat the butter and milk in a jug until the butter is just melted. Make a well in the centre of the flour and pour in the milk and butter, gradually bringing the flour in from the sides. When the flour is all incorporated, you should have a soft dough. Knead the dough for at least 5 minutes on a floured surface, until it is stretchy. If the dough is too sticky, add a little more flour. This process can also be done in the bowl of an electric mixer or food processor using the dough hook.

2 Wrap the dough in plastic wrap and allow to rest at room temperature for about 30 minutes. Divide the dough into 12 pieces (or more, if you want smaller flatbreads) and roll out on a floured surface as thinly as you can. I am never able to achieve perfect circles so I have decided that I like irregularly shaped flatbread better – it's rustic!

3 Heat a generous splash of olive oil in a frypan over medium-high heat. When the oil is hot, place 1 piece of flatbread in the base. It will immediately start to bubble up. When the edges are starting to look golden and the bread is becoming less floury looking around the edges (about 40 seconds to 1 minute), flip the bread carefully with a spatula. Cook for a further 40 seconds to 1 minute then remove to a piece of paper towel. Repeat to cook remaining

pieces. Once cooked, the flatbread can be stored in plastic wrap for a day or so, but it's really better cooked and eaten fresh.

Tear and share pizza scrolls

Makes 12 scrolls   Prep time: 20 minutes + rising time
Cooking time: 30 minutes

3 cups plain flour
2 teaspoons (7 g/1 sachet)
  dried yeast
1½ teaspoons salt
1¼ cups lukewarm water
1 tablespoon olive oil
⅓ cup tomato paste

½ cup grated tasty cheese
½ cup grated mozzarella cheese
Handful of baby spinach leaves
4 shallots (spring onions), finely
  sliced
100 g shaved hot salami
1 egg, beaten

1 Make the dough a few hours in advance. In a large bowl, combine the flour, yeast and salt and mix thoroughly. In a separate bowl, combine the water with the oil and pour into the dry ingredients. Mix thoroughly again. Knead in the bowl for a few minutes, until all the ingredients are combined. Cover and put in a warm place for at least an hour, or until the dough doubles in size. (If the weather is cold, we sit ours under the heat lamps in the bathroom.)

2 Preheat the oven to 200°C and line a baking sheet with baking paper.

3 Sprinkle some flour on the bench top and roll the pizza dough out into a rectangle about 25 x 35 cm. Lay the dough so that the long edge is aligned with the edge of the bench. Using a spoon, spread the tomato paste over the dough, right to the edges. Scatter the 2 cheeses evenly over the top. Spread the spinach and shallots over the cheese then top with the salami.

4 Starting at the edge closest to you, roll the dough into a Swiss-style roll. Carefully lift onto a cutting board and slice into 12 even pieces.

5 Place the slices on their side on the baking tray, just touching. Brush with egg and bake for 30 minutes or until golden brown.

Note: This recipe is easily varied – put your own favourite topping in the scroll as you would if making a pizza.

Tear and share pizza
scrolls, recipe page 228

Boston bun

Makes 12 pieces   Prep time: 10 minutes
Cooking time: 30 minutes + rising time

7 g sachet dried yeast
4 cups plain flour, plus extra
    for dusting
¼ cup caster sugar
½ cup warm milk, plus extra
    1 tablespoon milk, for glazing

100 g cold butter, diced
1 cup warm water
⅓ cup sultanas

For the icing
190 g butter, at room temperature
1 teaspoon vanilla bean paste
1 tablespoon coconut essence

3 cups icing mixture, sifted
½ cup moist coconut flakes

1 Combine the yeast, 1 teaspoon flour, 1 teaspoon sugar and ½ cup warm milk in small bowl. Cover and stand in a warm place for about 10 minutes or until the mixture is frothy.

2 Place the remaining flour and sugar into the bowl of a food processor and add the diced cold butter. Blitz until the mixture is crumbly and resembles breadcrumbs. Add the yeast mixture and water and pulse until the dough just comes together. Add the sultanas and pulse until just mixed.

3 Turn out the dough onto a floured surface, and knead for 5 minutes or until it is smooth and elastic. Return the dough to a large greased bowl, cover with plastic wrap and stand in a warm place until doubled in size – about an hour. Turn out again on a lightly floured surface, punch the dough to expel air then knead until smooth. Shape into a large oval.

4 Preheat the oven to 220°C. Line a large baking tray with baking paper and place the dough onto the tray. Stand uncovered in a warm place for about 10–15 minutes or until the dough is well risen. Brush the dough with the extra milk.

5 Bake for 10 minutes, then reduce the heat to 180°C and bake for a further 20 minutes or until golden brown and cooked. Remove the bun from the oven and place on a wire rack to cool completely.

6 For the icing, cream the butter in the bowl of an electric mixer until lighter in colour. Add the vanilla and coconut essence and mix for a moment to combine. Sift the icing mixture into the bowl and start to combine on low speed. When the mixture is all wet, increase the speed and beat until light and fluffy. Spread thickly on the completely cooled bun and scatter with coconut flakes.

Gluten-free white bread

Makes a 20 cm loaf   Prep time: 15 minutes
Cooking time: 45 minutes + rising time

1 cup milk
¼ cup caster sugar
1¼ teaspoons dry yeast
1¼ cups rice flour
1¼ cups potato starch

3 teaspoons xanthan gum
1 teaspoon salt
60 g butter, cubed, at
  room temperature
2 eggs

1 In the microwave or in a small pot on the stove, gently heat the milk until it is about blood temperature. (Just warm to touch.) Remove from the heat and add the sugar and yeast. Stir and set aside.

2 In the bowl of an electric mixer with a paddle attachment, combine the rice flour, potato starch, xanthan gum and salt. Gradually add the milk and yeast mixture, scraping down the sides of the bowl occasionally. Add the butter and the eggs. Increase the speed to high and beat for 3 minutes or until smooth. Cover the bowl with plastic wrap that has been sprayed with cooking oil and allow the dough to rise in a warm place for an hour.

3 Preheat the oven to 180°C. Grease a 10 x 20 cm loaf tin. Stir the dough and place into the tin, levelling the top. Loosely cover with greased plastic wrap and set in a warm place for a further 30 minutes or until the dough rises to just above the top of the tin.

4 Bake the loaf for 50 minutes, until it sounds hollow when tapped. Remove from the loaf tin and cool completely on a wire rack before cutting.

Hot cross buns

Makes 12   Prep time: 20 minutes + rising time
Cooking time: 30 minutes

1¼ cups milk
¼ cup caster sugar
2 x 7 g sachets dried yeast
4 cups plain flour
2 teaspoons ground cinnamon
2 teaspoons mixed spice
1 teaspoon salt

60 g butter, at room temperature
1½ cups sultanas
½ cup mixed peel (optional)
2 eggs, lightly beaten
¼ cup self-raising flour
2 tablespoons apricot jam

1 In a microwave-safe jug, heat the milk for just over a minute or until warm. Add the caster sugar and stir until dissolved. Mix in the dried yeast. It is

important at this stage that the milk is warm enough to activate the yeast but not too hot. Leave this mixture for 5–10 minutes or until it froths up a little.

2 In a large bowl, sift together the plain flour, cinnamon, mixed spice and salt. Rub through the butter with your fingertips until it is evenly distributed. Add sultanas and mixed peel. Stir in the eggs and the yeast mixture with a wooden spoon until it comes together in a dough.

3 Turn out onto a floured work surface and knead by hand for 5–7 minutes until smooth and elastic. Alternatively, place in the bowl of an electric mixer with the dough hook attachment and knead for 5 minutes. Place the dough in a large, greased bowl loosely covered with plastic wrap. Place in a warm place for 45 minutes until the dough rises to almost twice its size.

4 Turn out the dough onto a work surface and knead the dough again for a couple of minutes, then divide into 12 balls. Place the balls on a greased baking tray, pressed up against each other. For tall hot cross buns, I put mine into a greased 26 cm springform cake tin. Cover and leave in a warm place for a further 15 minutes.

5 Preheat the oven to 180°C.

6 Combine the self-raising flour with 2 tablespoons of water and mix well. Place in a small piping bag with a narrow nozzle. Pipe a cross onto each of the buns.

7 Bake for 25 minutes or until the buns are risen and sound hollow when tapped. Heat the jam with a little water in the microwave and brush over the hot buns to glaze.

Pastry

Savoury shortcrust pastry

The secret to good pastry is to work with everything nice and cold, and to not overwork the dough.

Makes enough for the base and lid for a 23 cm pie dish or 6 individual pie bases
Prep time: 15 minutes + cooling time

1½ cups plain flour
125 g well-chilled butter,
  cut into cubes

¼ teaspoon salt
1 egg

1 Place the ingredients into a food processor and process until the mixture looks like fine breadcrumbs and there are no lumps of butter. With the processor running, add the egg and process until the dough comes together in a ball.

2 Turn the dough out of the food processor onto a cold surface. With cool hands, knead the dough a few times just to bring it together. Wrap the dough in plastic wrap, shape into a disc about 3 cm thick, and rest it in the fridge for 15 minutes.

3 To roll out the dough, place it between 2 sheets of baking paper. Roll very gently with a rolling pin. It needs to be done quite slowly and carefully so that it is being flattened, rather than stretched. Rest it again before using. At this stage, if the dough is too soft from a warm kitchen, it can be chilled on a tray in the fridge. If it goes too hard, it will need to be brought back to room temperature for a few minutes before use.

Sweet shortcrust pastry

Makes enough for the base and lid for a 23 cm pie dish or
6 individual pie bases
Prep and cooking time: 20 minutes + 30 minutes resting time

2½ cups plain flour
¼ cup icing sugar
¼ teaspoon salt

125 g butter cubed, cold
2 eggs

1 Preheat the oven to 180°C. Lightly grease your flan tin or pie dish.

2 Place the flour, icing sugar and salt in the bowl of a food processor with the butter. Process until a fine crumb consistency. Add the eggs and process until the dough comes together in a soft ball. Flatten into a thick disc (or a rectangular shape if using a rectangular pan) and wrap with plastic wrap. Rest in the fridge for 10–15 minutes.

3 Place the pastry between 2 sheets of baking paper and roll out to the desired shape and to about 3 mm thick. Leave the pastry to rest again for about 15 minutes. The reason for this is, it will shrink a little bit – you don't want it to shrink after you have lined your dish.

4 Using your rolling pin, loosely roll the pastry up and lift it over your tin. Drape it carefully over the tin, making sure it settles into the base well. You now have a choice whether to cut the excess pastry off, or leave it draped over the edge and cut it off after baking. The advantage of the second method is that the end result will not have shrunk at all. Prick the pastry with a fork all

over the base. This allows hot air to escape and avoids big bubbles in the floor of your pie.

5 Cut a circle of baking paper the same size as the base of the dish and place it on the pastry. Weigh the paper down with rice, dried peas or beans, or baking weights. (Rice or legumes can be put into a container and used over and over again as your blind baking weights.)

6 Bake for 15 minutes. Remove the weights and the paper and bake for a further 10 minutes or until light golden brown. Cool in the tin before turning it out.

Note: If you want to make chocolate shortcrust pastry, exchange ¼ cup of flour for cocoa powder.

Rough puff pastry

Makes enough pastry to fit a 25–30 cm tart tin
Prep time: 20 minutes + resting time

1 ⅓ cups plain flour,
  plus extra for kneading
½ teaspoon sea salt

180 g unsalted butter
80 ml ice cold water

1 Place the flour and salt in a large bowl and grate the cold butter into the bowl. Mix well with your hands to distribute the butter evenly.

2 Add the water and gently mix. Tip onto a lightly floured work surface and bring together just enough so that the dough is lumpy and butter is still visible. It is important not to overwork the dough with too much kneading.

3 Shape the dough carefully into a square shape and dust the top and bottom of the pastry lightly with a small amount of flour. Roll out to form a rectangle about 30 cm long and 15 cm wide. Dust off excess flour with a pastry brush – this is to prevent trapping too much flour every time the dough is folded.

4 Fold the dough in thirds so the top and bottom overlap to form an envelope-like rectangle. Turn the dough by a quarter of a turn and roll out again to a 25 cm long and 15 cm wide rectangle. Fold into thirds again, then dust lightly with flour and brush off excess with the pastry brush. Repeat the rolling and folding 4 more times so that you have done this step 6 times. Your rectangles will get neater and neater every time you fold and roll out.

5 After the sixth and final fold, tap the edges with the rolling pin to make an even square shape. Place onto a plate and cover in plastic wrap then chill

in the fridge for 2 hours. Allow the pastry to sit at room temperature for 30 minutes before using.

Note: This dough is best to make on a cool day or in a cold kitchen. If the kitchen is too warm, the butter will begin to melt and the dough will become greasy and not form separate pastry layers when cooked. To prevent this from happening, after each fold, cover the dough and refrigerate for 10 minutes or until the butter is firm before rolling out.

Beef pasties

Makes 18 small pasties (serves 6)   Prep time: 20 minutes
Cooking time: 40 minutes

2 tablespoons olive oil
2 brown onions, diced
2 cloves garlic, chopped
400 g beef mince
2 medium potatoes,
   diced into 1 cm pieces
1 carrot, peeled and
   diced into 1 cm pieces
¼ cup tomato paste
2 tablespoons Dijon mustard

¼ cup Worcestershire sauce
1 teaspoon sugar
1 cup beef stock
2 quantities rough puff pastry
   (see page 234)
1 egg, beaten

1 Preheat oven to 200°C. Line 2 large baking sheets with baking paper.

2 Heat the oil in a chef pan or large, heavy-based frypan over a high heat. Sauté the onions and garlic for about a minute, until softened, then add the beef and cook for 5 minutes until cooked through.

3 Add the potato and carrot and stir through. Add the tomato paste and stir to coat all the ingredients in the pan. Sauté for 1 minute.

4 Add the mustard, Worcestershire sauce and sugar, and stir to combine. Stir in the stock and simmer for about 10 minutes until the potato has started to soften and the meat mixture is moist but not too wet. Set aside to cool.

5 Roll out the pastry 3 mm thick and cut with a 12 cm round cutter. Place large spoonfuls of the meat mixture in the centre of each circle. Brush the pastry edges with the beaten egg. Fold over and pinch the edges together all the way around.

6 Place the pasties on the 2 baking trays. Brush the pasties with egg and pierce a few small holes in the top. Bake for 25 minutes or until golden brown.

Caramel tarts

Makes 12   Prep time: 20 minutes + cooling and refrigeration time
Cooking time: 40 minutes

1 quantity sweet shortcrust pastry
   (see page 233)
3 x 395 g tins sweet condensed milk

⅓ cup golden syrup
75 g butter
100 g dark chocolate melts

1 Preheat the oven to 180°C (160°C fan-forced). Grease a 12-hole cupcake tin with cooking spray.

2 Using a 12 cm circular cutter, make 4 circles from each sheet of pastry. Press the pastry evenly into the base of the prepared tins, add a few pastry weights and bake for 12–15 minutes or until golden. Remove and set aside.

3 To make the filling, place the condensed milk, golden syrup and butter into a saucepan over medium heat and cook, stirring, for 20 minutes until the mixture is light golden brown.

4 Pour the filling into the pastry cases and return to the oven. Bake for 15 minutes. Remove and allow to cool.

5 When the tarts have cooled, place the chocolate in a heat-proof bowl set over a small saucepan of simmering water and stir until melted. Place into a piping bag with a very fine nozzle and drizzle the chocolate in a zigzag motion over the tarts. Refrigerate for at least 3 hours before serving.

Dark chocolate and raspberry tart

Serves 10   Prep time: 30 minutes
Cooking time: 50 minutes + resting and cooling time

3 punnets raspberries
½ cup caster sugar
1 quantity chocolate sweet
   shortcrust pastry (see page 233)
270 g dark chocolate melts

60 g butter, diced
1¼ cups thickened cream
4 eggs, lightly beaten
⅓ cup raspberry jam

1 Preheat the oven to 180°C.

2 Place 2 punnets raspberries with the sugar in a small pot over medium heat.

Bring to the boil and boil for 5 minutes or until the raspberries have broken down and they become a rich sauce. Remove from the heat and chill in the fridge.

3 Grease a rectangular flan tin and line with the pastry. Rest in fridge for 15 minutes. Line with baking paper and fill with pastry weights. Bake for 10 minutes, then remove the weights and paper and bake for a further 10 minutes. Remove from the oven and chill.

4 Reduce the oven to 160°C.

5 Place the chocolate and butter in a heat-proof bowl. Place the cream in a pot and bring to the boil. Pour the cream over the chocolate and stir until smooth. Allow to cool slightly and stir in the eggs.

6 Spread the raspberry jam in the chilled base of the tart and place the remaining whole raspberries on top. Pour the chocolate mixture carefully into the pastry shell and bake for 25 minutes.

7 Remove from the oven and refrigerate until completely chilled. Serve with the raspberry coulis.

Lemon lime meringue tarts

Makes 12   Prep time: 20 minutes
Cooking time: 35 minutes + chilling time

2 quantities sweet shortcrust
  pastry (see page 233)
½ cup lemon juice (about 2 lemons)
¼ cup lime juice (about 2 limes)

1 cup caster sugar
⅔ cup thickened cream
5 eggs, lightly beaten

For the meringue topping
6 eggwhites

1⅔ cup caster sugar

1 Preheat the oven to 180°C (160°C fan-forced). Grease twelve 10 cm fluted, loose-based tart tins.

2 Roll out the pastry 3 mm thick and drape it in pieces over the tart tins, pressing carefully. Trim the excess pastry. If you need to fill any gaps in the pastry, use the trimmings. Put the tart tins on a tray in the fridge to rest for a few minutes.

3 Line the tart cases with baking paper and fill with baking weights or rice. Bake for 10 minutes. Remove the baking paper and weights, and bake for a further 10 minutes or until lightly golden brown.

Peach pie recipe,
page 239

4 Combine the lemon juice, lime juice, sugar and cream in a bowl. Whisk in the beaten eggs, a little at a time, until well mixed. Pour the mixture into the pastry cases and bake on the tray for 20 minutes or until the filling is set. Remove from the oven and set aside.

5 In the bowl of an electric mixer, whip the eggwhites until they are white and doubled in volume. Rain the sugar into the eggwhites as they whip. When stiff peaks form, place the mixture into a large piping bag with a star-shaped nozzle.

6 Pipe the meringue generously onto the tarts and return to the oven for 10–15 minutes or until the meringue has firmed up a little. Allow to cool then refrigerate the tarts until needed.

Peach pie

Serves 8–10   Prep time: 20 minutes   Cooking time: 40 minutes

2 kg peaches, peeled,
  stones removed, cut into sixths
⅔ cup caster sugar
2 quantities sweet shortcrust
  pastry (see page 233)

¼ cup cornflour
1 egg, lightly beaten
Extra caster sugar, for sprinkling

1 Combine the peaches and sugar in a bowl and set aside, covered, for an hour or until the peaches are softened and have released some fluid.

2 Preheat the oven to 180°C.

3 Grease a 22 cm pie dish. Roll the pastry out to 3 mm thick. Line with 1 sheet of pastry, trimming the edges and using them to fill any gaps. Cut the other sheet of pastry into 1 cm wide strips.

4 Strain the peach and sugar juice into a small saucepan and whisk in the cornflour. Bring to the boil and boil until the cornflour cooks and the liquid is thickened. Allow to cool then add the peaches back to the cornflour mixture and stir through.

5 Spoon the peach mixture into the pie base and lay the strips of pastry over the top in a lattice pattern. Seal the edges with a fork. Brush with the egg and sprinkle with sugar. Bake for 40 minutes or until the pastry is golden and the filling bubbling.

Mille-feuille

2 quantities rough puff pastry
  (see page 234)
600 ml milk
3 strips lemon peel, made
  using a vegetable peeler
1 vanilla pod, seeds scraped,
  or 1 teaspoon vanilla extract

6 large egg yolks
120 g sugar
⅓ cup cornflour
50 g butter, cubed
1½ cups icing sugar mixture
Pulp of 2 passionfruit

1 Preheat the oven to 220°C (200°C fan-forced).

2 Roll pastry into 3 rectangles slightly larger than a 20 x 30 cm lamington tin. Place each rectangle on a lined baking sheet and prick thoroughly with a fork. Place another sheet of baking paper on top and put a tray on top to keep pastry flat. Bake for 20 minutes or until golden brown. Remove from the oven.

3 In a saucepan, place the milk, lemon peel and vanilla. Bring to the boil and remove from the heat.

4 In a bowl, beat the egg yolks and sugar with electric beaters until pale and thick. This will take a few minutes. Add the cornflour and beat again.

5 Strain half of the scalding milk into the eggs, beating all the while. Then return all the egg mixture back to the saucepan and bring to the boil, beating. The custard will thicken considerably. Reduce the heat a little and cook for a further 2–3 minutes, beating all the while, and making sure the custard does not catch and burn.

6 Remove from the heat and continue to beat to release as much of the heat as possible. Allow to cool down to 'blood temperature' – a little hotter than room temperature. Beat in the cubed butter.

7 Trim 1 pastry sheet to fit the bottom of the lamington tin. Pour over half the custard and spread evenly. Trim the other pastry sheet to fit neatly on top. (This will be slightly bigger than the one on the bottom.) Repeat with the remaining custard and top with the last sheet of pastry. Place in the fridge for at least an hour.

8 Combine the icing sugar mixture and passionfruit pulp in a bowl. When the slice has chilled, pour the icing over the top and return to the fridge.

9 To serve, cut the slice into 12 pieces using a very sharp knife and taking care to cut all the way through the bottom.

Cakes and muffins

Buttercream icing

Makes enough for 24 cupcakes or 1 large cake   Prep time: 5 minutes

190 g butter, at room temperature
1½ teaspoons vanilla extract
3 cups icing sugar mixture, sifted

3–4 drops food colouring
 (optional)

1 Cream the butter in the bowl of an electric mixer until lighter in colour. Add the vanilla or other essence, and mix for a moment to combine. Sift the icing sugar mixture into the bowl and start to combine on a low speed. When the mixture is all wet, increase the speed and beat until light and fluffy. If you like, put a few drops of food colouring into the bowl and mix for a delicate colour.

2 Place the icing in a piping bag with a 1 cm star-shaped nozzle and pipe onto cooled cupcakes or spread on a large cake. Decorate as you wish.

Variations: You can vary the flavours in this buttercream. Instead of vanilla extract try 2 tablespoons of rose water, orange blossom, coconut water or whatever flavour you like.

Cream cheese icing

Enough for 1 cake   Prep time: 5 minutes

250 g cream cheese
½ cup icing sugar mixture

1 teaspoon vanilla extract

1 Combine the cream cheese, icing sugar mixture and vanilla in a bowl. Beat with electric beaters until light and fluffy.

Victoria sponge cake

Serves 10   Prep time: 30 minutes   Cooking time: 25 minutes

6 medium eggs
½ teaspoon salt
1 cup caster sugar
¾ cup self-raising flour, sifted
½ cup cornflour, sifted

500 ml thickened cream
½ cup strawberry jam
Strawberries (optional) or
    icing sugar, for decoration

1 Preheat the oven to 180°C. Grease two 20 cm cake tins and line with baking paper.

2 In the bowl of an electric mixer fitted with the balloon whisk, beat the eggs with the salt for 5 minutes until pale and fluffy. Gradually sprinkle in the sugar while still beating. Continue beating for a further 5 minutes.

3 With a metal spoon, gently fold in the sifted flours. Pour into prepared tins.

4 Reduce the oven to 160°C and bake for 20 minutes or until the cakes are well risen, pale golden and spongy in the centre. Immediately turn out of tins onto a cooling rack.

5 When the cakes are completely cool, whip the cream. Spread the jam on top of one cake then top with cream. Stack the second cake on top. Spread the remaining cream on top and decorate with strawberries if you wish. Alternatively, just sprinkle a little icing sugar over the top.

Melt-and-mix cupcakes

Makes 24   Prep time: 15 minutes   Cooking time: 45 minutes

4 eggs
2 cups caster sugar
2 cups plain flour
2 teaspoons baking powder

¼ teaspoon salt
1 teaspoon vanilla extract
1 cup milk
125 g butter

1 Preheat the oven to 160°C (140°C fan-forced). Line two 12-hole cupcake tins with paper patty cases.

2 In an electric mixer with the paddle attachment, beat the eggs and vanilla extract for 4–5 minutes or until pale and creamy. With the mixer still running, gradually add the caster sugar and continue to beat for 3–4 minutes. The mixture is ready when it 'forms a ribbon'. This means when the paddle or a

Victoria sponge cake,
recipe page 242

spoon is lifted out of the mixture, a trail is left across the surface for a moment before it sinks.

3 In a bowl, sift together the flour, baking powder and salt. Fold through the egg mixture.

4 In the microwave or in a small saucepan on the stovetop, heat the milk and butter until just melted. Gently fold this through the batter.

5 Divide the batter between the patty cases. Bake for 20 minutes or until slightly risen and light golden brown. A skewer inserted into the centre will come out clean. Cool in tins for 10 minutes before turning out onto a wire rack to cool completely then ice with buttercream icing (see page 241).

Banana cake

Serves 6–8   Prep time: 10 minutes   Cooking time: 1 hour

3 very ripe bananas
125 g butter, melted
2 eggs, beaten
2 teaspoons vanilla extract
¾ cup brown sugar
1½ cups self-raising flour

¼ teaspoon cinnamon
2 quantities cream cheese icing
  (recipe page 241)
1 quantity candied walnuts
  (recipe page 167)

1 Preheat the oven to 180°C (160°C fan-forced). Grease and line two 23 cm cake tins.

2 In a large bowl, mash the bananas thoroughly. Add the butter, eggs, 1 teaspoon vanilla and sugar and mix well. Fold through the flour and cinnamon.

3 Pour the batter into the cake tins and bake for about 45 minutes or until risen, dark golden and coming away from the edges of the tin. A skewer inserted into the centre will come out clean, but this is a very moist dense cake. Cool in the tin for 10 minutes before turning out onto a wire rack.

4 When completely cooled, cut each cake in half horizontally to create 4 layers.

5 Spread bottom layer with ¼ of icing and stack next layer of cake and repeat with the rest of the icing until you have icing on top. Sprinkle with candied walnuts.

Little carrot cakes

Serves 12   Prep time: 20 minutes   Cooking time: 1 hour 10 minutes

1 cup self-raising flour
½ cup plain flour
1 teaspoon bicarbonate of soda
½ teaspoon cinnamon
3 carrots (about 300 g), grated
150 g walnuts, roughly chopped
½ cup brown sugar
¾ cup olive or vegetable oil

½ cup golden syrup
3 eggs, lightly beaten
1 teaspoon vanilla extract
2 quantities cream cheese
  icing (see page 241)
1 quantity candied walnuts
  (see page 167)

1 Preheat the oven to 160°C. Place 12 straight-sided paper patty cases on a baking tray.

2 In a large bowl, combine the flours, bicarbonate of soda and cinnamon and mix well. Stir through the carrot and walnuts.

3 In a separate bowl, combine the brown sugar, oil, golden syrup, eggs and vanilla. Pour the wet ingredients into the dry and stir until just combined.

4 Use an ice cream scoop to divide the mixture between the 12 cases. Bake for 40 minutes, or until dark golden and set. Remove from the oven and place on a wire rack to cool completely before icing.

5 Place the cream cheese icing in a large piping bag fitted with a 1 cm star-shaped nozzle and pipe onto the cakes. Top each cake with some candied walnuts.

Lime coconut cupcakes

Makes 12   Prep time: 15 minutes   Cooking time: 10–15 minutes

100 g unsalted butter, softened
¾ cup caster sugar
½ teaspoon vanilla extract
2 eggs

Zest of 4 limes
1⅓ cups self-raising flour
½ cup milk

For the icing
125 g unsalted butter, softened
2 cups icing sugar mixture
2 tablespoons lime juice
1 teaspoon coconut essence

1 drop green food colouring
  (optional)
1 cup moist coconut flakes

1 Preheat the oven to 180°C. Line a 12-hole ⅓-cup capacity cupcake tin with paper patty cases.

2 In a bowl, cream the butter and sugar using electric beaters. Add the vanilla, then the eggs one at a time, beating well after each addition, then add the lime zest.

3 Stir in half the flour, then half the milk. Repeat with remaining flour and milk. Transfer the batter into the patty cases.

4 Bake for 10–15 minutes, until the cakes are golden. Remove from the oven and place on a wire rack to cool completely before icing.

5 For the icing, mix the softened butter into the icing sugar mixture and gradually add the lime juice and the coconut essence until the icing is at piping consistency. If you like, you can add a drop of green food colouring. Place in a piping bag with a 1.5 cm star-shaped nozzle. Pipe onto the cooled cakes and sprinkle with coconut flakes.

Variations: Substitute lemons or oranges for the limes. Instead of lime juice in the icing, use milk and 2 tablespoons of cocoa for chocolate buttercream icing. Cut the tops off the cupcakes and cut the tops in half. Pipe passionfruit lime curd (see page 220) on the cupcakes then place the halved tops back on so they look like wings.

Zucchini cake

Serves 8–12   Prep time: 20 minutes   Cooking time: 1 hour 10 minutes

1 cup self-raising flour
½ cup plain flour
1 teaspoon bicarbonate of soda
½ teaspoon cinnamon
3 large zucchini (about 300 g), grated
150 g pistachio kernels,
   roughly chopped

½ cup brown sugar
¾ cup olive oil
½ cup golden syrup
3 eggs, lightly beaten
1 teaspoon vanilla extract
1 quantity cream cheese
   icing (see page 241)

1 Preheat the oven to 160°C. Grease a 24 cm springform cake tin and line the base with baking paper.

2 In a large bowl, combine the flours, bicarbonate of soda and cinnamon and mix well. Stir through the zucchini and pistachios.

3 In a separate bowl, combine the brown sugar, oil, golden syrup, eggs and vanilla. Pour the wet ingredients into the dry and stir until just combined.

4 Pour the batter into the tin and bake for 1 hour 10 minutes or until dark golden and set. Remove from the oven and cool in the tin for 10 minutes before turning out onto a wire rack to cool completely. Ice with cream cheese icing.

Fruit cake

Serves 12   Prep time: 20 minutes   Cooking time: 2 hours 40 minutes

330 g butter
330 g sugar
5 eggs
500 g sultanas
60 g mixed peel
Grated zest and
  juice of 2 lemons

Pinch of salt
200 g glace cherries,
  roughly chopped
330 g plain flour
165 g self-raising flour

1 Preheat the oven to 200°C. Grease a 20 cm square cake tin and line the base and sides with baking paper.

2 Cream the butter and sugar until thick and pale. Add the eggs one at a time, beating after each addition. Stir in the sultanas, mixed peel, lemon zest and juice, salt and cherries. Gently fold the flours through.

3 Spoon the mixture into the cake tin. Use damp hands to smooth out the top of the cake. Bake for 10 minutes, then reduce the heat to 150°C and bake for a further 30 minutes. Reduce the heat again to 120°C and bake for a further 2 hours or until a skewer inserted comes out clean. Cool in the tin for 10 minutes and then turn out onto a wire rack.

4 When completely cooled, wrap the cake in foil, then plastic wrap, then store in a cake tin.

Orange poppy seed cake

Serves 8–12   Prep time: 15 minutes   Cooking time: 45 minutes

4 eggs
2 cups caster sugar
2 cups self-raising flour
¼ teaspoon salt

4 oranges, zested and juiced
⅓ cup poppy seeds
200 g butter

For the icing
375 g cream cheese
¾ cup icing sugar mixture

¼ cup orange juice

1 Preheat the oven to 160°C. Grease two 20 cm cake tins and line the base with baking paper.

2 Using an electric mixer with the paddle attachment, beat the eggs for 4–5 minutes or until pale and creamy. With the mixer still running, gradually add the caster sugar and continue to beat for 3–4 minutes. The mixture is ready when it 'forms a ribbon'. This means when the paddle or a spoon is lifted out of the mixture, a trail is left across the surface for a moment before it sinks.

3 In a bowl, sift together the flour and salt. Stir through the orange zest and poppy seeds. Fold the flour mixture through the egg mixture.

4 Melt the butter and gently fold the butter and ¾ cup orange juice through the batter.

5 Divide the batter evenly between the prepared tins. Place the tins side by side on the centre shelf of the oven and bake for 45 minutes or until golden brown and starting to come away from the sides of the tins. A skewer inserted into the centre will come out clean. Cool in the tins for 10 minutes before turning out onto a wire rack to cool completely before icing.

6 For the icing, place the cream cheese, icing sugar mixture and orange juice in a bowl and beat together until smooth.

7 To assemble the cake, spread the icing on the first cake and top with the second cake, then ice the top.

Swiss roll

Serves 10   Preparation time: 20 minutes   Cooking time: 15 minutes

6 medium eggs
½ teaspoon salt
1 cup caster sugar
¾ cup self-raising flour
½ cup cornflour

Icing sugar, for dusting
  and decoration
500 ml thickened cream
1 cup strawberry jam

1 Preheat the oven to 180°C. Grease a 24 x 30 cm Swiss roll pan and line with baking paper.

2 In the bowl of an electric mixer fitted with the balloon whisk, beat the eggs with the salt for 5 minutes until pale and fluffy. Gradually sprinkle in the sugar while still beating. Continue beating for a further 5 minutes. Using a metal spoon, gently fold in the sifted flours.

3 Pour the mixture into the prepared tin. Reduce the oven to 160°C and bake for 15 minutes or until pale golden and spongy in the centre. Lay a tea towel on a wire cooling rack and top it with a piece of baking paper. Dust the baking paper with icing sugar and turn the cake out of the tin onto the paper.

4 When the cake is completely cool, whip the cream. Spread the jam evenly all over the cake then top with cream. Using the tea towel to lift it, remove the cake from the rack and lay it vertically on the bench top. Start rolling the cake, using the baking paper but ensuring none of it gets rolled into the cake. Keep the roll as tight as possible. When done, wrap the baking paper tightly around the roll and place the cake seam side down on a serving tray. To serve, remove the paper and sprinkle a little icing sugar over the top.

Chocolate cake

Serves 16–20   Preparation time: 20 minutes   Cooking time: 40 minutes

1¼ cups cocoa powder
1½ cups boiling water
180 g unsalted butter, chopped
2½ cups caster sugar

3 eggs
¾ cup sour cream
½ teaspoon salt
3 cups self-raising flour, sifted

For the ganache icing
½ cup thickened cream
250 g dark chocolate
  – grated or choc bits

Chopped roasted peanuts,
  for the top

1 Preheat the oven to 180°C. Lightly grease a 30 x 40 cm baking tin and line the base and sides with non-stick baking paper.

2 Sift the cocoa powder into a heat-proof bowl and gradually add the boiling water, stirring until smooth, then set aside to cool.

3 Using electric beaters, beat the butter and sugar in a bowl until light and creamy. Add the eggs one at a time, beating well after each addition. Stir the sour cream for a moment before using, to thin it out. Add the salt, 1 cup flour and ¼ cup sour cream to the butter mixture, and stir to combine. Repeat with the remaining flour and sour cream, then stir in the cocoa mixture. Transfer the mixture to the prepared tin.

4 Bake for about 35–40 minutes, until the cake springs back when gently touched and pulls away from the sides of the tin. Cool in the tin for 10 minutes, then turn out onto a wire rack to cool completely before icing.

5 For the ganache icing, place the chocolate in a heat-proof bowl. Place the

cream in a microwave-safe jug or a small saucepan on the stovetop. Heat the cream to scalding point – almost boiling but not quite. Pour over the chocolate and stir until fully melted and combined. Allow to cool and thicken slightly, then spread over the cake. Sprinkle with peanuts. The ganache will set as it cools completely.

Flourless chocolate cake

Serves 12   Preparation time: 20 minutes   Cooking time: 40 minutes

200 g dark chocolate, grated
200 g unsalted butter, at room
   temperature
1 shot (30 ml) espresso coffee
   or 1 teaspoon dry instant coffee

8 eggs, at room temperature
1½ cups caster sugar
1¼ cups almond meal
¼ cup cocoa, plus extra
   cocoa, for dusting

1 Preheat the oven to 170°C. Spray the base and sides of a 24 cm springform cake tin and line the base with baking paper.

2 Place the chocolate and butter in a microwave-safe glass bowl, and cook on high for 30 seconds at a time, stirring after each time, until melted. Add the shot or teaspoon of coffee. Stir to combine and set aside to cool.

3 In the bowl of an electric mixer, beat the eggs at high speed for 5 minutes, until they are pale and frothy. Trickle the caster sugar in slowly, still beating, until all the sugar is incorporated. Gently fold the chocolate through the egg mixture.

4 In a separate bowl, combine the almond meal and ¼ cup cocoa, and fold through the wet ingredients.

5 Gently pour the mixture into the cake tin and cook on the middle shelf of the oven for about 40 minutes. It should have formed a crust but still be dense and fudgy in the middle. Cool on a wire rack.

6 When cooled, sift extra cocoa over the top.

Flourless citrus syrup cake

Serves 16   Prep time: 10 minutes   Cooking time: 3 hours

4 large navel oranges
1 lime
1 lemon
6 eggs

2 cups caster sugar
400 g almond meal
1 teaspoon baking powder

For the syrup

Juice of 2 oranges, 2 lemons and 2 limes   1 cup caster sugar

1 Boil the whole oranges, lime and lemon in a large pot of water for 2 hours. Top up the water if needed. Drain carefully. The fruit will be very soft and pulpy. Place into a food processor and blitz until completely smooth.

2 Preheat the oven to 170°C (150°C fan-forced). Grease and line a 26 cm springform cake tin with baking paper.

3 Place the eggs and sugar in the bowl of an electric mixer and beat until light and fluffy. Fold through the pureed fruit. Place the almond meal and baking powder on top and fold through.

4 Pour the mixture into the cake tin and bake for 1½ hours. Place foil loosely over the top if it is browning too quickly. It is cooked when a skewer inserted into the cake comes out mostly clean.

5 To make the syrup, combine the juices and sugar in a saucepan. Bring to the boil and boil for about 5 minutes, or until the syrup has thickened and reduced slightly.

6 When the cake is cooked, cool for 15 minutes in the tin. While the cake cools, 'feed' it by drizzling the syrup over the top, a little at a time, allowing each spoonful to soak in before adding more.

Orange gingerbread cake

Serves 12   Prep time: 15 minutes   Cooking time: 1 hour

2 cups caster sugar
60 g butter
3 oranges
50 g butter, at room temperature
1 cup brown sugar
2 eggs

1 cup milk
2 tablespoons golden syrup
2 cups self-raising flour
1 tablespoon ground ginger
1 tablespoon cinnamon
Double thick cream, for serving

1 In a large saucepan, heat the sugar with ½ cup of water. Stir until the sugar dissolves, then leave to boil. Boil for about 10 minutes, keeping a close eye on the pot. The sugar and water will turn a lovely caramel brown colour. At this stage, add the butter and stir briskly with a metal spoon. Be prepared for the mixture to froth up.

2 Preheat the oven to 160°C.

Orange gingerbread cake,
recipe page 251

3 Zest the oranges, then peel them, removing all the white pith. Cut each one in half from top to bottom then cut out the middle in a V-shape to remove the sinewy part of the segments. Cut into slices about 1 cm thick. Arrange the orange slices to cover the bottom of an unlined 22 cm non-stick cake tin. Pour the caramel over the orange slices.

4 For the gingerbread batter, cream the butter and brown sugar in a large bowl with electric beaters. Mix in the orange zest. In a separate bowl, beat the egg with the milk and golden syrup. Add gradually to the butter mixture, beating to combine.

5 Sift together the flour, ginger and cinnamon. Gently fold into the wet ingredients.

6 Pour the batter carefully over the oranges and spread to level. Bake on the middle shelf of the oven for 45 minutes or until the cake is coming away from the sides of the tin and springs back when touched in the middle. A skewer inserted into the middle of the cake should come out clean.

7 Cool in the tin for about 10 minutes, then place a plate on top of the cake tin and carefully turn upside down. The cake will drop onto the plate. Lift the cake tin off the top. Serve with double thick cream.

Lemon-scented scones with lemon curd

Makes about 20 small scones   Prep time: 5 minutes
Cooking time: 30 minutes

3 cups self-raising flour   1 cup lemonade
¼ teaspoon salt   4 eggs, beaten
3 lemons   1 cup sugar
1 cup thickened cream   125 g butter

1 Preheat the oven to 220°C. Line an oven tray with baking paper.

2 Sift the flour and salt into a large bowl and zest the lemons into it. Stir to combine. Make a well in the centre. In a jug, combine the cream and lemonade. Pour into the well in the bowl, stirring very minimally with a butter knife to draw the flour into the liquid. When all the flour is incorporated, tip out onto a floured bench and, using your hands, very gently bring the dough together. It's very important not to over-handle the dough at this stage, or the scones will be heavy.

3 When the dough has come together, flatten it to a disc about 3 cm thick. Use

a 5 cm cookie cutter to cut rounds in the dough. Once you have cut as many as you can, the remaining dough can be brought together once more and a few more rounds cut out.

4 Place the scones on the baking tray, just touching each other. Bake for 10 minutes or until they are puffed and golden on top, and sound hollow when tapped with a knife.

5 For the lemon curd, place the eggs and sugar in a bowl over a pot of barely simmering water. Whisk until sugar dissolves. Add lemon juice and butter and whisk constantly for about 20 minutes or until it thickens. Do not allow it to get too hot or to boil. Cool the lemon curd before serving with the scones.

Treacle scones

Makes 12   Prep time: 10 minutes   Cooking time: 15 minutes

3 teaspoons butter
2 tablespoons golden syrup
⅔ cup milk

2 cups self-raising flour
½ teaspoon salt

1 Preheat the oven to 200°C and line a large oven tray with baking paper.

2 Place the butter and golden syrup in a small pot over medium heat and stir until the butter is dissolved. Stir in the milk.

3 Add this mixture to sifted flour and mix to a soft dough. Knead very slightly – until the dough just comes together – then shape into an oval about 3 cm thick. Working on a floured bench, cut the scones with a 5 cm cookie cutter and place side by side on the tray, just touching each other.

4 Bake for 8–10 minutes or until golden brown on top. Remove the tray from the oven and cover with a clean tea towel. This will prevent a crust forming and will help the scones to finish cooking without browning further.

Vegemite cheese scones

Makes 12   Prep time: 10 minutes   Cooking time: 12 minutes

2 cups self-raising flour
¼ teaspoon salt
2 tablespoons butter, melted

1 cup milk
2 tablespoons Vegemite
1 cup grated tasty cheese

1 Preheat the oven to 220°C. Grease or line an oven tray with baking paper.

Treacle scones, recipe
page 254

2 Sift the flour and salt into a large bowl and make a well in the centre. Add melted butter to the milk and pour it into the centre of the flour. Using a butter knife, mix the wet and dry ingredients together. Tip out onto a floured bench and knead just a few times, enough to bring the dough together but no more.

3 Roll the dough out to about 1½ cm thick. Carefully spread the Vegemite over half the dough, and scatter half the grated cheese on top of the Vegemite. Fold the other half of the dough over the cheese. Spread the rest of the Vegemite and cheese on top.

4 Cut out the scones using a 5 cm cutter and place them, just touching each other, on the tray. Bake for 10–12 minutes or until golden and hollow-sounding when tapped.

Tiny mud cakes

Makes 24   Prep time: 15 minutes   Cooking time 20 minutes

1 cup milk
200 g butter, cubed
1⅔ cups caster sugar
200 g dark cooking chocolate
2 tablespoons strong black coffee
 (or 1 teaspoon instant coffee in
 2 tablespoons boiling water)

1 teaspoon vanilla extract
1¼ cups plain flour
⅓ cup self-raising flour
½ cup cocoa
2 large eggs, lightly beaten

Chocolate ganache
½ cup thickened cream

250 g dark chocolate
 – grated or choc bits

1 Preheat the oven to 170°C (150°C fan-forced). Line 2 trays of mini muffin tins with paper cases.

2 In a medium saucepan over medium heat, combine the milk, butter, sugar, chocolate, coffee and vanilla extract. Stir until melted together then remove from the heat to cool.

3 In a separate bowl, sift the flours and cocoa. When the chocolate mixture has cooled, pour it into the dry ingredients, stirring well. Add the eggs and stir again until well combined.

4 Pour the batter carefully into the prepared cases and bake for 30 minutes or until a skewer inserted into the middle comes away clean.

5 For the ganache, place the cream into a microwave-safe jug or a small saucepan on the stovetop. Heat to scalding point – almost boiling but not quite. Add the chocolate and stir until combined. Allow to cool completely then beat with electric beaters until fluffy. Place into a piping bag with a star nozzle and, when the cakes have cooled, top each one with a little swirl of ganache.

Apple walnut loaf

Serves 10–12   Prep time: 15 minutes   Cooking time: 1 hour

125 g butter, at room temperature
1 cup caster sugar
2 eggs
3 medium-sized Pink Lady apples,
   peeled, quartered and
   cut into thick slices

1¾ cups walnut pieces
¼ cup self-raising flour
¾ cup plain flour
1 teaspoon cinnamon
¼ teaspoon nutmeg
¼ teaspoon salt

1 Preheat the oven to 170°C. Grease a 13 x 23 cm non-stick loaf tin and line the base with baking paper.

2 Using an electric mixer or beaters, cream the butter and sugar until light and fluffy. Add the eggs one at a time, beating well after each addition. Stir through the apple and the walnuts.

3 In a separate bowl, sift the flours, cinnamon, nutmeg and salt and stir to combine. Stir the dry ingredients into the apple butter mixture. Stir the mixture only as much as you need to, to make sure it is well combined. This is quite a stiff mixture, but the apples release moisture as the cake cooks.

4 Bake for 1 hour or until golden, aromatic, and coming away from the sides of the pan. Invert onto a wire rack, then place a second wire rack underneath and flip the loaf so it is cooling right side up.

Dutch cake, recipe
page 259

Dutch cake

Serves 12   Prep time: 20 minutes
Cooking time: 35 minutes + chilling time

1 quantity sweet shortcrust pastry
  (see page 233)
¼ cup plum jam
170 g butter
½ cup caster sugar
2 eggs

2 cups self-raising flour
2 teaspoons mixed spice
½ cup milk
1 cup icing sugar mixture
1 teaspoon butter
Juice of ½ lemon

1 Preheat the oven to 180°C. Grease a 21 cm springform cake tin with spray oil and line the base with baking paper. Using the tin as a guide, cut a circle in the pastry. Line the base of the tin with the pastry and spread with the plum jam.

2 Using an electric mixer or beaters, cream the butter and sugar until light and fluffy. Add the eggs one at a time, beating well after each addition. Fold through half the flour and the mixed spice, then half the milk, and repeat.

3 Spread the batter over the pastry base and bake for 40 minutes. Remove from the oven and allow to cool in the tin for 10 minutes before removing to a wire rack to cool completely.

4 In a bowl, combine the icing sugar mixture, butter and lemon juice. When the cake is cool, spread the icing over the top.

Flourless almond and pistachio syrup cake

Makes 24 pieces   Prep time: 15 minutes + resting time
Cooking time: 35 minutes

3 cups almond meal
125 g pistachio kernels
  – 24 reserved, the rest ground
1 cup caster sugar
¼ teaspoon salt
1 teaspoon cinnamon

5 eggs
1 teaspoon vanilla extract
250 g butter, melted and cooled
¾ cup caster sugar for syrup
⅓ cup honey

1 Preheat the oven to 180°C. Spray a 21 x 31 cm baking tray with oil and line the base with baking paper.

2 In a large bowl, combine the almond meal, ground pistachios, sugar, salt and cinnamon. (Using a wire whisk is an easy way to do this.)

3 In a separate bowl, beat the eggs, then add the vanilla and butter and stir to combine. Pour the egg mixture into the almond mixture and stir to combine well.

4 Pour the batter into the prepared tin. Arrange the whole pistachios evenly over the top and bake for 35 minutes or until golden and coming away from the sides of the pan.

5 In a medium pot over medium-high heat, place the sugar, honey and ⅓ cup of water. Bring to the boil and boil for about 2 minutes, being careful not to allow the syrup to froth up over the sides of the pot.

6 When the cake comes out of the oven, carefully pierce the top with a toothpick and pour the hot syrup over the top. Leave the cake in the tin to allow the syrup to soak in. Cut into 24 pieces.

Pea, zucchini and feta muffins

Makes 12   Prep time: 15 minutes   Cooking time: 30 minutes

2 cups self-raising flour
1 cup frozen baby peas, thawed
2 large or 3 small zucchini,
   grated (about 1½ cups)
2 large brown onions, grated
   or finely chopped
1 tablespoon fresh thyme
   leaves, roughly chopped

200 g firm feta,
   cut into 1 cm cubes
1 cup grated tasty cheese
½ cup milk
3 eggs
60 g butter, melted

1 Preheat the oven 180°C (160°C fan-forced). Grease a 12-hole ⅓-cup capacity muffin tin with cooking spray. (Alternatively, line with muffin paper cases if you wish.)

2 Place the flour into a large mixing bowl and stir in the peas, zucchini, onion, thyme, feta and tasty cheese, reserving 12 cubes of feta. Mix well.

3 In a separate bowl, whisk the milk and eggs together and add the butter. Pour into the flour mixture and stir gently until just incorporated. Divide evenly in the muffin tin and top each muffin with a cube of feta. Bake for 25–30 minutes or until golden brown and cooked through. A skewer inserted into the middle should come out clean.

4 Cool in the tin before turning onto a wire rack to cool completely.

Biscuits and slices

Lavosh

This savoury bark is perfect for cheese boards and is so simple to make.

Makes 8 pieces   Prep time: 15 minutes   Cooking time: 20 minutes

1 cup plain flour
⅓ cup wholemeal flour
1 teaspoon salt
¼ cup olive oil

1 teaspoon sesame oil
½ cup water
½ cup sesame seeds

1 Preheat the oven to 180°C (160°C fan-forced) and line 2 large baking trays with baking paper.

2 In a mixing bowl, combine the flours and salt. Add the olive oil, sesame oil, water and sesame seeds and mix well. The dough will be quite wet and very stretchy.

3 Tear off about one-eighth of the dough and place between 2 large sheets of baking paper. Roll out in a long, narrow oval shape as thinly as possible.

4 Flip the baking paper onto the prepared tray and peel it from the back of the lavosh. Continue with the dough, baking in batches for about 10 minutes or until golden brown and crisp.

Parmesan crackers

Makes 12 pieces   Prep time: 20 minutes   Cooking time: about 12 minutes

50 g block parmesan
150 g plain flour
1 teaspoon sea salt flakes

50 g butter
¼ cup cream

1 Preheat the oven to 200°C and line a baking tray with baking paper.

2 Break the block of parmesan into 3–4 pieces and place in the bowl of a food processor. Blitz until powdered. Add the remaining ingredients and blitz until it comes together in a dough.

3 Place a large piece of baking paper on the bench, with the dough on top, and

cover with another large piece of baking paper. Use a rolling pin to roll the dough out to about 3 mm thick. If the dough is too soft to work with, put it in the fridge for half an hour or until it firms up.

4 Dock the pastry all over with a fork and use a sharp knife or a pizza wheel to cut the dough into 4-cm squares. Lift the squares with an icing spatula onto the prepared tray. Leave at least 1 cm around each square. Bake for 12 minutes or until golden. Allow to cool on the tray for a few minutes before transferring to a wire rack to cool completely.

Variations: Add some fresh thyme or rosemary leaves to the food processor, or half a teaspoon each of smoked paprika and ground chilli.

Apple crumble slice

Makes 18 pieces   Prep time: 15 minutes   Cooking time: 35 minutes

2 eggs
1 cup caster sugar
125 g butter, melted
1 teaspoon vanilla extract
3 Granny Smith apples, peeled,
    cored and cut into 1 cm pieces

¾ cup self-raising flour
¼ teaspoon cinnamon
½ teaspoon ground ginger
¼ teaspoon salt
¼ cup milk

Crumble topping
25 g butter
¼ cup firmly packed brown sugar
¼ cup flaked almonds

¼ cup rolled oats
¼ cup shredded coconut

1 Preheat the oven to 180°C (160°C fan-forced). Grease and line a 19 x 30 cm lamington tin.

2 Beat the eggs in the bowl of an electric mixer until pale and creamy. Add the sugar and continue to beat for 5 minutes or until the mixture is thick and forms a ribbon. Stir in the butter and vanilla.

3 Add the flour, cinnamon, ginger, salt and milk, stirring through gently. Add the apples and stir to make sure all the apples are coated in the batter. The batter will be quite runny. Pour into the prepared tin.

4 For the topping, rub the butter, sugar, almonds, oats and coconut between your fingers until well combined. Sprinkle evenly over the batter in the tin. Bake for 35 minutes or until golden brown.

Triple choc macadamia blondies

Makes 12 pieces   Prep time: 20 minutes   Cooking time: 45 minutes

250 g butter
250 g white chocolate melts
2 teaspoons vanilla extract
4 eggs
1¾ cups caster sugar

1½ cups plain flour
100 g milk chocolate melts
100 g dark chocolate melts
1 cup macadamia pieces

1 Preheat the oven to 160°C (140°C fan-forced). Grease and line a 19 x 30 cm lamington tin with baking paper.

2 In a medium pot over low heat, melt the butter. Add the white chocolate melts and stir until melted. Stir in the vanilla.

3 In the bowl of an electric mixer, beat the eggs for 5 minutes or until pale. With the mixer running, gradually add the sugar and continue to beat until the mixture 'forms a ribbon'. This means when the paddle or a spoon is lifted out of the mixture, a trail is left across the surface for a moment before it sinks.

4 Gently stir the melted chocolate mixture into the egg mixture. Sift the flour into the wet ingredients and gently fold through. Fold through the milk and dark chocolate melts and macadamias. Pour the mixture into the lamington tin and bake for 45 minutes. When ready, the brownies will have a delicate crust on top and still be dense and moist in the middle.

Melting moments

Makes about 24   Prep time: 15 minutes   Cooking time: 15 minutes

180 g butter, at room temperature
½ cup icing sugar
1½ cups plain flour
⅓ cup custard powder
2 cups icing sugar mixture

100 g butter
1 orange, zested and juiced
1 tablespoon orange
  blossom water

1 Preheat the oven to 180°C (160°C fan-forced) and line a baking tray with baking paper.

2 Using an electric mixer or beaters, cream the butter and sifted icing sugar until light and fluffy. Add the sifted flour and custard powder and mix to a soft dough.

Gingerbread with royal
icing, recipe page 265

3 Roll walnut-sized balls of the dough in your palms and press onto the prepared tray with a fork.

4 Bake for 10–15 minutes or until starting to colour slightly at the edges. The biscuits will still be soft when they come out of the oven. Leave them to cool for a few minutes on the tray before removing to a wire rack to cool completely.

5 For the filling, place the icing sugar mixture, butter, orange zest, 1 tablespoon orange juice and the orange blossom water into a bowl and beat with electric beaters until light and fluffy. Spoon the filling into a piping bag with a 1 cm plain nozzle. Pipe a walnut-sized blob onto 12 of the completely cooled biscuits and sandwich with the other 12.

Gingerbread with royal icing

These little gingerbread shapes are perfect for decorating with icing. The longer they cook, the crisper they are.

Makes about 36 medium-sized gingerbread shapes
Prep time: 10 minutes   Cooking time: 10 minutes per batch

3 cups plain flour	1 teaspoon bicarbonate of soda
1½ cups caster sugar	200 g butter, melted
1 tablespoon ground ginger	1 tablespoon golden syrup
2 teaspoons ground cinnamon	1 egg, lightly beaten

Royal icing
1 eggwhite	1 tablespoon water
2¼ cups icing sugar	

1 Preheat the oven to 180°C. Line 2 baking trays with baking paper.

2 Combine dry ingredients in a large bowl.

3 Combine wet ingredients in a small bowl. Stir the wet into the dry ingredients to form a dough. Wrap the dough in plastic wrap and refrigerate for 15 minutes.

4 Roll out the dough between 2 sheets of baking paper to a thickness of about 3 mm.

5 Cut out shapes with Christmas-themed cookie cutters and lift with a palette knife onto the lined baking trays. Bake for 10 minutes or until golden brown. Remove from the oven and cool on a wire rack. Biscuits must be completely cool before icing.

6 To make the royal icing, using electric beaters, beat the eggwhite until frothy. Add the sugar a little at a time and beat until stiff peaks form. Thin with water if needed. Spoon into a piping bag and use immediately. It will dry to a hard, glossy finish.

Macadamia shortbread

Makes about 30   Prep time: 10 minutes
Cooking time: 10 minutes per batch

250 g unsalted butter
¾ cup icing sugar mixture
1 teaspoon vanilla essence
½ cup cornflour
2 cups self-raising flour

Good pinch of salt
250 g salted macadamias,
   roughly chopped
Extra caster sugar, for dipping

1 Preheat the oven to 180°C and line 2 large baking trays with baking paper.

2 Using electric beaters, beat the butter and icing sugar mixture in a large bowl until light and creamy. Beat in the vanilla essence.

3 Sift the cornflour, self-raising flour and salt together. Stir the macadamias through the flour. Add to the butter mixture and use a butter knife to mix together thoroughly.

4 Roll the dough into small balls about the size of a walnut. Dip the tops in the sugar and put onto the prepared trays, about 5 cm apart. Flatten slightly with a fork.

5 Bake for about 8–10 minutes, or until just starting to colour underneath (the biscuits will still be soft, and pale on top). Leave on the trays to cool for 10 minutes to become firm, then transfer to a wire rack to cool completely. Store in an airtight container.

Anzac biscuits

Makes 36   Prep time: 10 minutes   Cooking time: 20 minutes

1 cup rolled oats
1 cup plain flour
1 cup sugar
¾ cup desiccated coconut

125 g butter
2 tablespoons golden syrup
½ teaspoon bicarbonate of soda
1 tablespoon boiling water

1 Preheat the oven to 150°C (130°C fan-forced). Line 2 large baking trays with baking paper.

2 In a large bowl, combine the oats, flour, sugar and coconut.

3 In a small saucepan over medium heat, melt the butter and syrup and stir together.

4 Mix the bicarbonate of soda with boiling water then stir into the melted butter mixture. Pour into the dry ingredients and stir to combine.

5 Shape the mixture into walnut-sized balls and place on the prepared trays, allowing room for spreading. Bake for 20 minutes. Allow the biscuits to cool on the trays for 10 minutes before transferring to a wire rack to cool completely. The biscuits will firm up as they cool.

Note: For a more crispy biscuit, bake for an extra few minutes.

Basic chocolate fudge

Makes 18 pieces   Prep time: 2 minutes
Cooking time: 3 minutes + chilling time

395 g tin sweetened
  condensed milk
375 g dark choc bits or melts,
  or grated cooking chocolate

1 teaspoon vanilla bean paste

1 Grease and line a 20 x 30 cm lamington pan with non-stick baking paper, making sure it overhangs the edges.

2 Place the ingredients in a large microwave-safe glass bowl (such as Pyrex) and microwave on high for 3 minutes, stirring once during cooking. Pour the mixture into the pan and set aside to cool completely before cutting into 18 pieces. Store in an airtight container in the cupboard.

Variations: This can be made with white or milk chocolate. You can also add your choice of nuts or lollies before cooling.

Rocky road

Makes 24 squares   Prep time: 10 minutes   Cooking time: 2 minutes

1½ cups mini marshmallows
1 cup shredded coconut,
  lightly toasted
1 cup walnuts, toasted and
  coarsely chopped

1 packet gummi bears
  or soft jubes
400 g milk chocolate, diced

1 Line a 20 x 30 cm lamington tin with baking paper, allowing a 5 cm overhang on the longest sides.

2 Place the marshmallows, coconut, walnuts and gummi bears in a bowl and mix together.

3 Melt the chocolate in a heat-proof bowl over a saucepan of simmering water. Remove and stir into the marshmallow mixture, making sure the ingredients are thoroughly mixed.

4 Tip into the tin and press until evenly distributed. Cover with plastic wrap and refrigerate for 1–2 hours before cutting into squares.

Giant choc chip cookies

Makes about 12 cookies   Prep time: 10 minutes   Cooking time: 12 minutes

185 g unsalted butter
1¼ cups caster sugar
1 egg
½ teaspoon vanilla essence
2 cups self-raising flour

¼ teaspoon salt
290 g packet choc melts (white, milk or dark)

1 Preheat the oven to 180°C (160°C fan-forced). Line 2 large baking trays with non-stick baking paper.

2 Using electric beaters, cream the butter and sugar in a large bowl until pale and fluffy, then beat in the egg and vanilla. Gently mix in the sifted flour and the salt. Stir in the choc bits until they are combined.

3 Divide the mixture into 12 pieces and roll each into a ball. Place 6 balls on each tray and, using damp hands, flatten the cookies. They will spread during cooking and touch each other, but that's ok if you don't mind them being odd shapes. If you want perfectly round cookies, bake them in batches of 2 cookies per tray. Press 5–6 chocolate melts into the top of each cookie.

4 Bake for about 12 minutes. For a softer, chewier cookie, remove them from the oven when they are just golden around the edges. For a crisper, lighter cookie, wait until they are golden all over. Cool the cookies on the trays for a couple of minutes until they firm up slightly, then transfer to a wire rack to cool completely. Store in an airtight container.

Peanut butter cookies

Makes about 36 cookies   Prep time: 10 minutes   Cooking time: 12 minutes

185 g unsalted butter
1¼ cups caster sugar
¾ cup crunchy peanut butter
1 egg

½ teaspoon vanilla essence
2 cups self-raising flour
¼ teaspoon salt

1 Preheat the oven to 180°C (160°C fan-forced). Line 2 large baking trays with non-stick baking paper.

2 Using electric beaters, cream the butter and sugar in a large bowl until pale and fluffy, then beat in the peanut butter, egg and vanilla. Gently mix in the sifted flour and the salt.

3 Shape the mixture into walnut-sized balls and place on the prepared trays, allowing room for spreading. Flatten gently with a fork.

4 Bake for about 12 minutes. For a softer, chewier cookie, remove them from the oven when they are just golden around the edges. For a crisper, lighter cookie, wait until they are golden all over. Cool the cookies on the trays for a couple of minutes until they firm up slightly, then transfer to a wire rack to cool completely. Store in an airtight container.

Meringue kisses

Makes about 50   Prep time: 10 minutes   Cooking time: 2½ hours

4 eggwhites
1 cup caster sugar
A couple of drops of
  food colouring, optional

Sprinkles, multicoloured or in
  your choice of colour

1 Preheat the oven to 80°C on the fan-forced setting. Line 2 oven trays with baking paper.

2 In the bowl of an electric mixer, beat the eggwhites until they form soft peaks. With the beaters running, add the sugar in a slow, steady stream. Beat until stiff peaks form and the sugar has dissolved. You may need to scrape down the sides of the mixing bowl a couple of times. At this stage, the meringue can be coloured with a couple of drops of food colouring if you like.

3 Place a 1.5 cm star-shaped nozzle into a large piping bag. Fill the bag and pipe meringues onto the prepared trays. Use a double movement – first, pipe a blob, then press down lightly and pipe a second blob on top. Lightly top with the sprinkles.

4 Bake for 2½ hours, switching the trays around halfway through cooking. They will be light as a feather and crisp all the way through. Remove from the oven and cool on wire racks before storing in an airtight container.

Desserts

Introduction

I'm a little bit obsessed with the beautiful food photos people post on Instagram, Facebook, Twitter, Pinterest, you name it … (not to mention Foodgawker and Tastespotting … you may want to try these too if you are a true appreciator of food pictures!) Anyway – my obsession with looking at beautiful food quite often drives me into the kitchen to create my own version of something I have seen. I find it inspiring in quite a tangible way.

This is especially true of desserts. For many years I focused on family meals and savoury cooking and didn't spend much time on desserts. Now that I have the enormous privilege of running a cooking school and spending many more hours in the kitchen than I used to, my desserts repertoire has grown enormously.

In this chapter you will find some simple go-to ideas, some classics, and some of my favourites and hopefully yours as well.

Basic pavlova

Makes 1 big pavlova   Prep time: 20 minutes
Cooking time: 1 hour 10 minutes

6 eggwhites
¼ teaspoon salt
1¾ cups caster sugar
600 ml cream, whipped

2 punnets strawberries, hulled
and halved
Pulp of 4 passionfruit

1 Preheat the oven to 160°C. Grease a 25 x 38 cm baking tray and line it with non-stick baking paper.

2 Beat the eggwhites and salt in an electric mixer until soft peaks appear. Begin adding the caster sugar a little at a time, until it is all incorporated. Continue to mix until the eggwhites form stiff, glossy peaks. Spread the mixture onto the baking tray, leaving a 2 cm space around the edges.

3 Bake for 30 minutes, then reduce the temperature to 120°C and bake for a further 1 hour. Turn the oven off and prop the door open an inch. Allow the pavlova to cool in the oven. When it is completely cool, top with whipped cream and fruit before serving.

Note: This is the simplest of pavlovas, and doesn't use any vinegar or cornflour to stabilise it. If the pavlova is starting to brown, reduce the temperature. There should be quite a thick crisp shell and fluffy interior.

You can sweeten the cream with 1 teaspoon vanilla extract and 1 tablespoon icing sugar if you wish. I choose not to as the pavlova itself is very sweet.

Banoffee pavlova roulade

Serves 10–12   Prep time: 20 minutes   Cooking time: 30 minutes

8 eggwhites
2 cups caster sugar
1 tablespoon cornflour
1 tablespoon white vinegar

1 teaspoon vanilla extract
600 ml thickened cream, whipped
4 ripe bananas, sliced ½ cm thick

For the caramel sauce
125 g butter
½ cup brown sugar

½ cup thickened cream

For the candied macadamias
½ cup macadamia nut pieces

¼ cup icing sugar

1 Preheat oven to 160°C. Grease and line a 26 x 34 cm baking tray with baking paper.

2 In the bowl of an electric mixer, whip the eggwhites until soft peaks form. Add the sugar a little bit at a time, whipping continually, until the sugar is dissolved and stiff peaks have formed.

3 Sprinkle over the cornflour, vinegar and vanilla and gently fold through the egg whites until combined. Do this very gently so as not to knock the air out of the mixture. Spread the mixture into the baking dish and bake for 20 minutes or until just firm.

4 When the meringue comes out of the oven, allow to cool for 5 minutes. Sprinkle a fresh sheet of baking paper with cornflour and lay over the top of the meringue. Lay a clean tea towel on the bench, and carefully invert the baking dish so that the meringue comes out on top of the baking paper and on top of the tea towel. Carefully remove the baking paper from the bottom of the meringue.

5 Spread half the cream in a line along the long edge of the meringue closest to you. Press half the sliced bananas into the cream. Now the fun part: carefully, using the tea towel as a helping hand, roll the meringue over the cream until it looks like a log. Carefully lift onto the serving plate, putting the join at the bottom.

6 For the caramel sauce, heat a large frypan over medium heat and melt the butter and brown sugar together. Add the cream to the pan and bring to the

boil, stirring, for 2 minutes or until slightly thickened. Remove from the heat and allow to cool (at room temperature – don't refrigerate).

7 For the candied macadamias, place the nuts and icing sugar in a frypan over medium-high heat. Stir until the icing sugar melts and turns golden. Stir to coat evenly and tip the mixture onto a tray lined with baking paper. Allow to cool and bash gently with the base of a glass or a rolling pin to crush just a little.

8 Immediately before serving, spread the remaining cream over the roulade. Spread the remaining banana over the top, drizzle generously with caramel sauce and sprinkle with the macadamias.

Passionfruit crepes

Serves 4   Prep time: 5 minutes   Cooking time: 20 minutes

1 cup self-raising flour
1 teaspoon caster sugar
¼ teaspoon salt

1¼ cups milk
2 eggs
50 g butter, melted

Passionfruit filling

1 quantity passionfruit
   and lime curd (see page 220)
300 ml thickened cream,
   whipped

2 tablespoons icing sugar,
   for serving

1 Place the flour, sugar and salt in a bowl and combine with a wire whisk. In a jug, whisk together the milk and eggs. Pour the milk mixture into the flour and whisk well to ensure there are no lumps. Cover and set aside to rest for 30 minutes at room temperature.

2 Brush the base of a 16 cm non-stick crepe pan or frypan with butter and place over medium-high heat. When hot, pour in just enough batter to cover the base. Tilt the pan so the batter covers the base in a thin film and pour any excess back into the bowl. Cook the crepe for about 1 minute until the underside is golden, then use a metal spatula to flip. Cook the other side for less than 1 minute until golden.

3 Transfer to a plate and cover loosely with foil to keep warm. Repeat for the remaining crepe mixture, stacking the crepes on the plate as you go.

4 To serve, spread each crepe with passionfruit and lime curd then whipped cream before folding over. Sift the icing sugar over the top.

Banoffee pavlova roulade,
recipe page 275

Basic pancakes

Makes 8   Prep time: 10 minutes   Cooking time: 3 minutes per batch

1 cup self-raising flour
1 egg

1 cup milk
Olive oil cooking spray

1 Place the flour in a bowl. Make a well in the centre. In a small bowl or jug, whisk the milk and egg together and pour into the flour, whisking well to ensure there are no lumps.

2 Heat a frying pan over medium-low heat and spray with oil. Pour ¼ cup batter into the pan and swirl. Cook for 2 minutes or until bubbles form on the surface. Turn and cook for a further 1 minute, or until cooked through. Remove to a plate and cover with a clean tea towel. Repeat with the remaining mixture.

Suggested toppings

· Maple syrup and whipped cream

· Lemon juice and caster sugar

· Bananas and butterscotch sauce (see page 150)

· Raspberries and chocolate sauce (see page 150)

· Fresh berries, natural yoghurt and honey

· Mascarpone and passionfruit syrup (see page 152)

Ricotta pancakes

Makes 8   Prep time: 10 minutes
Cooking time: about 25 minutes

1 egg
1 cup milk
125 g ricotta

1 cup self-raising flour
Cooking spray

1 Separate the egg. In a large bowl, mix the yolk with the milk and ricotta, then stir in the flour. In a separate bowl, whisk the eggwhite for a short time until it is frothy, and fold through the flour mixture.

2 Heat a non-stick frypan over medium-high heat. Place ⅓ cup batter in the pan. Thin out by swirling with the back of a spoon, if you like. Cook for about 2 minutes or until bubbles appear on the surface and the underside is golden

brown. Flip and cook for a further minute or so. Remove to a plate and cover with a clean tea towel. Repeat with the remaining mixture.

Note: See basic pancakes (see page 278) for topping suggestions.

Banana fritters

Serves 4   Prep time: 10 minutes   Cooking time: 5 minutes per batch

4 bananas, halved lengthways
   then sliced across
250 g flour   ·

375 ml beer
Oil, for deep-frying
Ice cream, for serving

1 Preheat the oil to 190°C in the deep-fryer.

2 Place the flour in a bowl and add the beer, stirring to ensure there are no lumps. Dip the banana pieces into the batter and allow the excess to run off, then place them directly into the oil. Only cook 4 at a time so the temperature of the oil does not drop too far. Cook for 3–4 minutes or until golden brown. Remove from the oil and drain on paper towel. Repeat with remaining banana pieces. Serve hot with ice cream.

Note: These go very well with the butterscotch or caramel sauces (see page 150).

Apricot jam bread and butter pudding

Serves 8   Prep time: 10 minutes + 20 minutes standing time
Cooking time: 40 minutes

300 ml thickened cream
300 ml milk
6 eggs, beaten
¾ cup caster sugar
1 teaspoon vanilla extract
12 slices white bread,
   crusts removed, cut in half
   into rectangles

½ cup butter, at room
   temperature
1 cup apricot jam
½ teaspoon cinnamon
Whipped cream, for serving

1 In a large mixing bowl, combine the cream, milk, eggs, sugar and vanilla extract.

2 Spread the bread with butter and jam. Roll up the bread rectangle with the jam on the inside and stand the roll on its edge in a 20 x 25 cm baking dish. Repeat with all the remaining bread.

3 Pour over the egg mixture to just cover the bread. Sprinkle the cinnamon over the top. Stand for 20 minutes before baking to allow the custard to soak into the bread.

4 Preheat the oven to 180°C. Bake the pudding for 40 minutes. Remove from the oven and serve warm with cream.

Coconut crumble

This is a lovely way to dress up fresh or stewed fruit and ice cream.

Makes about 1½ cups   Prep time: 5 minutes   Cooking time: 10 minutes

¼ cup caster sugar
½ teaspoon ground cinnamon
½ cup plain flour

1 cup shredded coconut
½ cup slivered almonds
80 g butter

1 Preheat the oven to 180°C and line a baking tray with baking paper.

2 Combine all the ingredients in a bowl and mix until just combined. Tip onto the baking tray and bake for 8–10 minutes or until golden brown and fragrant. Remove from the oven, allow to cool, and store in an airtight container.

Honey poached pears with walnut crumble

Serves 4   Prep time: 15 minutes   Cooking time: 20 minutes

½ cup plain flour
¼ cup caster sugar
½ teaspoon ground cinnamon
½ teaspoon ground ginger
½ cup walnuts, chopped
½ cup rolled oats
80 g butter, at room temperature

1 cup honey
1 cm knob ginger, sliced
1 cinnamon stick
4 Packham or Williams pears, peeled, quartered and cored
Crème fraiche, to serve

1 Preheat the oven to 180°C. Line a baking tray with baking paper.

2 Combine the flour, sugar, ground cinnamon and ginger, walnuts and oats in a bowl. Add the butter and use your hands to mix it thoroughly through the dry ingredients. Tip onto the baking tray and bake for 8–10 minutes or until golden brown and fragrant. Remove from the oven and allow to cool.

3 In a large saucepan over medium heat, combine 4 cups of water with the honey, sliced ginger and cinnamon stick. Bring to the boil and lower the pears into the mixture. Reduce the heat and simmer for 15 minutes or until the pears are tender. Remove from the syrup with a slotted spoon and place straight into serving bowls.

4 Increase the heat of the syrup and boil rapidly for about 5 minutes or until the syrup reduces. Strain the syrup and pour some over the pears. Top with the crumble and serve with a dollop of crème fraîche.

Vanilla ice cream

Makes about 1.5 litres   Prep time: 10 minutes
Cooking and chilling time: 40 minutes

600 ml thickened cream
400 ml milk
2 strips lemon peel,
    made using a vegetable peeler

10 egg yolks
250 g caster sugar
1 vanilla pod or 1 teaspoon
    vanilla bean paste

1 Place the milk and cream in a large pot over medium-high heat and add the lemon peel. Stir and bring to the boil. Pour into a jug and wipe out the pot.

2 In a large bowl, beat together the eggs and sugar until thick and fairly pale. Pour the milk in a slow stream into the egg mixture, whisking the whole time. When all mixed together, pour the mixture back into the pot and place over a low heat. Split the vanilla bean and scrape out the seeds or add vanilla bean paste. Add both to the pot and stir continuously with a spatula.

3 It's important not to let the mixture boil. Be patient – it takes about 20 minutes of stirring for it to reach the right consistency. You will know when it's ready when you can dip a wooden spoon into the custard, run your finger through it, and the custard doesn't bleed back into the trail. Remove the pot from the heat and strain the custard into a bowl to remove the vanilla pod (if using).

4 Chill in the fridge or freezer until completely cold. Churn in an ice cream maker until frozen, then leave in the freezer for a little while to set and harden.

Note: If you don't have an ice cream maker, cool the mixture in a container

Ginger and caramel pudding,
recipe page 283

then place it in the freezer with plastic wrap covering the surface. Give it a good whisk every 30 minutes, until it's getting too hard to put the whisk through. You will need to do this several times, but it means there will be no gritty ice crystals in the ice cream.

Variations: Coffee and walnut: Combine 1 tablespoon dried instant coffee with the milk mixture, and then stir through candied walnuts (see page 167) in the final minutes of serving.

Caramel macadamia: Stir through 1 cup caramel sauce (see page 150) and chopped macadamias before the setting stage.

Honey joy: Add 2 tablespoons honey to the milk at heating stage, and then crumble honeycomb through the ice cream before the setting stage.

Mint choc chip: Add 1 tablespoon mint essence to the milk plus 2 drops green food colouring (optional), and then stir through fresh chopped mint and crumbled Flake bars before the setting stage.

Ginger and caramel pudding

Makes 4   Prep time: 15 minutes   Cooking time: 20 minutes

1 tablespoon butter
½ cup brown sugar
1 egg
½ cup milk
1 tablespoon golden syrup

1 cup self-raising flour
2 teaspoons ginger
2 teaspoons cinnamon
Vanilla ice cream, for serving

For the sauce
125 g cold unsalted butter, chopped
½ cup brown sugar

2 cm knob ginger, peeled and sliced thinly
½ cup pouring cream

1 Preheat the oven to 160°C. Grease four 1-cup capacity dariole moulds.

2 In a bowl, cream the butter and brown sugar using electric beaters.

3 In a separate bowl, beat the egg with the milk and golden syrup. Add gradually, stirring, to the butter mixture.

4 Sift together the flour, ginger and cinnamon. Gently fold into the wet ingredients.

5 Pour the mixture into the greased moulds, about three-quarters full. Bake

for 15 minutes or until coming away from the sides and springy when touched on top. Remove from the oven and turn out of the moulds.

6 While the puddings are cooking, make the sauce. In a medium saucepan over medium heat, add the butter and sugar and stir until melted. Stir in the sliced ginger and bring to the boil. Stir in the cream and bring back to the boil. Cook for about 5 minutes. Strain the sauce into a jug to remove the ginger pieces. The sauce will thicken a little as it cools.

7 To serve, cut a slice off the top of the sponges if they are not level. Place them upside down on individual plates and douse generously with caramel sauce. Serve with vanilla ice cream.

New York style baked cheesecake

Serves 10–12   Prep time: 20 minutes
Cooking time: 35 minutes + 6 hours chilling time

For the base
1 packet Butternut Snap biscuits   125 g butter, at room temperature

For the filling
1 ⅓ cups caster sugar   2 eggs
500 g cream cheese at room   2 teaspoons vanilla bean paste
   temperature

For the topping
½ cup sour cream   1 teaspoon vanilla bean paste
2 tablespoons caster sugar

1 Preheat the oven to 180°C (160°C fan-forced).

2 To make the base, place the biscuits and butter in the bowl of a food processor and blitz until it comes together in a ball. Press the mixture firmly into a 20 cm non-stick springform cake tin. Bring the mixture about 3 cm up the sides of the tin. Chill in the freezer while making the filling.

3 Place the sugar and cream cheese in the bowl of an electric mixer. Beat until very well mixed. Add the eggs, one at a time, then the vanilla, mixing well after each addition. Pour the filling into the chilled base and bake for 25 minutes.

4 Remove from the oven and raise the temperature to 200°C (180°C fan-forced).

5 To make the topping, combine the sour cream, caster sugar and vanilla then pour evenly over the cheesecake. Return to the oven for a further 10 minutes.

6 Refrigerate the cheesecake for at least 6 hours before serving.

Note: If you don't have 6 hours to wait for the cheesecake to set, chill it for 30 minutes in the freezer before refrigerating.

No-bake lemon cheesecake

Serves 12   Prep time: 30 minutes
Cooking time: 10 minutes + chilling time

250 g packet Butternut
  Snap biscuits
100 g butter, melted
1 tablespoon caster sugar
1½ teaspoons powdered gelatine

500 g cream cheese at room
  temperature
395 g tin condensed milk
Zest and juice of 3 lemons
1 cup thickened cream, whipped

1 In the bowl of a food processor, process the biscuits to a rough crumb. Add the butter and sugar and mix well. Press firmly into the base of a 26 cm springform cake tin and refrigerate.

2 Sprinkle the gelatine over ⅔ cup lukewarm water and stir until dissolved.

3 In the bowl of an electric mixer, beat the cream cheese until light and fluffy. With the mixer running, pour in the condensed milk. Remove the bowl from the mixer and stir through the gelatine mixture, the lemon zest and ⅓ cup juice, then gently fold through the whipped cream. Pour into the biscuit base.

4 Chill the cheesecake in the fridge for 6 hours or overnight.

Crème brûlée

Makes 6   Prep time: 20 minutes
Cooking time: 5 minutes + 6 hours chilling time

600 ml thickened cream
1 teaspoon vanilla bean paste
  (or 1 vanilla pod, seeds scraped)
3 strips lemon peel, made using
  a vegetable peeler

8 egg yolks
⅓ cup caster sugar
Caster sugar for the top

1 Place the cream, vanilla (pod and seeds if using) and lemon peel into a

medium saucepan over medium-high heat and bring almost to the boil.

2 In a large bowl, whisk the egg yolks and sugar until thick and pale.

3 Strain the cream into the eggs, stirring constantly. Wash and dry the saucepan, and return the mixture to it. Stir continuously over low heat for about 5 minutes, until the custard thickens. To test the correct thickness, dip a wooden spoon into the custard. Run your finger along the back of the spoon. If the trail left by your finger stays intact, the custard is thick enough. If it runs, or if the custard 'bleeds' into the mark left by your finger, it needs longer.

4 Pour the custard into six 150 ml ramekins. Refrigerate for at least 6 hours, until set and well chilled.

5 Just before serving, sprinkle caster sugar over the whole surface of the custard, making sure there are no gaps. Depending on the surface area of your ramekin, you will need about 1½–2 teaspoons per dish. Using a kitchen blowtorch, heat the sugar until it bubbles and turns golden brown. If you like a nice thick caramel topping, repeat this process. Leave the toffee for a few minutes to cool and set before serving.

Note: Once you have scraped out the vanilla pod and used it, it can be rinsed clean, dried and stored in your sugar canister for vanilla-scented sugar.

Crème caramel

Makes 6   Prep time: 20 minutes
Cooking time: 40 minutes + 6 hours chilling time

1½ cups caster sugar
400 ml thickened cream
1 teaspoon vanilla bean paste
  or extract

3 strips lemon peel, made using
  a vegetable peeler
8 eggs

1 Preheat the oven to 160°C.

2 Place half the sugar with ½ cup of water in a saucepan over medium-high heat. Stir until the sugar dissolves then bring to the boil. The sugar will turn a lovely caramel colour. Divide the caramel between six 1⅓-cup capacity ceramic ramekins.

3 Whisk the eggs and the remaining sugar in a bowl until pale and fluffy.

4 In a saucepan over medium-high heat, combine the milk, cream and vanilla

and add the lemon peel. Bring the cream mixture to scalding point – almost, but not quite boiling. Using tongs, remove the lemon peel from the mixture.

5 Carefully pour the cream mixture into the egg mixture, whisking constantly. If you don't have a spare pair of hands in the kitchen at this stage, dampen a tea towel and wrap it around the base of the bowl to help hold it steady while you are pouring and whisking.

6 Divide the custard mixture between the 6 ramekins. Place the ramekins in a deep baking dish and carefully pour boiling water into the baking dish until it is halfway up the sides of the ramekins. Bake for 30 minutes or until just set, topping up the water bath if needed. Remove the ramekins from the baking dish and set aside to cool.

7 When cool enough to put in the fridge, refrigerate overnight or for at least 5 hours. To serve, run a knife around the edge of each ramekin and invert onto a serving plate.

Hot chocolate fondant

Serves 4   Prep time: 10 minutes   Cooking time: 25 minutes

Cocoa, for dusting moulds
125 g unsalted butter
200 g dark cooking chocolate, chopped

2 eggs plus 2 egg yolks
½ cup caster sugar
¼ cup plain flour

1 Preheat the oven to 180°C. Grease four 1-cup capacity pudding moulds and dust with cocoa.

2 Place the butter and chocolate in a bowl over a saucepan of simmering water. Make sure the bowl is not touching the water. Stir until melted and combined, then remove from the heat.

3 Place the eggs, egg yolks and sugar in a large mixing bowl and, using electric beaters, beat until thick and creamy. The mixture should 'form a ribbon' or 'hold a figure of 8'. Stir the melted chocolate and butter mixture into the egg mixture, then sift in the flour and gently fold through.

4 Divide the batter between the pudding moulds and bake for 15 minutes. Cool in the moulds for a few minutes then gently invert onto the serving plates.

Sherry trifle

I like to use McWilliam's Cream Apera (once known as McWilliam's Cream Sherry) in this recipe because it was my nan's favourite.

Serves 20   Prep time: 30 minutes + jelly setting time

2 x 400 g jam roll cakes,
  sliced 1 cm thick (or make
  your own Swiss roll, see
  page 248, and slice it up)
500 g cherries, pitted
2 x 125 g punnets raspberries
⅓ cup sherry
2 packets raspberry
  flavoured jelly, made to
  directions and cubed

600 ml custard, either homemade
  or thick store-bought
600 ml thickened cream,
  whipped to soft peaks
Icing sugar, for dusting

1 In a very large bowl, lay the slices of 1½ of the jam rolls in the base and halfway up the sides.

2 On top of this, place one-third of the fruit. Using a spoon, sprinkle about half the sherry over the fruit and sponge. Place half the jelly over the fruit then top with half the custard. Place the remaining sponge slices on top of the custard. Layer again with fruit, sherry, jelly and custard. Dollop the whipped cream over the custard and spread with a spoon. Top with the last of the fruit and refrigerate. Sift some icing sugar over just before serving. Serve nice and cold.

Chocolate trifle

Serves 20   Prep time: 30 minutes + jelly setting time

2 punnets strawberries,
  hulled and sliced
¼ cup caster sugar
2 x 400 g chocolate swiss roll
  cakes, sliced 1 cm thick
2 x 125 g punnets raspberries
⅓ cup Frangelico (or use coffee,
  if you prefer no alcohol)
2 packets raspberry flavoured
  jelly, made to directions
  and cubed

600 ml chocolate custard, either
  homemade or thick store-
  bought
600 ml thickened cream,
  whipped to soft peaks
1 Cadbury Flake chocolate bar

1 Place the strawberry slices in a shallow dish and scatter with sugar. Allow to soften for 10 minutes.

2 In a very large transparent bowl, lay the slices of 1½ of the swiss rolls in the base and halfway up the sides. On top of this, place one-third of the macerated strawberries and one-third of the raspberries. Using a spoon, sprinkle about half the Frangelico over the fruit and sponge. Place half the jelly over the fruit then top with half the custard. Place the remaining sponge slices on top of the custard. Layer again with fruit, Frangelico, jelly and custard. Dollop the whipped cream over the custard and spread with a spoon. Top with the last of the fruit, crumble the Flake over the top and refrigerate. Serve nice and cold.

Sticky toffee pudding

Serves 8–10   Prep time: 20 minutes   Cooking time: 30 minutes

60 g butter
¾ cup brown sugar
¼ cup golden syrup
2 eggs

1⅓ cups self-raising flour
200 g pitted dates
300 ml boiling water
1 teaspoon bicarbonate of soda

For the sauce
300 ml thickened cream
120 g butter

½ cup brown sugar
½ cup golden syrup

1 Preheat the oven to 200°C and grease a 20 cm square cake tin.

2 In the bowl of an electric stand mixer fitted with the balloon whisk attachment, cream the butter and sugar until pale and fluffy. Add the golden syrup and eggs and mix well. Add the flour a little at a time and beat until combined.

3 Place the dates and boiling water into a food processor and blitz to a puree. Stir in the bicarbonate of soda then fold the date mixture immediately into the batter. The batter is quite loose and pale. Pour into the tin and bake for 30 minutes or until golden brown and lightly springy in the middle. Turn out onto a wire rack.

4 For the sauce, place all the ingredients in a saucepan, stir and bring to the boil. Boil for 5 minutes then place in a serving jug ready to pour over the pudding.

5 Serve warm with generous lashings of the sauce.

Christmas wreath, recipe
page 291

Christmas wreath

Serves 24   Prep time: 20 minutes
Cooking time: 1 hour + cooling time

For the choux puffs

120 g butter, cubed

¼ teaspoon salt

1½ cups plain flour

5 eggs, lightly beaten

For the crème pâtissière filling

2 cups caster sugar

10 egg yolks

1 cup plain flour

50 g butter

3½ cups milk

½ cup Grand Marnier

1½ teaspoons vanilla extract

3 strips orange peel, made using
  a vegetable peeler

For assembly

2 cups caster sugar

250 g white choc bits

Assorted decorations: cachous,
  gold and silver edible glitter

1 In a medium saucepan over medium-high heat, bring 1½ cups of cold water to the boil with the butter and the salt. Remove from the heat and add the flour, beating hard with a wooden spoon. Return to a low heat and cook, constantly stirring, for about 5 minutes. A dough will form into a ball around the spoon and come away from the sides of the pan. This will cook out the flour. Don't rush this process – it is important to successful choux puffs.

2 Preheat the oven to 200°C (180°C fan-forced). Line 2 baking trays with non-stick baking paper.

3 Beat the choux mixture with a whisk to speed the cooling process. When the mixture has cooled to a little above room temperature, beat in the eggs a little at a time. The mixture should be smooth, glossy and thick.

4 Place the mixture into a large piping bag with a 1 cm plain nozzle. Pipe little piles of mixture about 3 cm in diameter and 3 cm high onto the lined baking trays. With a wet finger, smooth down any little peaks on top of the puffs.

5 Bake for 10 minutes, then swap the top and bottom trays and bake for a further 10 minutes. Reduce the heat to 160°C (140°C fan-forced) and bake for a further 30 minutes. Ten minutes before the end of cooking time, remove the puffs from the oven and, using a small knife or a 5 mm sharp piping nozzle, pierce the base of the puffs and lay them on the side for the last 10 minutes of cooking to allow the insides to dry out. When the total baking time is up, the puffs should be golden brown and hollow in the centre.

6 For the crème pâtissière, place the sugar and egg yolks in the bowl of an electric mixer and beat for 5 minutes on high speed until light and creamy. Add the flour and beat for a further minute until well combined.

7 In a large saucepan, bring the milk to the boil with the vanilla, Grand Marnier and orange peel. Remove the orange peel and pour the milk over the egg mixture in a steady stream, beating on low speed.

8 Return the mixture to the saucepan and bring to the boil. Reduce the heat and stir continuously with a whisk. The custard will thicken and darken to a yellow colour. Continue to stir for 4–5 minutes or until the flour has cooked out. Taste the custard before removing it from the heat. When the custard is cooked, remove from the heat and allow to cool for a few minutes. (To speed the process, you can beat it with a whisk.) While still slightly warm, beat through the butter. Place in a tray and cover the surface with plastic wrap to avoid a skin forming on top. Refrigerate until ready to fill the profiteroles.

9 To fill, place the crème pâtissière into a piping bag with a 4 mm nozzle. Insert the nozzle into the hole at the bottom of each puff and fill slowly and carefully, until the profiterole has a decent weight and you feel resistance when piping.

10 To assemble the wreath, place the sugar in a non-stick frypan over medium-high heat. It will begin to brown on the bottom. Swirl the pan occasionally to prevent the sugar from burning. When it is a deep golden colour, remove the pan from the heat. Dip the top of half of the filled profiteroles into the toffee and leave to set. If the sugar in the pan starts to harden, place it back on the heat until it's loose again.

11 In a heat-proof bowl over a pot of barely simmering water, melt the white chocolate. Dip the tops of the remaining half of the profiteroles in white chocolate and while it is still wet, decorate with cachous or glitter. Allow to set.

12 Place a dinner plate on a large, round cake board. Dip a toffee-covered profiterole sideways into the liquid toffee and 'glue' it to the side of a chocolate-covered one. Alternating between the toffee-coated and chocolate-coated profiteroles, work your way around the plate until you have a full circle. Remove the plate before building the second level. One at a time, dip the bases of the remaining profiteroles in the toffee and position on top of the first layer.

13 When the wreath is assembled, dip a fork into the cooling toffee and wave it above the wreath to form spun sugar.

Choc malt baked cheesecake

Serves 16   Prep time: 15 minutes   Cooking time: 35 minutes + chilling time

For the base
50 g packet plain chocolate biscuits   125 g butter, at room temperature

For the filling
500 g cream cheese at room   375 g milk chocolate melts
   temperature   2 eggs
1⅓ cups caster sugar
¼ cup malted milk powder

For the topping
2 tablespoons cocoa   37 g packet Maltesers

1 Preheat the oven to 180°C (160°C fan-forced).

2 For the base, place the biscuits and butter in the bowl of a food processor and blitz until it comes together in a ball. Press the mixture firmly into a 20 cm non-stick springform cake tin. Bring the mixture about 3 cm up the sides of the tin. Chill in the freezer while making the filling.

3 For the filling, place the cream cheese, sugar and malted milk powder in the bowl of an electric mixer. Beat until very well mixed.

4 In a microwave-safe glass bowl, heat the chocolate for 1 minute on high. Stir, then heat for 30 seconds – repeat until the chocolate is melted. Stir some of the cream cheese mixture into the chiocolate, then tip all the chocolate into the mixer bowl. Mix until combined.

5 Add in the eggs, one at a time, mixing well after each addition.

6 Pour the filling into the chilled base and smooth the top. Place the tin on a baking tray in case of leakage and bake for 25 minutes.

7 Refrigerate the cheesecake for at least 6 hours before serving. Just before serving, place the cocoa in a wire mesh sieve and sprinkle it all over the top of the cheesecake. Top with Maltesers.

Note: If you don't have 6 hours to wait for the cheesecake to set, chill it for 30 minutes in the freezer before refrigerating.

Apricot cheesecake

Serves 12   Prep time: 30 minutes
Cooking time: 10 minutes + chilling time

750 g (about 12) ripe fresh
  apricots, halved and
  stones removed
¾ cup white sugar
250 g packet plain biscuits
100 g butter, melted
1 tablespoon caster sugar

¼ cup apricot jam
1½ teaspoons powdered gelatine
500 g cream cheese at room
  temperature
395 g tin condensed milk
1 cup thickened cream, whipped

1 In a medium frypan over medium-high heat, place the apricots and white sugar. Cook, stirring, for 10 minutes or until the sugar has dissolved and the apricots are soft and sticky. Remove to a container and refrigerate to cool.

2 Process the biscuits to a rough crumb in a food processor. Add the butter and caster sugar and mix well. Press firmly into the base of a 26 cm springform cake tin and refrigerate. When cool, spread the jam evenly over the biscuit base.

3 Sprinkle the gelatine over ⅔ cup of lukewarm water and stir until dissolved.

4 In the bowl of an electric mixer, beat the cream cheese until light and fluffy. With the mixer running, pour in the condensed milk. Remove the bowl from the mixer and stir through the gelatine mixture, then fold through the whipped cream. Pour into the biscuit base. Refrigerate for several hours (preferably overnight) until set.

5 Just before serving, spoon the apricot mixture evenly over the cheesecake.

Baked molten jam pudding

Serves 4   Prep time: 10 minutes   Cooking time: 40 minutes

100 g butter
100 g caster sugar
2 eggs
Zest of 1 lemon
100 g self-raising flour

¾ cup jam (strawberry and
  apricot are lovely but use
  your favourite)
Thick cream, for serving

1 Preheat the oven to 180°C.

2 Grease a 500 ml capacity pudding basin. If you don't have a pudding basin, a Pyrex bowl works as well.

3 Using an electric mixer or beaters, cream together the butter and sugar in a bowl until light. Add the eggs, one at a time, beating well after each addition. Stir through the lemon zest and gently fold through the flour.

4 Place the jam evenly into the base of the pudding basin and pour the pudding mixture on top. Cover the basin with buttered foil, remembering to fold a pleat across the middle to allow for expansion. Bake for 35–40 minutes. The pudding is cooked when a skewer inserted into the centre comes out clean.

5 Turn the pudding out onto a warmed dish and serve hot, with thick cream.

Rum and raisin baked cheesecake

Serves 10–12   Prep time: 20 minutes
Cooking time: 35 minutes + chilling time

For the base

250 g packet Butternut
   Snap biscuits

¼ teaspoon ground nutmeg
125 g butter, at room temperature

For the filling

¼ cup rum
½ cup raisins, roughly chopped
1⅓ cups caster sugar
500 g cream cheese at room
   temperature

2 eggs
1 teaspoon vanilla extract
   (or vanilla bean paste)

For the topping

125 g dark chocolate melts

1 cup thickened cream

1 Preheat the oven to 180°C.

2 For the base, place the biscuits, nutmeg and butter in the bowl of a food processor and blitz until it comes together in a ball. Press the mixture firmly into a 20 cm non-stick springform cake tin. Bring the mixture about 3 cm up the sides of the tin. Chill in the freezer while making the filling.

3 Heat the rum for 1 minute on high in the microwave, or until scalding point in a pot on the stove. Add the raisins and leave to soak.

4 Place the sugar and cream cheese in the bowl of an electric mixer. Beat until very well mixed. Add the eggs, one at a time, then the vanilla, mixing well after each addition. Drain any excess liquid from the raisins and fold them through the cream cheese mixture.

5 Pour the filling into the chilled base and bake for 25 minutes.

6 For the topping, place the chocolate melts in a heat-proof bowl. In a microwave-safe jug in the microwave, bring the cream to boiling point and pour over the chocolate, stirring with a metal spoon or silicone spatula. Pour evenly over the top of the cheesecake and refrigerate for at least 6 hours before serving.

Note: If you don't have 6 hours to wait for the cheesecake to set, chill it for 30 minutes in the freezer before refrigerating.

Raspberry ripple cheesecake slice

Makes 18 pieces   Prep time: 20 minutes
Cooking time: 35 minutes + chilling time

For the base
250 g packet Butternut Snap   125 g butter, at room temperature
   biscuits

For the filling
500 g cream cheese at room   1 teaspoon vanilla extract
   temperature   ½ cup raspberry jam
1⅓ cups caster sugar   Icing sugar, to dust
2 eggs

1 Preheat the oven to 180°C (160°C fan-forced). Grease and line a 19 x 30 cm lamington tin.

2 For the base, place the biscuits and butter in the bowl of a food processor and blitz until it comes together in a ball. Press the mixture firmly into the base of the prepared tin. Chill in the freezer while making the filling.

3 Place the cream cheese and sugar in the bowl of an electric mixer. Beat until very well mixed. Add the eggs, one at a time, then the vanilla, mixing well after each addition.

4 Spread half the jam over the chilled biscuit base. Pour the filling into the

base and dollop the remaining jam throughout the tin. Bake for 25 minutes. The slice will puff up, but as it cools it will sink back down.

5 Refrigerate for 2–4 hours and dust with icing sugar before serving.

Jaffa chocolate pots

Makes 6   Prep time: 20 minutes   Cooking time: 1½ hours + chilling time

½ cup caster sugar
1½ cups milk
1½ cups thickened cream
1 vanilla pod, cut in half,
   or 1 teaspoon vanilla bean paste

Peel from 1 orange, removed in
   strips using a vegetable peeler
250 g dark chocolate melts
6 egg yolks

For the ganache
125 g dark chocolate melts
1 cup thickened cream

1 tablespoon Grand Marnier
   or Triple Sec

1 Preheat the oven to 120°C.

2 In a medium pot, combine the sugar, milk, cream, vanilla and orange peel and stir over a medium heat until scalding but not quite boiling. Add the chocolate and stir until melted.

3 In a large bowl, whisk the egg yolks until pale and frothy. Slowly strain the hot chocolate mixture into the eggs, stirring vigorously. Whisk until all the ingredients are well combined.

4 Pour the mixture into six 150 ml ramekins or ovenproof dishes. Place the ramekins in a deep baking tray and fill the tray with cold water to about half depth. Bake for an hour. When done, the custards will still seem slightly liquid, but they will set further in the fridge. Refrigerate for several hours until firm.

5 For the ganache, place the chocolate in a heat-proof bowl. In a microwave-safe jug or in a pot on the stovetop, bring the cream to boiling point and pour over the chocolate, stirring with a metal spoon or silicone spatula. Set aside at room temperature while the custards bake and cool.

6 When the custards have set in the fridge, pour the ganache over them in a layer about 3 mm thick. Return to the fridge for a further hour or so until the ganache has set.

Orange self-saucing pudding

Serves 6   Prep time: 15 minutes   Cooking time: 40 minutes

1¼ cups self-raising flour
1¼ cups caster sugar
3 oranges, zested and juiced
½ cup milk

1 egg
75 g butter, just melted
1 tablespoon cornflour
Vanilla ice cream, for serving

1 Heat the oven to 170°C (150°C fan-forced). Grease a 20 cm square ceramic or glass baking dish.

2 In a large bowl, combine the flour, ½ cup sugar and orange zest. In a jug, whisk together the milk, egg and melted butter.

3 Make a well in the flour and pour in the wet ingredients. Stir gently until combined. Pour the batter into the baking dish.

4 In a small saucepan, combine ¾ cup of water and the orange juice. Bring to the boil for 1 minute and remove from the heat.

5 In a bowl, combine the remaining sugar with the cornflour and sprinkle over the batter. Carefully pour the juice over the top.

6 Bake for 40 minutes, or until the pudding is lightly golden on top and a skewer inserted into the middle comes out clean. Serve hot, with vanilla ice cream.

Steamed plum pudding

This pudding is best made 2–3 months ahead of Christmas.

Serves 10–12   Prep time: 20 minutes   Cooking time: 3 hours

200 g butter
¾ cup brown sugar
2 eggs
1 cup white breadcrumbs
500 g raisins
150 g currants
¾ cup plain flour

½ teaspoon bicarbonate of soda
1 tablespoon all-spice
2 teaspoons nutmeg
2 teaspoons cinnamon
¼ cup brandy and add an extra
    ½ cup brandy, to serve

1 Place a large pot on the stove over medium heat. Make sure the pot is big enough that its lid can fit with the pudding steamer inside. Put an inverted saucer or small wire rack on the bottom, and half fill with water. Bring to the simmer.

2 In the bowl of an electric stand mixer with the balloon whisk attachment, beat the butter and sugar until light and creamy. Add the eggs, one at a time, beating well after each addition. Stir in the breadcrumbs, then stir in the fruit. Add the sifted dry ingredients and stir through. Finally, stir in the ¼ cup brandy.

3 Lightly grease a 1.8 litre capacity pudding steamer and place the mixture in it, spreading the mixture level. Fit the steamer lid tightly.

4 Place the pudding steamer in the pot. Ensure that the water is halfway up the side of the pudding steamer.

5 Simmer with the lid on the pot for 3 hours. Remove the pudding and cool for a few minutes before turning out onto a wire rack. When completely cooled, wrap the pudding with plastic wrap and refrigerate or freeze until required.

6 To reheat, repeat the process of boiling the pudding in the steamer in a pot for 1 hour. If the pudding is frozen, make sure you remove it from the freezer the night before serving.

7 To serve, pour ½ cup warmed brandy over the pudding and set it alight.

Note: A pudding steamer is a metal bowl with a tight-fitting lockable lid. You should be able to find it in a homewares store.

Desserts

299

Hot cross bun and butter pudding

Serves 8   Prep time: 10 minutes + 20 minutes standing time
Cooking time: 40 minutes

300 ml thickened cream
300 ml milk
6 eggs, beaten
¾ cup caster sugar

1 teaspoon vanilla extract
6 hot cross buns
Cream, for serving

1 In a large mixing bowl, combine the cream, milk, eggs, sugar and vanilla extract.

2 Cut the hot cross buns in thirds crossways.

3 In a 20 x 25 cm baking dish, arrange slices of bun to cover the base. Pour over the egg mixture to just cover the slices. Add another layer of bun slices and cover with egg mixture again. Place the last of the bun slices on top. Pour the remaining egg mixture evenly into the dish. Stand for 20 minutes before baking to allow the custard to soak into the bun.

4 Preheat the oven to 180°C. Bake the pudding for 40 minutes. Remove from the oven and serve warm, with cream.

Hot cross bun and butter pudding, recipe page 300

Notes

My hope for this book is that it will foster a love of cooking and sharing of food among families and friends. I have provided some of my most precious recipes, tips and tricks gained over the years – however, this book remains incomplete. What it needs to fully complete it is your input: your favourite recipes, your advice to those you will hand this book on to, even some of your favourite food memories and traditions. This chapter is for you, to make this *Essential Cookbook* truly and fully belong to you, and the people you love.

Notes

Notes

Index

Acknowledgements

It's incredible how many people are involved in creating a book. My heartfelt thanks go to the team at Hachette: Karen the editor and Jordan the publicist; Tom in marketing and Chris and Katrina in Sales, also Lewis in design. Thanks to the food and photography team – Steve for the pictures, Tracey for the styling and Liz for the wonderful cooking. Special thanks to Robert who guides me, humours me and forgives me, and who has become far more than my publisher – he is my friend.

Thanks to the teams who prop me up in other areas of my life as well.

Lisa and Caitlin and the team at One Management, who wrangle my chaotic life and have done for many years.

Thank you Shelley, Janny, Leah and Renee and all the team at Julie's Place, my cooking school. Much of my test cooking goes on here and the team put up, clean up and eat up the results. Thanks for all you guys do.

Thanks to Rabbit, Shayne, Moltz and all the team at Star 104.5, my radio colleagues, for giving me the best start to each day and for your total support and understanding of my schedule which usually has me racing round like a madwoman.

To my friends who don't see that much of me but are always there when needed; and to my extended family, thanks and love to you all.

And of course to Mick and my three beautiful boys who are the loves of my life and the reason for it all.

Gratitude and love to each and every one of you.

Julie Goodwin first came to the attention of the Australian public as the winner of the hit television show *MasterChef Australia* in 2009. Formerly an IT professional running a successful family business, Julie now writes a monthly column for *The Australian Women's Weekly* and is a bestselling cookbook author. She opened her highly successful cooking school, Julie's Place, in 2014. In 2015 Julie was a contestant on Channel 10's *I'm a Celebrity … Get Me Out of Here!* A tireless charity worker, Julie lives on the Central Coast of New South Wales with her husband and three sons.

Also by Julie Goodwin:

Our Family Table
Heart of the Home
Gather
Julie Goodwin's 20/20 Meals
Homemade Takeaway

Follow Julie online:

juliegoodwin.com.au

 juliegoodwincooklivelove

 _JulieGoodwin

 _JulieGoodwin

hachette
AUSTRALIA

Published in Australia and New Zealand in 2017
by Hachette Australia
(an imprint of Hachette Australia Pty Limited)
Level 17, 207 Kent Street, Sydney NSW 2000
www.hachette.com.au

10 9 8 7 6 5 4 3 2

National Library of Australia
Cataloguing-in-Publication data:

Goodwin, Julie, author.

Julie Goodwin's essential cookbook / Julie Goodwin.

ISBN 978 0 7336 3711 7 (paperback)

Cooking.
Cookbooks.

Cover and internal design by Lewis Csizmazia
Photography by Steve Brown
Food preparation by Elizabeth Chapman
Styling by Tracey Pattison
Colour reproduction by Splitting Image
Printed in China by 1010 Printing Group Limited